On the Edge of Mystery

Religions and Discourse

Edited by James Francis

Volume 8

PETER LANG

Oxford · Bern · Berlin · Bruxelles • Frankfurt a.M. · New York · Wien

Gill Goulding

On the Edge of Mystery

Towards a Spiritual Hermeneutic
of the Urban Margins

Regis College Library
15 ST. MARY STREET
TORONTO ONTARIO, CANADA
M4Y 2R5

PETER LANG
Oxford · Bern · Berlin · Bruxelles • Frankfurt a.M. · New York · Wien

Die Deutsche Bibliothek – CIP-Einheitsaufnahme

Goulding, Gill:
On the edge of mystery : towards a spiritual hermeneutic of the urban
margins / Gill Goulding. – Oxford ; Bern ; Berlin ; Bruxelles ; Frankfurt
a.M. ; New York ; Wien : Lang, 2000
(Religions and discourse ; Vol. 8)
ISBN 3-906758-80-X

British Library and Library of Congress Cataloguing-in-Publication Data:
A catalogue record for this book is available from *The British Library*, Great
Britain, and from *The Library of Congress*, USA

ISSN 1422-8998
ISBN 3-906758-80-X
US-ISBN 0-8204-5087-1

© Peter Lang AG, European Academic Publishers, Bern 2000
Jupiterstr. 15, Postfach, 3000 Bern 15, Switzerland; info@peterlang.com

Printed in Germany

Acknowledgements

My debts of gratitude are extensive, but far from onerous. In particular my thanks are due to the following:

Peter Lang publishers and especially Jim Francis, the series editor, whose enthusiasm encouraged me to undertake this book and Denise Brunton who gave so much of her time and energy to typing it.

Dr Michael Northcott, Professor Duncan Forrester and Rev Dr Fergus Kerr OP enabled my original doctoral thesis while Dr Peta Dunstan believed in the work so much she proof read the text.

Rev Joseph Veale SJ whose interest, comments upon the text and ongoing care and support have sustained this enterprise from its inception.

Finally, an inadequate expression of gratitude must go to the present and past members of the Hope Community, and to the many men and women on the Heath Town Estate who willingly shared their time and life experience with me; also to the men and women in Britain and Ireland whom it has been my privilege to accompany over these years.

I acknowledge with gratitude the scholarship granted by the Divinity Faculty of the University of Edinburgh and the Postdoctoral Fellowship to which I was later elected. Combined with a grant from the Christendom Trust this has enabled me to progress this work into a new area of exploration and a deeper dimension of probing the mystery.

Gill Goulding IBVM
March 2000

Contents

Foreword

The boundaries of discourse are like the compositional structure of a symphony. The composer aims to fulfil musical vision by including the different instruments according to the patterns of imagination and insight. All instruments designated by the musical score are vital for the true performance of the work, and they have their appointed parts to play. Under the conductor's baton the musical score becomes a whole symphony of sound. But for a truly great work it is necessary not merely for the instruments to perform with accuracy and precision the notes allotted to them which may be more or less harmonious or discordant according to the taste of the composer and the effect he is trying to convey. A work of true greatness, and particularly a performance of such, must draw forth the commitment of the players to the extent that they reach into the very depths of themselves and call upon the reserves of mature interpretation of which they may be capable. The resulting effect is immensely powerful and challenging.[1] Such a performance may also have transformative effects upon members of an audience and upon those who perform such a work. For particularly when there is an acknowledged faith dimension to the work, there can be the invitation to touch what is divine within those who listen.

A not dissimilar process may be said to apply to this book. The boundaries of discourse I have set are in place in order to assist the conversation. The whole enterprise was conceived to address a specific question and in pursuing certain lines of enquiry very different participants are drawn into the converse. Like the different instruments each has their part to play. There is the part allotted to those who work on the urban margins – members of a particular community. There are the many different people with whom they work on a peripheral housing estate. Apparent within the work is the influence of important Philosophers like Hans Georg Gadamer and David Tracy. A significant theme throughout the work is my reflective engagement with the work of Karl Rahner. The

---

1   This paragraph was inspired while listening to a performance of Triduum by James MacMillan.

11

Roman Catholic Church has a particular function to perform within the work and of prime importance have been certain Vatican II documents and many of the Papal Encyclicals. Finally the conversation is not complete without interaction with those from the Spiritual Tradition ranging from Francis of Assisi to Thomas Merton each of whom in a significant way assist the construction of the whole work. And within the final movement there is a challenge for the future – what transformative effect may this work have on those who read it?

The final contributor to the discourse is the reader's interaction with the spiritual hermeneutic, which has been outlined throughout the work. In the crossing of the boundaries of discourse which occur, the living reality of the presence of God in the voice of the people is heard. It finds expression in their words, as included, and it is – as it were – an echo of much within the spiritual tradition. It is given added veracity in the experience of those who live and work on the urban margins. And it is an ongoing source of reflection and resonance for contemporary theologians. It is the cumulative effort of those involved in this construction and primordially the work of the Holy Spirit which gives an indication of the presence of God amongst those upon the margins of our contemporary society.

Gill Goulding IBVM
April 2000

Introduction

This book originated in personal experience working with marginalised individuals and groups in four British cities. In Birmingham, Bristol and Brixton I worked with teams of lay people and religious in fields as diverse as prostitution, race relations, unemployment and homelessness. In Glasgow, I was employed in a drug rehabilitation unit, dealing with both drug abuse and the inevitable problems of H.I.V. and A.I.D.S. Working in such stressful circumstances, with individuals who faced severe problems, awakened very deep questions for many team members. These included reflecting upon what the reality of God meant for themselves and for the people with whom they worked. These questions arose in each team with which I worked and were considered important by all members, whether individuals had a firm or vague Christian commitment.

Reflecting upon my own experience, I was conscious of God at work within marginalised groups and individuals in a way often embarrassingly direct and simple for our more complicated Christian formats. Most people I worked with inhabited no specific religious tradition and yet demonstrated a spiritual vitality, openness and exploration of real depth and quality which puts many of those of us who do inhabit such traditions to shame. Since they showed no sign of being susceptible to conversion it occurred to me to ask, what can the tradition offer to them, and what more importantly, can they offer to us? Given that the "spiritually alive of no fixed abode" may be on the increase, how do we relate to them? Also, given the breakdown of shared frameworks of discourse how can individuals or a community share and communicate their values, perspectives and prescriptions with those who inhabit different frameworks? How does one achieve either prophetic witness or courteous transition in such a world? Ultimately one focus emerged. Is it possible to have a shared spirituality between those who work on the margins and the people with whom they work and what factors might assist such a reciprocal sense of depth exchange at that level of experience? It seemed to me these considerations were fundamental for any Christian social outreach.

Given the contentious nature of two words, which will occur frequently throughout this work, it seems appropriate to assist the discourse by giving a preliminary explanation.

"Spirituality" has become an over-exploited contemporary term, which can cover a wide spectrum of possibilities from New Age meditation in pyramids through shades of occult practice to the most orthodox Sunday worship. Within the Christian tradition particular forms of contemporary spirituality can render a degree of elitism, such that if you do not visit a spiritual director and preferably have a therapist as well, keep a journal, know your Enneagram number, have your Myers Briggs profile and make a regular retreat, you are falling short somewhere. However, spirituality is always grounded in a context and particular experiences. May working definition of spirituality has been that which is most deeply personal – is me – is most precious to me. This is not just the "me" which may so often be alienated, distracted and inauthentic, but also what is the most genuine, often most simple and certainly the most profound "me" that exists. This is the depth of an individual where we meet God and other real human beings. Here we touch the place where spirituality is more than what shapes and guides us. It is also what moves us, what resonates deep within, the place of our deepest desires. This centre, this focal point, this deep silence within, is the source of our lived response to God and to others. From here come the actions that really count. Here, the source of faith, is the inspiration of our vision – the fusion of prayer and action – for each individual in each specific context.

The term "marginalised" encompasses an enormous spectrum of marginality including the old, the very young, the handicapped, the sick, the incapacitated in many different forms, and ethnic groups. In terms of this book it has been specifically focused on marginality in the inner city and peripheral housing estates and has included: problems associated with bad housing conditions and homelessness, issues of ethnicity and racist violence, drug abuse and problems associated with H.I.V. and A.I.D.S., unemployment, prostitution and all other problems associated with multiple deprivation in urban areas.

The actual acquisition of data involved participant observation and a form of sampling. I was concerned that the location for this should be some area or areas where it might be possible to see the interaction between those who chose to work on the margins and the people with whom they worked. My own background as a religious sister meant I was conversant with some of the initiatives being undertaken by religious women in this sphere, and consideration of these appeared a likely possibility and a relevant focus both within the Roman Catholic tradition and the wider church. Given the constitution of such communities, it seemed that the possibilities of contributing to the understanding of the ministry of women, and the particular contribution of women within the field of spirituality, was also a feature.

The primary placement for participant observation involved a religious community living and working in Wolverhampton on a peripheral housing estate, who are endeavouring to assist Community development. The Hope Community have four flats on the estate within near proximity and during my time with them the Community comprised three religious sisters and three lay women.[2] Here I spent ten months in periods of one, two, or three months at a time, living as a member of the Community and engaged in their regular programme of activities. I was accepted by the Community as another member of the team and by the residents as another religious sister who arrived for periodic involvement with the Community.[3] During this time I also conducted a series of informal interviews with forty individuals and recorded details of numerous group meetings involving members of the Community and residents of the estate. Engagement with the Community and residents was thus widespread, but the primary focus was the spirituality emerging and interactive within these groups. In accordance with an agreement entered into with the Community and local residents, in what follows, no personnel are identified by name or substitute names.

From the accumulated primary data the seeds of an analytical framework began to emerge. Such grounded theory[4] is both derived from the primary data and illustrated by characteristic examples from the data. This process is followed throughout the book and thus there is an ongoing interaction with the voices of the participants which both adds to the sig-

---

2   There has been a change of personnel since my last visit to the Community.
3   My initial contact was the leader of the Community. My purpose was initially explained to the Community members and residents, but this was quickly forgotten as I became for the majority just another member of the religious sisters within the Community.
4   Here I am indebted to the work of Glaser B. and Strauss A., *The Discovery of Grounded Theory: Strategies for Qualitative Research*, New York, Aldine, 1967.

nificance of the emergent theory and contributes to its validity.[5] Reflection on the information acquired revealed a predominant emphasis on the importance of conversation and dialogue between Community members and residents and the prerequisite of a listening disposition on the part of Community members. The primordial feature of the life and work of the Community was the willingness and ability to exercise this listening faculty. Indeed I assert that, it is the easy and natural engagement of the Community with the affairs of daily life which is a vital ingredient in any potential shared spirituality. Thus conversation as the natural mode of interaction between Community and residents appeared most useful as a starting point for a model to analyse the primary data. Here Hans Georg Gadamer's dialogical hermeneutics and his emphasis on conversation proved most helpful.

As Gadamer describes genuine conversation it is open-ended. It is characterised by the fact that all participants are led beyond their initial positions towards a richer more comprehensive view. Gadamer refuses to foreclose on such interaction, emphasising that it is always possible for dialogic encounters to develop. Understanding, for Gadamer, is primarily coming to an understanding with others. This requires profound and indeed uninterrupted listening which is the rigour of hermeneutical experience. Indeed there is a particular dialectic implied in hearing. 'It is not just that he who hears is also addressed, but also that he who is addressed must hear whether he wants to or not'.[6] One cannot 'hear away' in a similar manner to the way one 'looks away' if refusing to observe any particular phenomenon. Rather there is a certain primacy in hearing. It is to such a model of listening that the church might look in order to become aware of the urban margins, in a way that does not deny them or is threatened by them but that can enter deeply into conversation with them, and thus have the potential to embrace the richness of areas of experience outside its present domains. Here it will be important to bear in mind Gadamer's emphasis that, 'Experience is always actually present only in the individual observation'.[7] This requires an open disposition.

---

5   "Generating a theory from data means that most hypotheses and concepts not only come from the data, but are systematically worked out in relation to the data during the course of the research." *Ibid.* p. 6.

6   Gadamer H. *Truth and Method*, trans. Weinsheimer J. and Marshall D., London, Sheed & Ward, 1989, p. 462.

7   *Ibid.* p. 351.

The reality of such an open disposition involves personal vulnerability and the voluntary admissibility of potentially negative knowledge. This is necessitated if the other in a dialogue is actually to have the real status of other.[8] In this way reverence for each participant is guaranteed, it is not that one person 'understands' the other.

The classic illustration of a dialogue between two individuals might be analogously related to the reality of the institutional church and the marginalised. The question here posed is – does the church really wish to envisage the kind of genuine human bond portrayed above? A positive answer to this question is a necessary prerequisite for real conversation to occur. What is being proposed is that the church enters into a reciprocal dynamic with the marginalised, not engage in a benevolent monologue. Neither interlocutor in any mutual exchange has possession of the language of the exchange by ordained right. Rather, in the reality of the conversation that occurs a deeper bond is forged and a transformation of both participants. In order to effect such a transformation, a degree of renunciation is required in order to effect a form of transposition into 'the other', and thus acquire comprehension of a different experience and understanding.

Hermeneutical conversation as Gadamer explicates involves finding a common language, the search for which coincides with the very act of understanding and reaching agreement. However, a problem arises in the very familiarity of a particular language structure, which for those who live within it appears peculiarly appropriate, indeed linguistically unsurpassable. It seems impossible that another language could have an equally positive effect in describing experiences. In the same manner, the ecclesiastical subculture with its esoteric in-language can appear equally closed and exclusive in its relationship with the urban margins. Thus to search for a common language may involve a real agony on the part of the institution to widen a fore-shortened view and willingly embrace what is seen as alien and possibly inferior. Gadamer's solution to the linguistic dilemma is to highlight the hermeneutical experience as the corrective by means of which the thinking reason escapes the prison of language, and is itself verbally constituted. This is the form of discourse he advocates.

---

8   *Ibid.* p. 362 gives further elaboration of the openness and reverence of such a genuine human bond.

It is not that experience begins by being wordless and subsequently becomes an object of reflection, is named, and then subsumed under the universality of language. Rather, experience of itself seeks and finds words that express it. Though such words may be limited in vocabulary, they may still convey something of the essence of the experience. More than that, the most unsophisticated speech may potentially still convey something of the mysterious reality of both what is said and unsaid.[9]

For the church as institution, as for all individuals, the possibility exists to widen the horizons of understanding by being open to exterior insight, and therefore to the expansion of its own vision of the world. This might then result in a wider availability to include both its traditional membership and the marginalised. 'As verbally constituted, every world is of itself always open to every possible insight and hence to every expansion of its own world picture and is always available to others.'[10]

The only true reality of language lies in dialogue, that is, in the reality of understanding being achieved. If this is indeed so and the language of the church is alien to people on the margins such that there is no real dialogue, then there is no real understanding. Genuine understanding is rooted in truth rather than in a concern to adhere to presupposed criteria of belief.

In analysing the interaction of the Community and the residents, it became evident that a discovery had been made of the transcendent human dignity of individuals and the reality of grace in the daily life of the people. Here the work of Karl Rahner proved particularly appropriate – in interaction with the primary source material – with his emphasis on the dynamic drive towards divine mystery inherent within humanity. Thus our experience of God is given with and through human experiences in the world. This emphasis when applied to the concrete circumstances of the life of the people of the Heath Town estate is able to authenticate the experience of grace at work in the lives of individuals and the corporate celebration of that in the paraliturgical gatherings. When reflectively considered, this experience achieves a dynamic evangelistic thrust in the lives of Hope Community members, such that there is an acknowledged sense of being evangelised by the residents of the estate. Here also, the experience of God at work amongst the people presents a challenge for

---

9   *Ibid.* p. 469 for further discussion of this issue.
10   *Ibid.* p. 447.

reflective evaluation at all levels within the churches. Moreover, it is at this juncture that the involvement of this irregular group of women who have chosen to enter the marginal status of the residents of the estate become also marginalised within the institutional church. The experienced reality provokes a question, if not a challenge, to the church to seek a more effective communication with its own marginal members – for in the experience of the latter lies a potential source of blessing. It is from the conviction that the mystery of God is already at work upon the urban margins that commitment is made to a mode of profound critical listening within the ordinary conversation and dialogue of daily life. This is seen as imperative not merely for the members of the Hope Community working on the Heath Town estate but also for the institutional church to both confirm and incorporate.

The conversation advocated is not only between individuals and between the institutional church and the urban margins but also involves reflective engagement with the Christian tradition. Here the work of David Tracy[11] proves particularly important. Tracy argues[12] that the heart of any hermeneutical position is the recognition that all interpretation is a mediation of past and present, the tradition and the contemporary world in which that tradition ongoingly develops. Here his use of the 'classic' is invaluable. It is important hermeneutically as an example of both radical stability become permanence and radical instability become excess of meaning through ever-changing receptions. For Tracy there is the conviction that if the religious classics are classics at all, they can be trusted to evoke a wide range of responses including the shock of recognition of God, which in religious terms is named faith. He states that explicitly religious classic expressions will involve a claim to truth as the event of a disclosure-concealment of the whole of reality by the power of the whole – as in some sense, a radical and finally gracious mystery. Though the classic referred to by Tracy is predominantly a text, analogously I argue it may be used in reference to the experience of those on the margins of society. Here, just as in a text, there are demands necessitating constant interpretation. The experience here manifested is such as is apprehended

---

11   Of particular importance have been Tracy D., *The analogical: Christian Theology and the Culture of Pluralism*, London, SCM, 1981. Tracy D., *Plurality and Ambiguity.*

12   Tracy D., *The Analogical Imagination, op. cit.*, p. 99ff.

by those who have chosen to live and work there, and involves a transformative truth, if approached in openness and reverence.

Within the hermeneutical tradition priority is given to understanding in the process of interpretation, yet there is an essential dialectic of understanding-explanation-understanding. However, a prior dimension is that of listening in order to hear in order to understand. The actual form of this listening is from the depths of the human heart. At this level may be experienced the powerlessness and helplessness which is a daily reality for those who live on the margins. Here in that position of essential vulnerability within an individual's own contemplative depths, the clarity of resonance with others – particularly the marginalised – is peculiarly powerful. It is from the wellspring of the contemplative dimension that true compassion is born, and this provides the existential dynamism for action and orientates the disposition towards a spiritual hermeneutic of the urban margins.

Thus the empirical work, engaging with a community who are a living embodiment of that tradition of Christian involvement with the marginalised, leads through a process of analysis emphasising the importance of conversation and dialogue into a realisation of the vital prerequisite of a critical listening faculty. The facilitative tool for such an attuned listening is seen to be the willing openness to the contemplative dimension. At all stages it is emphasised that this process has both an individual and institutional applicability. It does appear that a shared spirituality on the urban margins is possible, and the Hope Community have made major strides in this direction.

The format of what follows is in sections. The first gives consideration to the sociological context – outlining the factors which gave rise to the building of the estate, its chequered career and the contemporary living conditions. There follows a brief historical perspective, indicating the involvement of the churches with the urban margins. Against this background the coming of the Hope Community to the Heath Town estate and their life and work is outlined. Section one concludes with an indication of the way in which the Hope Community is viewed by the churches at local and hierarchical levels, and the particular nature of that regard in the light of the all female composition of the Community. The second part enters into an analysis of the primary data utilising the work of Hans Georg Gadamer, Karl Rahner and David Tracy. Here it becomes apparent that the core listening dimension which the Community brings to its

20

involvement with the residents and which is of critical importance with regard to a shared spirituality, may be facilitated by deeper engagement with the contemplative dimension.

The last section furthers the contemplative dimension and includes both concluding evaluation and wider conclusions, in an outward orientation indicating where further study might be appropriate. Firstly, by re-engagement with the spiritual tradition, it becomes evident that much within the tradition points to the peculiar fecundity of contemplation in its outward working in discerned action. Secondly, engagement with contemporary spirituality, through the work of Merton, reveals the importance of a renewed spirituality and a renewed asceticism not only for those who work on the urban margins but also at all levels within the churches. Here the emphasis within the tradition upon the need for on-going purification of desire in order to authenticate discerned action is interlinked in contemporary mores with the co-inherence of humility and integrity. Thus these chapters indicate the need for further investigation to be made of the spiritual tradition and its contemporary applicability, particularly as related to the peculiar dynamic of this listening mode. Such an exploration could deepen the preconditions for a renewed spirituality and a renewed asceticism – leading inevitably towards a spiritual hermeneutic of the urban margins.

Chapter 1

A Sociological Context

'Tis all in peeces, all coherence gone'[1] 'Heath Town a tinder box' 'a breeding ground for criminals'.[2]

What sort of society are we aiming to build together? ... A substantial minority swollen by mass unemployment, feel they have no stake at all. Many more are troubled that their life chances appear to be determined by impersonal economic forces and distant bureaucracies over which they have little or no control.[3]

'Underclass' is a destructive and misleading label that lumps together different people who have different problems. It is the latest of a series of popular labels that focuses on individual characteristics and thereby stigmatises the poor for their poverty.[4]

Imagine grey: a grey day reflected in the mirror image of the buildings, grey-soaked and sodden concrete, marked by millions of tiny rivulets of water, rain beating upon reinforced concrete and ill-fitting window panes, condensing into pools along walk-ways slippery with dog dirt. Grey faces as a few individuals scurry through the rain or walk more slowly with a disconsolate air, rain-soaked hair plastered to the head. A few mothers pushing baby buggies or clambering up stairs with push-chair and shopping and infant clutched in one flailing embrace. Two older children moodily kicking a tin around a patch of churned mud and turf, while a bedraggled dog looks on belligerently. This is Heath Town Estate one October afternoon.

Walking around the estate the eye is drawn to the number of blank boarded windows of the 'voids' – flats which have been left vacant and

---

1   Donne J., 1611 'An anatomy of the world', cited in Best S & Kellner D. [eds.], *Postmodern Theory*, London, Macmillan, 1991, p. viii.
2   *Wolverhampton Express and Star*, November 6, 1984, and 24 May, 1989.
3   Carey G., Archbishop of Canterbury, *The Times*, 6 October 1992.
4   McGahey R., 'Poverty's Voguish Stigma', *New York Times*, 12 March, 1982, cited in Jencks C., *Rethinking Social Policy: Race, Poverty and the Underclass*, Cambridge, Mass., Harvard University Press, 1992, p. 6.

whose windows are covered by boarding to protect them from vandals. Row upon row of interconnected flats empty and occupied, common entries to both. At the corners of corridors concealed stairs or lifts – which are frequently out of order – are the connecting lines for the inhabitants. The graffiti on the walls of stairways vary in its poignant portrayal of life on the estate from obscenity to political and racist issues. Passing a bin-chute room – all rubbish is sent through a series of chutes to a ground floor collecting room, unwanted pets pass that way too sometimes – a mattress and a pair of shoes indicate this as the sleeping place of one illegal resident. Suddenly, the loud rumbling of a train passing by is heard. The estate is only a few hundred yards from the main railway track in and out of Wolverhampton station. It is still raining! Such was the recollection of one visit to the estate.

Clearly evident are the physical constraints and inadequacies of the material fabric of the estate. A number of residents were asked the question – How would you describe what Heath Town looks like? The following replies were received: 'a box'[5] 'run down grey area full of derelict buildings'[6] 'a prison on stilts'[7] None of the replies elicited had a positive image of the estate with regard to the material fabric. All seemed to suffer from some problems both with individual flats, and in terms of sharing a common environment. The sense of being enclosed was paramount, and amongst some contributed to a real sense of claustrophobia. In particular the lack of access to play areas for children and indeed the absence of any childcare provision was acutely felt. The cliché – a concrete jungle – was one not infrequently used.

The Failure of the Modernist Dream

In the 1990s there seemed to be little good to say about the material circumstances of the estate. Yet at the time of its planning and commencement, it had held such promise in terms of a housing complex of the fu-

---

5   Resident Y.
6   Resident K.
7   Resident M.

ture, creating a new form of community, benefiting from the technological revolution. Many of the houses cleared to make way for the scheme were without internal water supplies or adequate facilities for the preparation of food. A good number had walls which were buckled and fractured, roofs which were sagging or leaking and brickwork which had perished.

What went wrong? How did the modernist dream of a prestigious new housing scheme disintegrate into the nightmare of contemporary life on the estate? The reality of single-parent families and elderly pensioners trapped in these flats in the 1990s was a particularly poignant ratification of the difficulties. Yet the vision which inspired the post-war provision of low rental housing coupled with slum clearance must be acknowledged. However, the attempt to provide a material Utopia, with little or no reference to the people who would inhabit such an environment, the lack of appreciation of the deep communitarian ties which already existed, and the use of space in a way which was predominantly utilitarian with no thought for the deeper needs of individuals and families, all this contributed to the evacuation of the spiritual dimension from this new possibility, which became in effect a distilled material essence cemented in concrete.

Dilapidation and Disrepair

The scale upon which the Heath Town estate began was both unprecedented and over-ambitious. Increasing expense led to the use of inadequate materials in building. The result of this was that the new flats which proved initially such a delight to their inhabitants quickly deteriorated into novel 'vertical slums' as maintenance repairs were only spasmodically addressed. It was certainly noticeable that the properties, which received most attention, tended to be those closest to the main road, and more visible to passing motorists. The unseen inhabitants of the interior of the estate, and particularly those on the inner edge were seemingly forgotten or ignored in terms of priority rating for repairs.

The flaws in the Heath Town dream became apparent as faults in the design began to erode the reputation of success. A shopping centre that was hidden from the main road soon died with no real means of generating income from outside. Stairways that were enclosed and poorly lit left individuals vulnerable to attack, open-air car parks, often out of view, lefts cars at the mercy of vandals, the long walkway across the estate with no exit points except at either end meant many refused to cross it alone after dark, and an estate-wide-heating system that functioned inefficiently and was prohibitively expensive all began to cause friction amongst residents. Meanwhile the completely illogical layout, though perhaps prematurely postmodernist, continued to cause disruption and sometimes danger to life. 'Mrs M of 87... was asked where number 85 was, but she didn't know. 'I have lived here for 18 months and I have never found it. I presume it is on another floor somewhere, but I don't know which one.'[8] The issue of noise was one that was raised by one of the Community, when in an interview, I asked what she most disliked about life on the estate. 'The worst thing about living here I guess is the noise, at times, like 2 am. People don't have regular hours, they come awake and alive at times when people who work all day are asleep.'[9]

Who lives on the estate

'I'd say there is a majority of single women with young children except in the tall blocks where the elderly live'[10] From observation, there are few middle age[11] residents and this was verified by the local housing office.[12] The particular difficulties for young women on the estate proves an ongoing source of concern both to the social services and the Hope Community. The estate has become a dumping ground for individuals and families who have been labelled 'problem'. Such families are placed in

8   *Wolverhampton Express and Star*, 8 November 1972.
9   Fieldworker D.
10   Fieldworker A.
11   Between the ages of 45-60.
12   The local housing office was reluctant to give any official figures.

this category by local officials. 'They can be expected to treat their houses inefficiently if not badly, and will therefore have allotted the worst houses available.'[13]

Another problem category involves individuals who have been released from long-term psychiatric care. Here the laudable aim of endeavouring to absorb them into the local community with the maintenance of appropriate support structures has not been realised. Increasingly the difficulties such individuals encounter in endeavouring to lead an independent existence are compounded by the lack of after-care provision.

On the Heath Town Estate a day centre (New Start) was opened specifically to support ex-psychiatric patients living within the community. An inability to cope, and an increasing sense of isolation and alienation amongst those with psychiatric problems has led at times to violence or other forms of anti-social behaviour. The local community comprising others who in different ways are particularly vulnerable, has received no assistance in dealing with these new problems. Consequently a degree of hostility has been created with regard to ex-psychiatric patients amongst some members of the community, although it is notable how supportive others, with few resources themselves, can also be. The following extracts from a conversation discussing this issue illustrate some of the difficulties. 'I wouldn't like to live with them people.'[14] 'New Start already helps. You can have someone who moves in just as dangerous if not more so than someone coming out of the psychiatric hospital.'[15] 'If they came out to a caring community who were prepared to help them and be lenient because of their strange behaviour that would be brilliant.'[16] Of the suicides which occurred during my times visiting the estate, and those that were recounted to me by members of the Community, or residents, it became clear that most involved individuals with some form of psychiatric disorder.

---

13   *Condemned*, A Shelter Report on Housing and Poverty London, Shelter, 1971.
14   Resident Y.
15   Resident K.
16   Resident T.

The National Context

The developments on the Heath Town estate reflected in microcosm what was taking place in macrocosm in the wider national context. As Middleton states, 'We moved people in great numbers from intolerable conditions into accommodation which we needlessly allowed to become intolerable.'[17] There was a growing awareness of the self-perpetuating poverty which stretched across generations in deprived areas. At the same time racial tension began to be a recognised feature of inner city life.

The lack of co-ordination amongst government departments with regard to the inner cities has been a constant feature of the last two decades. No wonder then that the National Audit Office, the governmental watchdog body, commented in September 1989, 'Government support programmes are seen as a patchwork quilt of complexity and idiosyncrasy. They baffle local authorities and business alike. The rules of the game encourage compartmentalized policy approaches.'[18]

The Local Scene

In the 1990s unemployment levels were particularly acute in the inner city area of Wolverhampton. The particular social deprivation, which accrues to long-term unemployment, was something that was evident on the Heath Town estate. Discussing with residents on the estate about the issues of employment and unemployment, the following comments were responses to the question of what people did with their time. 'Majority spend their day sitting in the house.'[19] 'up town looking for jobs'[20] 'I've

---

17 Middleton M., *Cities in Transition, op. cit.* p. 34.
18 *Urban Regeneration and Economic Development: the Local Government Dimension*, National Audit Office, September 1989, cited in Middleton M., *Cities in Transition, op. cit.*, p. 43.
19 Resident Y.
20 Resident K.

been through phases when I watched telly all night and didn't get up till late.'[21] According to the leader of the Hope Community, on the estate 80% of residents were on social benefits of some form,[22] and a tiny minority were earning a salary that was sufficient for their living requirements. According to one resident this latter group, 'Are people who can live with dignity on what they get. Others if they have work, it's because they're forced to take it. Ones who do have cars, it's generally on the never/never, apart from the drug dealers and pimps.[23] 'When I had a job, the money was pretty pathetic. I was on £140 for Mon-Fri and now I'm on £135 on the dole.'[24] 'Those who do get a job and make money leave the estate, they cut themselves off.'[25]

Certain inner city residents were seen to be disadvantaged as a result of personal characteristics, which affect assessment of their employability. Among these were young, unskilled, ethnic minorities, those without formal qualifications, and those with lower educational achievements.

When asked how people acquired the money they lived on, the following answers were typical of the replies received from residents of the estate. 'We sign on.'[26] 'With great difficulty.'[27] 'I don't sign on I'm on the sick.'[28]

Changes in the social security system during the 80s and 90s have drastically effected those who live on the margins. The problem of debt can be particularly crippling. Loans from loan 'sharks' are notorious. One resident said, 'The worst thing is seeing people worried and hungry.

---

21   Resident M.
22   This information was based partly on observation, and on good contacts with the Social Services.
23   Prostitution and drug dealing are important parts of the local economy.
24   Resident K.
25   Resident S.
26   Resident Y.
27   Resident O.
28   Resident L.

You go to people's flats and you know they haven't eaten, the evidence speaks for itself. The giro ran out well before the next one was due.'[29]

Both the reduction in the expected value of benefits and the reduction or loss of entitlement have undermined the effectiveness of welfare provision in ameliorating the most brutal effects of poverty.[30] The following comment is from the experience of one resident who had previously been employed, but has not worked for a considerable time. His experience of the last ten years has been of a steady deterioration in living conditions. The grim note on which his comments end, indicate the cumulative effect of the cutbacks in benefit provision, coupled with an increase in the cost of living, and the additional pressure of alternative taxation.

> I used to be sceptical. I used to think if people can't afford to live off their giro then they must be doing something wrong. Up till 4 or 5 years ago I used to get on quite well with my giro. I used to buy electricity tokens and all that. My giro would last from one fortnight to the next for food and that, I'd not be short of anything, never in debt. It seemed then that the same amount of food was costing more and more every fortnight. It was getting more difficult, till I ended up with a choice, I could buy food to eat, or some food and some electric tokens to cook it with, or I could leave the electric tokens and buy food you could eat cold. So that's what I did, I forgot about the electric. They cut me off and I just bought food... I feel they're all closing in on me. I feel that everyone who lives here is threatened as well.[31]

---

29   'A terrible thing of living here is to see people suffering, people crying without actually crying. You can see that crying inside, see it in their faces but they can't cry out in the open, can't let their emotions come out. They can be accused of spending all their giro at the pub or on drugs. They talk about criminal elements. What they do to us is far worse, they make people break the law. There's a breaking point. If you see your children hungry and there's no way you can get money legally, social says you've had your giro, they don't care about you. A parent will go and get food for the children some other way, that's their first duty. That's the injustice.' Resident P.

30   In 1991 London Weekend Television and MORI undertook a survey entitled Breadline Britain – 1990s Researchers agreed on 44 items which were highlighted as ones people should not have to do without in Britain today. They grouped them into seven categories, adequate housing, essential clothing, adequate food, essential household items (e.g., fridge), financial security (i.e., could save £10 per month), important items for children (e.g., money for a school trip), something 'extra' (e.g., birthday present, holiday). Taking these categories as a guide the researchers found that 11 million people (including 3 million children) lacked three or more of these categories, 6 million lacked five or more, and 3.5 million lacked all seven and were classed as living in intense poverty.

31   Resident M.

The oppressive sense of being enmeshed in a deteriorating situation is one which is communicated here with real poignancy. It does appear that contemporary government policies have had a particularly insidious effect upon the prevailing ethos, by communicating a basic tenet that there is no alternative. Such a proscription upon alternative ways of conceiving reality increase demoralisation amongst communities such as those on the estate.

Ill-Health and Inadequate Medical Provision

Given the nature of the experience of poverty which includes lack of nutritional food, warmth, and stimulus (particularly deleterious long-term with regard to children), and the stress involved in the physical housing conditions, the concentration of vulnerable individuals, and personal relationships – health problems abound. The vulnerabilities of poverty are also aggravated by transition in the neighbourhood and heterogeneity among neighbours. This aggregate of disasters leads to an increasing likelihood of illness of one form or another, physical or psychological or a combination of both. Accordingly, the medical services in their turn come under pressure from increasing number of demands. At the same time the limited resources available to local practitioners appear at times inadequate to deal with the many demands made upon them.

During the course of my time on the estate I encountered some horrific stories, not least the long wait of Q., a young single parent, to be diagnosed as having a form of non-Hodgkin Lymphoma, a somewhat rare cancer. Over a considerable number of months she had experienced pain which had mystified the medical staff, indeed she had spent weeks being told that the pain she was experiencing was psychosomatic!

Extracts from a conversation with local residents concerning medical provision indicated strong antipathy. The local people present were vociferous in their protests. From one resident, 'I was told face-to-face by an emergency doctor that it was lucky he came out to see our baby because some won't come onto Heath Town Estate at night.'[32]   Another

---

32   Resident K.

said, 'Basically, doctors on this estate are quacks. They send the trainees here.'[33] Yet another, 'I've walked in and the doctor's there with a prescription in hand before I've said anything.'[34]

Many of those present had at one time been prescribed tranquillisers. However, it is noteworthy that eventually most of those who had been so prescribed had refused further medication of this sort.[35] Also a sense of receiving second class treatment, and the infringement of the residents rights and dignity were common features of responses received.[36]

Policing – by consent or coercion?

The lack of employment possibilities for young people combined with family deprivation can lead inevitably into petty crime, which may escalate over time. A factor rarely taken into account is the dilemma facing young people, especially the unemployed, who are trying to survive in inappropriate flats that take little account of their poor financial position – as the comments above indicate. This could be a contributory factor to the disinterest and detachment from any sense of responsibility for their neighbourhood. The increased stress on law and order in the national sphere has led to serious consequences with regard to surveillance and policing priorities.[37] The majority of residents expressed a very jaundiced view of the local constabulary. The following extracts indicate the views of some of those willing to give their opinion. 'You're lucky if you see a

---

33   Resident R.
34   Resident K.
35   'The unemployed and their families have considerably worse physical and mental health than those in work. There is substantial evidence of unemployment causing deterioration in mental health with improvements being observed on re-employment.' Whitehead, M., 'The Health Divide' in *Inequalities in Health* Townsend, P. and Davidson, N. [ed.], 'The Black Report' and Whitehead, M., 'The Health Divide', London, Penguin, 1992, p. 394.
36   Regarding the availability of services there is poorer provision in more deprived areas and poorer quality in what is provided. c.f. Whitehead M., 'The Health Divide', in *Inequalities in Health, op. cit.* p. 396ff.
37   The connection of surveillance with policing policy can lead to an oppressive creation of 'deviants' against whom a policy of suppression must be pursued.

policeman round here, you used to, they don't bother anymore.'[38] From another resident, 'The police say there's crime here when they want a bit of fun. They move in, big publicity, heavy invasion, helicopters and all, gives them public credibility in the eyes of people outside Heath Town.[39] In fact they need Heath Town for that!'[40]

The vehemence with which the above remarks were delivered, and the personal histories of varied associations with the police, indicated the great need for reconciliation in any community policing policy. However, these remarks also indicate something of the legacy that needs to be overcome. From my own observation over the months living on the estate, it was rare to encounter policemen and never one alone. On one evening there was a drugs raid on the local pub, and the police moved in en masse with helicopters and many men. The reality of drug dealing and prostitution on the estate is well known. The reality of violence can be heard during the night, but a more frequent occurrence is the noise of cars entering and leaving the estate to make a deal at the local drug den, situated close to the Community flat. Yet the crime rate on the estate is not as high as other parts of the town, and, as one resident stressed, the form of police intervention might appear questionable in the light of the statistics available. 'If they were policing Earls Court and they weren't really present, the crime rate would be huge. Here, non-existent police and the crime rate is 7th on the Wolverhampton list as regards reported crime.'[41]

The public image of Heath Town is one which emphasises the aspect of violence and crime, associated by right-wing ideologues with the underclass. In a secret police report of 1987, made available to the local press in 1989, it was stated that attempts were being made to make Heath Town a 'no go' area for the police. This followed incidents in which police officers were apparently lured onto the estate and attacked – on occasions with petrol bombs. The most common occurrence is the problem of vandalism. A survey of young people in Wolverhampton in 1984 endeavoured to ascertain why people were vandalising the area and a num-

---

38   Resident S.
39   'Too many of the new policies represent an abnegation of the tradition of British policing [by consent] and the adoption of an alien style of paramilitary policing.' Waddington P., *The Strong Arm of the Law, Armed and Public Policing*, Oxford, Clarendon, 1991, p. 334.
40   Resident T.
41   Resident P.

ber of responses were made: boredom, lack of money, unemployment, were all mentioned. The types of vandalism mentioned by young people included: burglary, broken windows, broken security doors, broken intercom systems. Lifts were a particular target for vandals. The police response to vandalism has been an extension of community policing. However, there are particular difficulties in police protection for high rise flats and maisonettes with the numerous balconies and landings. Modernist architecture and the post war housing policies adopted by urban planners, created the kind of environment in which social malaise and crime were an almost inevitable daily phenomenon.

The views of some young black residents of the estate were sought with regard to their relationship with the police, and their views of police behaviour towards the black community on the estate. 'Lots of kids are stopped because they're black. When I was a teenager, I was stopped left, right and centre – not so much now I'm older.'[42] From another resident 'What really hurts is the way they're handled, it's degrading and the other guy is white and in a blue uniform. I feel the police are the worst disservice to racial harmony because of their attitude.'[43]

The major question of racist behaviour amongst the police force has become increasingly a National concern. The results of the Steven Lawrence Enquiry in 1999 only served to highlight the problem of racism within the police force.

Underclass or Marginalised?

The term 'underclass' is an emotive word, inevitably carrying ideological implications. Coined first in America and associated in a derogatory way with the so-called undeserving poor, the term had also particular ethnic connotations which in themselves border on the racist. It seems to have been employed mostly as a rhetorical device. Emerging definitions have

---

42   Resident T.
43   Resident P.

tended to be behaviourally-oriented ones although some commentators[44] have argued that a definition based on deprivation rather than behaviour would be more appropriate.[45]

Within Britain the divergent views of behavioural-related or deprivation-related definition can be identified with the names of Murray and Field respectively. An article written by Murray, which first appeared in the *Sunday Times Magazine* in 1989, and published in 1990 under the title *The Emerging British Underclass*,[46] outlines this behavioural mode. Murray's concern is to make a distinction between low income as such and the behavioural poverty that results from conduct which is anti-social. Field in *Losing Out*[47] sees the situation as more complex and is concerned to reduce inequalities of income and wealth, believing that without a return to full employment there can be no effective solution to the problem of the underclass. Murray's view does appear to attach blame to those who may be considered the victims of society; while Field asserts that it is vital to get away from the idea that the underclass of working age is in some way responsible for their own exclusion from the mainstream of society. Field also maintains there is no racial basis within the British underclass. He concedes that many black people are found within this group, but that this is because they are part of this particularly vulnerable section of society.

In an alternative presentation Mellor,[48] endeavours to critique the whole notion of an underclass associated with the inner city. She asserts that there has been a shift in the analysis of inner city problems to incorporate this notion of the underclass and the threat posed to the rest of society. Mellor herself insists that this adversarial model of the inner city in

---

44   e.g., R Aponte, 'Definitions of the underclass: a critical analysis' in Gans H. [ed.] *Sociology in America*, American Sociological association Presidential Series, California, Sage, 1990, pp. 117-137.

45   Aponte emphasises in his article that until the mid 1970s the few references to the underclass referred to the poor generally, or the poorest of the poor. After the mid 1970s, behavioural criteria came to be operative particularly when the term was taken up within the media. Thereafter the interrelationship of the term with specific problem behaviour, and increasingly with ethnic overtones, introduced a different dynamic. *Ibid.*

46   Murray C., *The Emerging British Underclass,* London, I.E.A., 1990.

47   Field F. *Losing Out*, Oxford, Blackwell, 1989.

48   Mellor R., *The Inner City as Underclass: A Critique and Restatement*, University of Manchester Sociology Department Occasional Paper, No. 23, 1989.

terms of an underclass ghetto is unhelpful and inappropriate to reality. The stereotype which is developing is an amalgamation of the deprived: those with no skills, husbands, health, or autonomy, along with the disaffected: the young, capable, and energetic who may often be black. In popular mythology the inner city has already emerged as a dangerous place where people are subject to indiscriminate violence. Within this view the underclass is one that threatens established values and potentially jeopardises key institutions. As opposers of this stereotyping, Mellor cites the work of Leech and Amin[49] whose work suggests that the term underclass is so ideologically loaded that this undermines its analytical potential. Indeed they agree the term has no validation within the contemporary discourse on marginalisation.

Exploring this issue against the context of the local estate, some young residents were asked what they did with their time – why they got up in the mornings and what time, and the following were some of the answers elicited. From one 'First to stop the dog chewing the postman's hand. I don't know why else I get up. I haven't got a programme for tomorrow say.'[50] A young mother indicated, 'Sometimes I get up at 6 am or 7 am or 8 am; the baby usually get up about 9 am.' [51] Another resident said, 'I get up about 11.30 am or noon.'[52]

These answers were compatible with a survey of social conditions of young people in Wolverhampton[53] where it was emphasised that the life style of the unemployed was unrelated to the public image of them as being more socially active or drinking. The long-term unemployed were more likely to be less active, more centred on the home and more socially isolated. There was a general feeling that society recognised neither their worth nor their existence. Paradoxically work was seen as becoming subjectively more important to the unemployed. Part of the oppression of unemployment seems to concern not only the poverty that being without wages brings, but worse, the fears that crucial aspects of their experience will be misunderstood or even totally inverted in other people's minds.

49   Leech K & Amin K., *A New Underclass?* London, Child Poverty Action Group, 1988.
50   Resident M.
51   Resident K.
52   Resident E.
53   Willis P., *Social Conditions of Young People in Wolverhampton 1984, op. cit.*

There was a sense within the group that the longer young people were unemployed, the more disillusioned they became about their prospects of success and this could contribute to a sense of hopelessness and loss of self-worth and dignity. However, some of the members of this group maintained a sense of their own worth in very distinctive ways and when asked what dignity meant to them the following replies were elicited. One said, 'Being respectable, have respect for yourself and wanting to respect other people.'[54] Another, 'For me personally, it's to dream really, to open my door to anybody. I spend most of my time checking whether it's a bailiff or the police. Dignity for me is to be able to walk down the road with no one pressuring me.'[55] Finally, 'I believe I have dignity, no money but my own self-esteem. I'm quite confident with myself.'[56] The link made between having enough money to live on and feeling a basic human dignity, appears peculiarly powerful.' Given the emotive and inadequate nature of the use of the term 'underclass' with reference to individuals who inhabit the inner city or deprived peripheral housing estates – allied with its ideological overtones – I suggest that the term marginalised is both more accurate and more applicable in this discourse. It is the contention of this book that the term 'underclass' though seen to describe a real situation of multiple deprivation, reinforces a categorisation which is essentially a stigmatisation. It gives further emphasis to an ethos which conceives of individuals as the 'dregs of society' or the 'waste products of the system'. What must be clearly differentiated are the social and economic processes which are accelerating the creation of an alienated section of society – known only by its alien status, and the individuals and groups which make up that section. The ready employment of the term, to refer to sections of the urban poor may be both ill-advised and potentially highly damaging.

By contrast, the term marginalised enables a degree of solidarity to be perceived to exist between deprived people – in the inner city, peripheral housing estates, within the drug culture, or in some form of abusive situation – and the rest of society. The honourable status of the marginal within Christian tradition is an important element in the use of the term marginalised. The chosen people of Israel were a marginalised group of

---

54 Resident A.
55 Resident M.
56 Resident T.

refugees for many years. Christ himself was a marginal member of his society coming from a marginalised area of the country, and the rumours of illegitimacy gave him a blemished social status. His own preference for association with the poor and marginalised has been enshrined – though at times obfuscated – in Christian tradition. Throughout that same tradition the voice of Christian prophecy, prophetic activity and sanctity have been most evidently associated with the margins. The reclamation of this term for use within contemporary society and particularly in association with these areas releases individuals from an imprisoned image and unleashes the potential for decisive action. It also enables further consideration to be given to the increased imposition of marginality and marginal status within contemporary culture and society.[57]

There are striking features about those who are marginalised. Very often they are in a position where they are not involved in the central factors which determine their lives. Dependency is an inevitable development, as they are educated to believe that others will always know best, and that some 'professionals' in social security, or housing, or education, or local planning, or possibly anybody other than themselves, will have the next determining voice in their lives. From the beginning then, possibly at the early age of childhood, they cease to be participatory subjects in life, but rather form objects of concern for one or another agency. Such a process ongoingly undermines the value and self-worth of an individual and progressively renders them more and more inadequate to cope with life. Considered economically irrelevant, and increasingly impoverished, marginalised individuals and groups present a shocking discontinuity to mainstream society. This process has received added momentum under successive governmental regimes, for the stress that there is no alternative has added a perverted benison upon what was conceived as necessity. Pushed to the margins by national and local government, maintained there by the attitude of police, social services and public media – it takes an individual of great character to refuse to accept the negative connota-

---

57   'With the redevelopment of inner cities to form cultural capitals, the poor who previously resided in these areas were moved out or driven into various small enclaves, to provide new living space for the incomers. In order to protect these new areas from what Featherstone terms 'the lower orders', increased security provisions are apparent. Thus the very liberty and licence granted to one group in cultural terms becomes the means of oppression and bondage of another.' Featherstone M., *Consumer Culture and Postmodernism*, London, Sage, 1991, p. 101ff.

tions of marginality as infallible criteria for life – that such characters proliferate on the margins may be evidence of something at work there beyond the confines of our consumer society. 'Every society has its boundaries and its margins just as it has its central roles and its establishments.' Hastings continues, 'In the end for a society to be understood aright, it has to be considered in the light of both: not only what is happening to the people on the margin – what they are doing and what is being done to them.'[58]

Grey is the colour of marginality as popular mythology conceives it – but such a colour has never received the imprimatur of Christian tradition. In this chapter with at times, considerable eloquence, residents have expressed their views about the material circumstances in which they find themselves. Through this we have begun to appreciate that the term 'marginal' may possess rich possibilities within the discourse.

---

58   Hastings A., *The Faces of God: Essays on Church and Society*, London, Geoffrey Chapman, 1975, p. 18.

Chapter 2

Historical Context

> ...the mass of the people in England do still regard themselves as Christian and a considerable injustice is done to their sensibilities when churchmen discount their, rather impure religious instincts as too diluted to be of value.[1]

The previous chapter outlined the grey social context of the Heath Town estate reflected in the physical environment and subject to increasing deterioration through the pressure of escalating social and economic pressures. There is no possibility of other than marginal existence upon the estate. Yet it is here that members of the Hope Community have chosen to live and to enter into that same condition of marginality. This is part of their vision: to be a Christian presence amongst the people.

> We are a reflective Christian community presence among the people of Heath Town, to nurture with them human community, which witnesses to the dignity and self-worth of each individual and which lives this out as communal responsibility and caring in the wider community.[2]

In this willingness to engage directly with those on the urban margins the Hope Community stands within a Christian tradition of such involvement. It is the purpose of this chapter briefly to examine the more recent history of the involvement of the church with the urban margins. Here it is necessary to explore: the continuance of some forms of religious belief – implicit religion – amongst this section of the population; and the particular contribution of Roman Catholicism and its close though diminishing ties with the working class during the twentieth century.

---

1   Norman E., *Church and Society in England 1770–1970*, Oxford, Clarendon Press, 1976, p. 424.
2   Hope Community Mission Statement 1994.

Historical Ambiguity

The Christian tradition of involvement with the working class is one marked by a certain ambiguity. One feature of this was the distinction made between the deserving and undeserving poor. This issue became particularly acute with the transition from a predominantly rural way of life to an increasingly urban one, as the eighteenth century gave way to the nineteenth.[3]

Such categorisation has a contemporary corollary in the distinction made between those who are considered deservingly dependent on assistance from benefits, and those who are seen as undeserving, generally associated with the stigma of 'underclass' [or more pejoratively as 'social security scroungers']. Thus the residents of the Heath Town estate, within this view, would comprise predominantly the latter with a minority representation of the former. It is the contention of this chapter that such a distinction is both unjustified and unhelpful.

The history of church involvement with the marginalised in Britain has been one well-chronicled by social historians and sociologists of religion. A notable ambiguity has been the apparent unwillingness of this group – historically associated with the working class – to attend church. This was of particular concern during the Victorian era. Victorian churchgoers believed that churches were important. Society it was claimed would fall apart without morality, morality was impossible without religion and religion would disappear without the churches.[4] A large part of the working class played little or no part in organised religious life in nineteenth century Britain and this trend was maintained into the twentieth century.

In urban and rural areas, the upper and middle classes were under far heavier social pressure than the poor to attend some kind of church. This highlighted the question of whether the poor could be fully integrated into congregations where the whole tone was set by their social superiors.

---

3   For further discussion of this point see Preston R., *Explorations in Theology 9*, London, SCM, 1981, p. 124.

4   'The greater a person's stake in social cohesion and social stability, the greater the appeal of the argument: society will collapse without the churches.' Cox, J., *The English Churches in a Secular Society*, Oxford, OUP, 1982, p. 271.

Indeed sermons and prayers spoke the language of the elite and echoed their concerns. It was a discourse far removed from working class life and understanding of religion. Thus the poor who did attend were liable to feel marginal members of the congregation. Developments in the first half of the nineteenth century emphasised this sense of marginality and led to further alienation of the poor from the Established Churches and also from many Free Church congregations. By the mid-nineteenth century it was clear that the churches had not persuaded the emerging urban working class to attend Sunday services en masse.[5] However, the unjustified sense of failure was the result of unrealistic expectations. By 1900 according to Cox,[6] churches had become accustomed to what had been the case for many years, that regular churchgoing was only for the minority of the population. Callum Brown[7] maintains that more generally working class women remained in close contact with religious ideas and institutions. Amongst the female population church-going appeared an integral factor of feminine respectability.[8]

However there continued to be religious activity amongst the working class and the established churches found new and significant social functions at both parochial and national level. Through sacramental rites of passage and the network of social welfare institutions with which it was involved, the rural and urban church maintained contact with the working class in ways which focusing attention on attendance at public worship fails to demonstrate. Indeed the churches created a vast parochial and philanthropic network which provided the sacraments and social services to the working class and the poor. Virtually all the activities of the welfare state were prefigured as the churches responded to urban social conditions.

With the advent of universal education and the legal necessity for some form of religious education by trained professionals, a diffusion of religious knowledge was promoted through the state school system. Indeed this in itself imposed a degree of knowledge of organised religion amongst working class children. In contemporary Britain this may be the

---

5 c.f. *Ibid.* p. 4.
6 *Ibid.* p. 273.
7 Brown C., *The Social History of Religion in Scotland since 1730*, London, Methuen, 1987, p. 251.
8 For elaboration of this point see *ibid.*

only source for many of religious knowledge if not of religious belief. Cox argues[9] that school rather than churches were responsible for a de-mystification of religion concerned more with ethical orientation. The technological developments of the latter part of the twentieth century have also seen the contribution of religious broadcasting which receives a wide audience. Both media activity and religious teaching in schools have served as a substitute for active church participation and sustains in diverse ways a form of diffusive Christianity.

Implicit Religion

The work of Ahern and Davie has been valuable in understanding the nature of this diffusive Christianity or as contemporary writers have pre-ferred to refer to it – implicit religion.[10] The evidence that there exists religion 'below street-level' is another way of describing what one re-searcher has termed 'subterranean theologies', 'that luxuriant theological undergrowth which provides the working core of belief more often than is realised.'[11] Studies in implicit religion and urban theology have also evinced a common belief in the paranormal, in one form or another – ghosts, fate, the occult, clairvoyancy, etc. – while at the same time there is a readiness to turn to the church in connection with specific events – notably death. Such inconsistencies are not perceived as such by indi-viduals, but rather part of everyday thought, indeed it is now a hackneyed statement that 'orthodox Christian theology plays little part in the every-day life of our nation.'[12] Work in this field has also emphasised the real-ity that religious beliefs are strongly related to a particular cultural in-heritance and are absorbed as a whole package of wisdom. They contain largely unexamined assumptions and indeed are almost unconscious parts

---

9   *Ibid.* p. 268ff.
10   There is also the contribution of the Religious Papers of the department of Sociol-ogy University of Leeds.
11   Martin D. cited in Ahern G. and Davie G., *Inner City God*, London, Hodder & Stoughton, 1987, p. 70.
12   *Ibid.* p. 38.

44

of an individual's thinking. It is only a major crisis, which will bring religious ideas to the fore, unless they are elicited in some less threatening manner. It is here that account must be taken of the profoundly inarticulate nature of much common religion,[13] and the gulf that exists between conventional religious language and a very large sector of the population who are excluded from the discourse. Indeed for many marginalised people the church is seen as one more 'authority', another 'them' to be mistrusted along with other authorities social, educational, etc., all of whom appear to communicate in a language which is unintelligible to those in the inner city.[14]

Davie argues that if the church's aim might be described as a need to create contexts in which 'belief' can emerge from a semi-conscious level and be gradually transformed into something closer to an authentic Christian faith, it does not always follow that this is achieved in a uniform way. Indeed, the role of the churches at the end of this century may well centre around this very important area of creating the conditions or contexts in which the unexpressed or inarticulate 'spirit' can surface and become a vital part of the discourse.

There is a clear discrepancy between believing and belonging which Davie perceives as most acute among the urban working class in Urban Priority Areas. Here belief persists but the reluctance to adopt religious practice involves also the mistrust of any kind of institutional life and involvement therein. In line with historical precedent, it is evident that on the urban margins belief is not equated with liturgical practice which at best is seen as unnecessary and at worst hypocritical. Various views were expressed about why people attended church by residents of the Heath Town estate. In one meeting at the Community flat, only one of those consulted was a regular churchgoer, but many had views on why others went to church. 'People go to church because they want to go to heaven.'[15] 'The only time I go to church is when I feel guilty. The other

---

13   'Folk' or 'common' religion can be defined as: 'those beliefs and practices of an overtly religious nature which are not under the domination of a prevailing religious institution.' Towler R., *'Homo Religiosus: Sociological Problems in the Study of Religion'*, London, Constable, 1974, chapter 8 cited in Davie G., 'The nature of belief in the inner city', Ahern G. and Davie G., *Inner City God, op. cit.*, p. 34.

14   See particularly *ibid.* p. 60.

15   Resident W.

thing why I don't go, when I need to go it's locked. I've been told to go round the back and peer in the windows, but it's not the same.'[16]

The very middle class organisational pattern of the churches reflect middle class ways of believing and are expressed in predominantly middle class language – this of its very nature is problematic for those who live on the urban margins. 'My view of church is that it's run by people with a good education. The majority are from middle class backgrounds. The church is sort of aloof from the poor.'[17] He went on to say, 'The church in Britain seems cut off from the people it's supposed to be representing. To me the church is people.'[18]

Faith in the City[19] echoes a similar concern about the middle class nature of much that occurs within the churches. 'It is the consistently middle class presentation of the gospel and style of church life which creates a gulf between it and most working class people.'[20] The comments here expressed appear to emphasise the reality that those involved in running the church are themselves drawn from the same narrow background as those whom they continue to spend their time serving.

The mixture of superstition and belief that generally appears to pervade much of the religious belief in inner cities leads to a certain policy dilemma on the part of the churches and Christian involvement. Recent studies indicate that the most sensible policy seems to be one which uses popular religion as a base upon which to build, but at the same time stresses the need to 'affirm' selectively; i.e., to strengthen those elements that are closest to an authentic Christian faith and to discourage those that are not. This strategy appears to give value to the expressions of faith arising from the people, but the attitude implies a judgement over and against established practice. It is not merely a question of semantics to argue that a real endeavour to listen to the reality of what religious experience is emerging from the people with an openness to consider it might be calling the establishment to some change, might seem a more positive

---

16   Resident O.
17   c.f., 'The clergy are seen in stereotype as well-fed, callous and reactionary.' *Faith in the City: A Call for Action by Church and Nation. The Report of the Archbishop's Commission on Urban Priority Areas*, London, Church House Publishing, 1985, p. 28.
18   Resident M.
19   *Faith in the City, op. cit.*
20   *Ibid.* p. 66.

attitude. This would be to affirm the right of those on the margins to participate in the discourse.

The Roman Catholic Phenomenon

Gill[21] maintains that over the period of 150 years for which data exists regarding church attendance figures, the Roman Catholic churches were consistently full. This phenomenon is in part due to the completely different practices of church building. Instead of providing more buildings to accommodate numbers, more services were provided.[22] Thus even in contemporary Britain it is not unknown for there to be five masses in a church on one Sunday.

The ordinary membership of the Roman Catholic Church, unlike other denominations, incorporated a substantial working class element. For Irish immigrants church membership was part of their patrimony and one of the ways in which identity could be maintained within an alien environment. Allied with this were the exacting demands which membership made on individuals, demands which of their very nature served to authenticate the church's claim to mediate the sacred. In addition the church was consistently able to incorporate different classes within its structured framework.[23] All might be found attending the mass, the central form of worship, celebrated throughout the world in the same manner, utilising Latin as a universal language and providing a means of personal and private sanctification within a corporate and universal setting. The emphasis upon 'the one true church' gave a certainty and confidence to Catholic identity. This was of particular importance in working class

---

21 Gill, R., *The Myth of the Empty Church*, London, SPCK, 1993.
22 Gill, R. notes the remark of Arthur Black in *The British Weekly*, 23 Feb, 1928. 'How wise has been this Church in limiting the number of its centres, using them more fully and concentrating strength in a few rather than dividing limited energies over many.' *Ibid.* p. 79.
23 Such incorporation was not always able to bridge class barriers and indeed it is debatable whether the cleavage between the mainly Irish urban working classes has ever been bridged completely.

areas where the basis of attachment to the church was first through the family and thereafter via communal solidarity.

According to Archer[24] one of the strengths of the Roman Catholic Church has been the ability to encompass a wide range of religious sensibilities including the non church going and a spectrum of specific ways of relating to the sacred in terms of ceremony, mystery, symbol and distinctive practices.

The watershed of the second Vatican Council had its consequent effect upon the urban Catholic community, but changes had been in motion already. The old working class communities had been breaking up as younger generations were moved out of the inner city areas and onto new peripheral housing estates. This dispersal of traditional Catholic communities meant that in many areas the church's symbolic function in old working class communities was ending as it was revealed that the bonds of these communities were related more to shared experience and values than involvement with definite church activity. Thus the nature of Catholic identity was in decline and as the once immigrant community was absorbed into British society, Catholicism was no longer seen as important and symbolic of difference.

Against this context, the changes wrought by the Conciliar fathers in no way served to stem this tide of change rather it received fresh stimulus as, it appeared that the former things of Catholicism were simply passing away.[25] Most marked were the liturgical changes which evoked passionate acceptance or rejection provoking dissension within congregations. The contrast with the former liturgy was marked. Whereas pre-Vatican II the old mass appeared to provide something distinctively out of the ordinary and Roman Catholic, the new mass appeared little different from other liturgical practices. The old mass had allowed the space for individuals to engage with the mystery of the sacred in their own way. By contrast the new liturgy allowed little room for individual withdrawal but was a more rational form adapted by certain intellectual conceptions of what was appropriate in this particular part of the universal church. According to Archer the new mass presupposed a gathered community whose members would be already known to one another but rarely was

---

24 Archer A., *The Two Catholic Churches – A Study in Oppression*, London, SCM, 1986.

25 *Ibid.* p. 133.

this the case in Britain. It endeavoured to transcend class barriers, but the very mode of its language was middle class. For working class people to take on the new religious dispositions meant adopting the values of another class and another form of discourse.

What was achieved Archer denigrates as 'the evacuation of meaning from the old symbolism and the emasculation of its gestures.'[26] Access to the transcendent, which lay at the heart of the mass, was not now apparent to confused congregations, and as a result numbers of Catholics felt unable to trust themselves to the new ritual. Meanwhile the paraliturgical forms, which had fed Catholic devotional practice, no longer seemed encouraged by the new dispensation. In particular the predominance of mystery, which encouraged reverential participation, appeared to have been swept away. Many for whom the devotional life of rosary, benediction, novena, and first Fridays had sustained their commitment found no attraction in the prayer groups, liturgy groups and discussion groups of the renewed paraliturgical forms. There appeared few remnants of the non-intellectual forms of piety to which such individuals could relate, and ostracism was the natural consequence. Within the post-Vatican II church the mass was required to be an engaged community experience.[27]

Within the Roman Catholic community, although the liturgy of the past was divorced from everyday reality, yet it assisted by giving meaning to that reality. Here symbol and mystery helped to convey the sense of a transcendent larger reality which in some mysterious way gave meaning to the present. Catholicism in this way was a vehicle for the working class conviction that there was some point in an insecure and uncertain life. With the demystification process which underpinned many of the Vatican II liturgical modifications, intelligibility undermined meaningful mystery to the diminishment of ordinary life. There seemed little emphasis on the mysterious symbolic security underpinning life, where space was provided for individual dreams and devotions, rather rational middle class forms and participative communitarian ideas came to dominate worship leaving little room for personal devotions.

Also, paradoxically those with only a loose connection with the church but who nevertheless had found some shelter within the broader Catholic fold, were further alienated by the changes. Under the pre-

---

26   *Ibid.* p. 144.
27   For further discussion see *ibid.* p. 194.

Vatican II dispensation which had appeared to some coercive, those Catholics who failed to attend church were regarded not as individuals who were deliberately opting out of their Catholic allegiance but somewhat indulgently as those whose return should be sought. In the new post-Vatican II era the drift away from the church comprised an increasingly large number of the working class population as a new orthodoxy demanded an uncompromising commitment or a recognised exclusion.[28]

The traditional supports of clergy and religious appeared more suspect. What had formally been seen to lie within the competence of the priest was now decided by the informed consciences of an increasingly educated middle class laity.[29] Meanwhile the relative respectful seclusion of religious life was now exposed to public gaze, to the confusion of laity and clergy alike.[30]

Anthony Archer sees the church of Vatican II as geared towards an intellectual elite, and consequently, eroding its own traditional base among the marginalised.[31] According to *Faith in the City*, Roman Catholicism still has a strong numerical base within Urban Priority Areas, which employ proportionately more than average clergy and religious. Yet according to Hornsby-Smith, English Catholics may be termed a 'domesticated denomination' unlikely to rock the boat of British complacency to any marked extent, content rather with the status quo and marginal social engineering to file down the most pointed injustices.'[32]

---

28   c.f. *ibid.* p. 156ff.

29   Hornsby-Smith notes evidence of, 'A process of laicization at both the individual and organisational levels. This process manifests itself in the increasing differentiation of religious belief and moral decision-making where previously the priest was the sole focus of legitimate teaching and arbiter of morality.' Hornsby-Smith M., *Roman Catholic Beliefs in England: Customary Catholicism and Transformations of Religious Authority*, Cambridge, CUP, 1991, p. 230. By contrast the thrust of the papal encyclical *Veritatis Splendor*, London, Catholic Truth Society, 1993, may be seen as one attempt to withdraw moral criteria from the particularity of individualistic interpretation and restore prominence to the guide-lines of the church.

30   'For the nun to clamber off her pedestal, exchange her habit for ordinary clothing with cardigans and sensible shoes and engage in theological controversy and general insubordination, was both confusing to the laity and a challenge to the clergy.' Hornsby-Smith M., *Roman Catholic Beliefs in England*, op. cit., p. 164.

31   In a not dissimilar way to the movement of the Labour Party, since 1945, away from its own working class base.

32   See Hornsby-Smith M., *Roman Catholics in England*, op. cit., p. 216.

The fastest growing churches are the Independent predominantly black churches, which not only draw people together for a particular form of worship but in addition provide a series of support mechanisms for the minority ethnic community. The majority of black Christians live in Urban Priority Areas, and most are of West Indian origin. Other denominations have targeted the urban areas as priority project areas: the Methodist 'Mission Alongside the Poor'; United Reformed Church and Baptist Union have developed missionary strategies; the Salvation Army has continued its own distinctive mission to the poorest. What *Faith in the City* clearly emphasised[33] was that the Church of England had never enjoyed a golden age in regard to urban Britain. Rather the predominantly middle class congregations have found the way of life of the urban poor simply repulsive.

Unrelated to daily life

Reactions to the church from the people on the Heath Town Estate were gauged from attendance at different meetings where opinions were voiced and from interviews with individuals. What emerged was a sense of loss of contact with the institution, which was seen as alien. At the same time paradoxically, there was still considerable feeling that the church should be speaking in favour of the poor. One resident indicated a seminal view amongst the fieldworker group that God is especially concerned with the poor. His notion that a 'true church' would in some way inaugurate the eschaton is both a challenge to, and critique of, the prevailing ecclesiastical situation. 'We're the poor people, all are God's people, but God's especially for the poor. God's people are the poor and God's tool is the church – that's how it's seen. The church should speak out against the government in favour of the poor.'[34]

The authoritarian nature of some of the mainstream churches with structured hierarchies proved problematic for another resident. 'The

---

33   *Ibid.* pp. 45-46.
34   Resident J.

church is very hierarchical. If God is good, if there is a God, there shouldn't be a church based on hierarchy, shouldn't be any positions.'[35]

When daily life includes reference to so many professional authorities whose determining voices enhance or disrupt life for the marginalised, other authority structures, however benevolent, are unwelcome. No member of the statutory professional agencies lives on the estate, although many work there during the week. Also there is no church or minister's house actually on the estate. Thus the presence of the Hope Community comprising both religious sisters and committed lay women is a peculiarly powerful expression of church in the midst of the people.

'The problem with church is that it's so different to what people do everyday.'[36] Within Heath Town, there is a stark lack of contact between what is thought or felt or known to go on in church, and the daily life of most of the individuals on the estate. It is so different from what people do everyday. The everyday activities and concerns of people involve: the daily grind of traversing fouled footpaths; of being subject to interminable ongoing noise; of coping with vandalised laundries; standing in long queues waiting to 'sign on' for benefits; looking after children; and for some the boredom of countless unoccupied hours. This lack of engagement of the church in the ordinary lives of individuals who do not make up a constituent membership is still a distinctive feature of most denominations. Not only is the church not seen as relevant to these daily activities, there is the conviction that church personnel have no idea what ordinary life on a peripheral housing estate might be like and little interest in finding out. 'The majority of the people who run [the church] have no idea actually what life's like in a place like this. Living here I feel the church is out of touch.' He went on to say, 'I think people running the church should be educated more about what's going on and should come into places like this more and speak to the people.'[37]

For those who do endeavour to enter any sacred portals, the practical difficulties they face with regard to services mitigates against the potential for the real sense of acceptance and belonging. My own experience of regularly attending a local church exemplified this point. The services although intelligible to those who attended, would prove relatively in-

---

35   Resident J.
36   Resident T.
37   Resident M.

comprehensible to any unversed in the particular rubrics of that denomination. The church itself was only twenty minutes walk away from the estate, but in terms of the reality of contact between the two venues they could have been continents apart.

This point was one of particular discussion with a resident who had lived on the estate for only two years. He had opted to come to this area, so in this way was unusual amongst the residents, most of whom were there by default, having been allocated by the Council. He was also a regular churchgoer. He raised the very simple point that even in the matter of following the service and knowing what page the congregation were reading when it came to a prayer book could be a difficulty. Not all clergy give a clear indication. Also for those whose reading is habitually tabloid newspapers, a book of any size may appear to be an obstacle, while the position of the illiterate is made even more untenable. 'Things like that make it very difficult for people to get involved in it.'[38]

One of the fieldworkers told of a time when she took one of the residents along to another local church, and the impact on the resident, herself, and the congregation of the new 'participant'.[39] 'She was terrified. I suppose we sang, the people there knew some songs she knows, and she enjoyed that but otherwise it was all words and books and you had to dress up and worst of all there were people looking at her. You could tell she wasn't a churchgoing person.'[40]

There can be very little opportunity for people to participate if they are not familiar with the liturgy. Those who are so familiar may find it very helpful, but those for whom it is unfamiliar find it difficult to attune to what is taking place. As this resident indicated: 'I'm sure some people would like to get involved but they're fearful of saying the wrong thing.'[41]

---

38   Resident Clergyman D.
39   c.f. 'Most people want to feel comfortable and secure in church. We want the people sitting next to us to be like us. Recently a gentleman told me that he would not be able to go to church and sit down next to people who wear black jackets with aluminium spangles. 'Those people frighten me' he said 'and I don't want to be frightened when I go to church.' Faucher T., 'Outsiders need not apply', *The Tablet*, 12 December, 1992, p. 1566.
40   Fieldworker C.
41   *Ibid.*

With regard to the possibility of change in present church structures to include those who might like to attend but who find the present format too difficult to cope with, this resident was somewhat dubious with regard to possibilities. There was little likelihood that established congregations would be willing to change to become more inclusive bodies. 'There's a lot of people who are very comfortable with the way things are. They will accept certain innovations but basically they don't want it to go too far from what they're familiar with.'[42] The clearly stated difficulties of: the unintelligibleness of ritual; a perception of the middle class nature of church membership; and a predominantly white grouping are features which were reiterated in talking with local residents. The question was asked of one black resident whether he liked going to any particular church? 'I prefer the Pentecostal Church; it's my sort of rhythm but what I don't prefer is that they knock the doctrines of the other churches which doesn't sit well with me. I don't feel comfortable, which is a shame.'[43]

This resident elaborated his own sense of unease with the very structure of the churches, in particular the hierarchical nature of a number of denominations. Here, the violence he is aware of in his own daily life seems to find an echo in the verbal violence he feels he has witnessed amongst adherents of particular religious affiliations. His conclusion has a seeming cynical inevitability – 'church lets you down'! 'I see the church as being too dogmatic and regimented. When I say this I mean the pope and the bishops and the pastors. Well not so much the pastors and the ministers but they are the first level of the hierarchy.' He went on to say 'You've all the people who don't believe in Christianity or anything standing there watching people verbally kicking the shit out of each other. People then say – hang on I'm better outside the church if that's what goes on in there.'[44]

The distinct sense of fair play, which causes this resident to rile in the face of prejudice and bigotry, serves as a poignant criticism of inter-denominational feuding. It also highlights for this resident a basic clerical authority structure that he finds incompatible with his own philosophy of life.

---

42   Resident Clergyman D.
43   Resident T.
44   *Ibid.*

One of the fieldworkers, summarising her own perception of the relationship of individuals with the churches during her seven years on the estate, was predominantly aware of the general feeling of alienation from the church. Yet it was not that the church was irrelevant to individuals, for many had strong views about why they did not attend. Poignantly for some their reasons focus in a lack of self-worth, as individuals feel themselves 'not good enough'. 'The chief feeling about church is one of alienation from it really. People don't understand its ritual. They associate it with something, middle-class. For the black people it's seen as predominantly white. She went on to explain the reasons people give for not going, 'I've no good clothes to wear. I've no money to put in the collection plate.' Yet at the same time 'They are very conscious of sin in their lives and yet they want to pray and to worship God. They want to be together.'[45]

The radical revisioning of the nature of church which has taken place for some individuals on the estate is connected to their involvement with the Hope Community. Here the forms of activity engaged therein has caused numbers to see this now as their particular form of church. It has a vastly different appeal from the traditional denominational forms. This revivified life appears in stark contrast to the worsening socio-economic position of many on the estate, a position clearly exposed in the follow-up report to *Faith in the City*. 'Our conclusion must be that for a considerable number of poor people the picture looks bleaker than it did in 1985. For many it is because their relative position is so much weaker.' The report went on to state, 'From a Christian perspective the experience of the poor and those who live in Urban Priority Areas remains a grave and fundamental injustice.'[46]

This report from the General Synod of the Church of England in 1990, gives some indication of the ongoing concern that has been generated amongst members of the hierarchy with regard to the poverty evinced in the Urban Priority Areas. It also indicates the attempt – on the basis of careful research – to inform national opinion and to bring to bear a degree of Christian pressure upon national policy-making. By contrast the work of the Hope Community is small-scale, local and individual in

---

45   Fieldworker A.
46   *Living Faith in the City*, London, General Synod of the Church of England, 1990, p. 89.

its outreach, but the effect in terms of some residents of the estate has been profound and substantial.

Marginality – chosen and imposed

Contemporary British history bears witness to the ongoing concentration of the working class and the marginalised within urban environments, and the problems confronting Christian ministry in these areas. Nowadays rather than the influx of Irish immigrants causing concern, the focus has shifted to consideration of immigrants of Asian and West Indian origin and their second and third generation families. The generic sense of distrust of the institutional church has developed into a sense of alienation based on the inability to relate the reality of everyday life to the way in which the church presents itself. The church today is rarely in the midst of marginalised people.

The failure of the vision of modernity, and the creation of marginality in a social economic and political context, has been reinforced by ecclesiastical structures, which have accommodated the prevailing emphasis of society.

Within contemporary society, the church holds a marginalised position. A fraction of society, less than 10% of the population have some regular involvement with any Christian church. Yet these self-same institutions appear to claim a certain monopoly with regard to Christian vision. The vision of the churches is confined within the respectable body of its membership, and is not seen as emerging from outside its own boundaries. This apparently claustrophobic grasp of the reality of God at work within the world appears at best short-sighted, and at worst positively debilitating. The effect is to emphasis the move towards ensuring continuing respectability and a measure of power within the framework of society for a respectable few, while neglecting to listen, hear or learn from the very marginal elements on whose behalf the churches so often claim to be working.

Accordingly, the marginality of the church is one from which the church appears to seek evasive action, not seeing it as an opportunity for dynamic impetus. Consequently, a primary concern still tends to be diminishing numbers, and the aim is to increase numbers in the pew, rather than to emerge from behind defensive walls into the uncomfortable reality of the everyday lives of individuals and groups on the margins. It is noteworthy how the myth of a golden age of full churches still seems to underlie much of the policy deliberations within the denominations. Such sterile debate focuses upon the search for an ideal form of liturgical life, which will draw numbers of people to return to the churches. In so doing the churches continue to distance themselves from particularly the most vulnerable on the urban margins. This inability to see marginal status as an opportunity to be welcomed, rather than a failure to be combated, engenders an inability to relate to those on the margins, those who have been forced into marginal status. It would appear then that the churches may be trampling upon their Christian vision in the pursuit of an illusion. The illusion that on some millenarian day in the future, great numbers will come pouring back into the churches which have faithfully maintained their practice. There is a vast discrepancy in terms of adherence to this view between those who are engaged in the church locally, and members of institutional hierarchies.

Finally, there is the situation of those who have chosen marginality, the religious Community living and working on the estate. Here, that very choice, and the willingness openly to interact with the people in the pragmatic reality of their lives has led to a new appreciation of the life of the marginalised, the work of God among them, and the possibilities to be learned from them. A potential further dimension of marginalisation emerges in consideration of the life and work of the Community. Here the willingness to risk steps into the unknown was a prime requisite both in the formation of the Community and in the continued maintenance and expansion of its life and work.

Within this chapter we have seen the contribution of history to understanding the interaction of the churches with the urban poor. The contemporary relationship between the Roman Catholic Church and the urban poor is founded on a clearer understanding of post-Vatican II development. Reappropriating the positive dynamic of marginality within the churches framework indicates vibrant possibilities for an enlarged discourse. However, the ambiguity of institutional response to the urban margins hampers church response.

Chapter 3

Living Embodiment of the Tradition

The contribution of women religious to the humanisation of the world and of the church... will be nothing less than the actual transformation of the gospel message today.[1]

To accept the effects seen in the very oppressive poverty of the people very seriously without judging or/and evaluating; the necessity of listening deeply to their experience, the meanings those experiences have for them and the interpretations they give them. In that way we come to understand them a little more deeply as persons who are poor, instead of the poor.[2]

Let there be love, peace and hope shared among us – those mean different things to different people but the sisters exude them for us in Heath Town.[3]

The previous chapter in exploring the recent history of church involvement with the marginalised indicated a contemporary malaise undermining such contact. This chapter gives consideration to the life and work of a community which has committed itself to living among marginalised people and sharing their everyday reality. In this process there is enacted, by virtue of need, something of that profound listening which Gadamer[4] asserts is the rigour of hermeneutical experience. It is listening to a person who has something to say and is seeking the words to make self intelligible. The words may well be most ordinary and commonplace and yet may still be able to express a meaning in what is said and unsaid. The consequences of such profound listening, as seen in the lives of marginalised individuals, is a growth both in self-confidence and in the ability

---

1   Pope John XXIII, cited in Azevedo M., *Vocation for Mission: The Challenge of Religious Life Today*, New York, Paulist Press, 1988, p. 168.
2   Coene S., 'Clinical pastoral education with the poor' *The Journal of Pastoral Care*, 37, 1983, pp. 90-97.
3   Resident L.
4   Gadamer H., *Truth and Method*, trans. Weinsdheimer J. and Marshall D., London, Sheed & Ward, 1989. c.f. Introduction.

actively to articulate, however tentatively, the presence of God in their lives. 'I used to be a bit of a loner before I knew the sisters. All people come whether they believe in religion or not, and we sit and we talk and we basically enjoy life. I've made many valuable friends through that.' This resident went on to say 'Through these friendships I've seen at first hand how God works, through helping, caring, sharing and praying when things are tough.'[5]

The Impact of Vatican II

The history of the coming of the sisters to Heath Town is part of the history of the Catholic Church in Britain after Vatican II. The desire to renew the church led the conciliar fathers to call for a major overhaul of religious life and practice. [6] The laconic terms in which this document on the renewal of religious life is phrased gave no premonition of the massive cultural shock it was to precipitate throughout the international community of religious. Nearly thirty years later, religious congregations are still trying to come to terms with the profound mythological shift which occurred as the once immutable body was seen to metamorphose. The Council that was to 'renew the wonders of Pentecost' was likened in an editorial in *The Times* to 'an earthquake which so substantially changed the landscape of Christian religion that maps previously drawn were irrelevant.'[7]

---

5   Resident M.
6   'In order that the church of today may benefit more fully from lives consecrated by the profession of the counsels and from the vital function which they perform, the holy synod makes the following provisions... The up-to-date renewal of the religious life comprising both a constant return to the sources of the whole of the Christian life and to the primitive inspiration of the institutes, and their adaptation to the changed conditions of our time. This renewal, under the impulse of the Holy Spirit and with the guidance of the Church.' *Perfectae Caritatis*, in Flannery A., [ed.], *Vatican Council II: The Conciliar and Post Conciliar Documents*, London, Geoffrey Chapman, 1975, pp. 611-706.
7   *The Times*, March, 1987.

The aftermath was variously described as a 'state of chaos', a time of 'ferment and flux' and the 'death-knell' of organised religion – if not of God himself. The Church had begun to recognise that if it were to continue to serve the people of God and bring contemporary people into contact with the vivifying and perennial energies of the gospel it must learn to speak in dialogue with them, using a language and idiom which would be comprehensible and relevant. A new vision, a new world view and a new discourse was sought which might dialogue with the modern world. In particular the question of justice appeared in a number of conciliar documents – and of greater significance – questions of injustice. The Council fathers recognised an increasing awareness of injustice within the world with regard to the tremendous inequalities existing between wealthy and poor which caused stark division among people. 'Many of these causes spring from excessive economic inequalities and from excessive slowness in applying the needed remedies. Other causes spring from a quest for power and from contempt for personal rights.'[8]

An emphasis upon the 'poor' and the 'little ones' was one which echoed a significant development in the church and particularly amongst religious orders. Constitutions of many religious congregations committed them to this integration which in recent times has commonly been specified in a decision to make an 'option for the poor'. Added impetus was given to this development by the 1971 Synod of Bishops. Here there was a clear call to consider the life of the poor in a manner previously unknown. The Synod outlined a detailed analysis of injustice in the world, and denounced a whole series of 'voiceless injustices'. Most memorable is the challenging declaration that: 'Action on behalf of justice and participation in the transformation of the world fully appear to us as a constitutive dimension of the preaching of the Gospel.'[9]

The Bishops had made it clear that the church must stand with the poor and oppressed if it were to be faithful to the gospel mandate. In the face of such a challenge, contemporary religious life appeared to demand the integration of faith with the search for social justice. Added impetus

---

8   *Gausdium et Spes*, para. 83, in Flannery A. [ed.] *Vatican II: The Conciliar and Post Conciliar Documents, op. cit.* pp. 903-1014.

9   Synod of Bishops, 30 November, 1971, in Flannery A. [ed.] *Vatican Council II More Postconciliar Documents*, New York, Costello, 1982, pp. 695-710.

was given in the same year by the publication of *Octogesima Adveniens*[10] on the eighteenth anniversary of *Rerum Novarum*[11] and the tenth anniversary of *Mater et Magistra*.[12] This encyclical urged the incorporation into every sphere of Catholic life that dimension of Christian responsibility in the world. It emphasised that action on behalf of justice was the responsibility of every Christian, and indeed every Christian organisation and institution. The principle of justice was extolled to be operative in personal, communitarian and all forms of social life, without exception. The attribution of such prominence to this principle further encouraged the development of liberation theology, particularly within the non-European church of Central and South America. Here the names of Gutierez, Segundo, Sobrino, Galilea, Boff have became synonymous with an alternative theological vision.[13] Over the years there has been a marked increase in practical concern for the poor and oppressed, and the attempt to translate into deeds an option of solidarity with the poor. In 1975 *Evangelii Nuntiandi* added further encouragement to this development when it gave emphasis to the move, 'to bring the good news from city to city and especially to the poor, who are often better disposed to receive it.'[14]

---

10   Pope Paul VI, *Octogesima Adveniens*, 1971.

11   *Rerum Novarum*, 1891, Pope Leo XIII in this encyclical spoke out against the inhuman conditions which were the normal plight of working people in industrial societies.

12   *Mater et Magistra* 1961. In this and *Pacem in Terris* 1963, Pope John XXIII 'set forth a number of principles to guide both Christians and policy makers in addressing the gap between rich and poor nations and the threats to world peace. Schultheis M., DeBerri E. and Henriot P., *Our Best Kept Secret: The Rich Heritage of Catholic Social Teaching*, London, CAFOD, 1988, p. 7.

13   Gutierez sees an 'irruption of the poor' into history such that society will never be able to ignore them again. The spirituality emerging in reaction to this irruption finds God in the midst of suffering.

14   Paul VI, *Evangelii Nuntiandi*, 8 December, 1975, para. 6, in Flannery A. [ed.] *Vatican Council II: More Post Conciliar Documents, op. cit.* pp. 711-761.

Acknowledgement of failure and the British 'option'

Within England and Wales fresh stimulus was given to the initiatives involving poor and marginalised people by the Declaration of the Justice Sector of the National Pastoral Congress held in Liverpool in 1980. Here, in an unprecedented statement, an acknowledgement was made of the failure of the church to combat the prevailing ethos of society and to proclaim the gospel message particularly with regard to the poor.[15] The principle stressed throughout this report was that of the need to hear the Word of God through the experience of the powerless, and for this to determine any apostolic action in the area of social concern. Indeed the tone of the report was to emphasise that it was the poor and the marginalised who must set the agenda for action, and who would be able to give authentic voice to their own needs and concerns. 'We must hear the Word of God addressed to us in the experience of our brothers and sisters in the world, and for us this means above all the powerless.'[16]

The form of listening advocated is resonant with the emphasis given by Gadamer,[17] particularly with regard to the importance attached to hearing what is coming from the other, and allowing that to transform our own understanding. For the Church of 1980 it was a challenging position to advocate and even more to consider adopting. The ringing admission

---

15   *Liverpool 1980: Official Report of the National Pastoral Congress*, London, St Paul Publications, 1981. p. 290 The Report began: 'On behalf of the Church of England and Wales, we in the Justice Sector of the National Pastoral Congress feel compelled to begin by placing on record our failure to proclaim the Gospel of Jesus Christ in all its fullness in this land. We regret our failure as a Church to combat the prevailing national mood of insularity, to identify with the poor in our midst and to work vigorously for a more peaceful world...We wish humbly to confess this failure to the poor who live amongst us in England and Wales and to the millions of our sisters and brothers in the Third World whose sufferings and oppression we have in good part caused and are still causing. May God give us the grace to make an entirely new attempt to face up to the demands of the Gospel and to put them into practice in our lives.' *Liverpool 1980: Official Report of the National Pastoral Congress*, London, St Paul Publications, 1981. p. 290.

16   *Ibid.* p. 294.

17   c.f. Gadamer H., *Truth and Method, op. cit.* p. 361.

of failure found no echo in *The Easter People*,[18] the response of the Bishops to the reports of the Congress. Concern for human rights and dignity was evident, but no clear focus on an option in favour of the poor.

The one central expression of this option in Britain as a whole through the decades of 80s and 90s has been the growing number of religious moving to live and work in deprived areas of this country, seeking to share in some measure the lives and struggles of those who are marginalised. This has been associated with the rediscovery of the original charism of orders and a conscious entry of some religious into the field of social analysis and critique with a concomitant impetus towards practical involvement.

There was a traditional missionary spirit among many orders which had led numbers of religious to seek service among the poor in other parts of the world. What was novel about the moves in this period was the concentration of attention and energy on deprived people within Britain. With a conscious withdrawal from more traditional apostolates, particularly schools, there began to emerge a pool of educationally trained personnel looking towards the inner cities, and peripheral housing estates.

The founding sister of the Community in Heath Town is exemplary of this movement. Her growing sense of a dissatisfaction with an apostolate which seemed to exclude the poorest, and a desire to confront more directly the issue of poverty, coincided with a term of office on the governing body of this sister's Province which enabled her to put her case more powerfully to the congregation's major superiors. Accordingly, in 1984 she was released from teaching and allocated to Wolverhampton with a mandate from her congregation 'to go and find what I was looking for'. Eventually a local parish priest approached the sisters with whom she was living at the time in search of someone to help in his parish on the other side of the town. Driving over to see the parish and the nearby psychiatric hospital, they passed the Heath Town estate. 'That was the first time that I saw Heath Town. Father had all kinds of ideas about hospital chaplaincy, work in the school. I hardly heard him. As we drove past Heath Town I kept saying 'Is that in your parish Father?'[19] The

---

18   *The Easter People*, The Reply of the Bishops of England and Wales to the Reports of the National Pastoral Congress of 1980. Both the Congress Reports and the Easter People may be found in *Liverpool 1980 op. cit.*

19   Fieldworker A.

prime interest of the parish priest was in having a sister to help in the parish and preferably also undertake the hospital chaplaincy. With a substantial degree of ingenuity this sister also managed to negotiate a 'census' of the Heath Town Estate as part of her job description and within a few days she had enlisted two of her congregation to help in the work. 'The three[20] of us marched in here with our pens ready to convert people.'[21]

Where you live determines what you see, whom you talk to determines what you hear

Their reception by the people of the estate was not of the most enthusiastic; strangers knocking on their doors were not welcome, but considered an intrusive presence. Strangers in Heath Town are often viewed with suspicion and might well be representatives of one or other of the Statutory agencies, the bailiffs, or possibly undercover police personnel. 'We didn't have much luck to begin with. In a tower block twenty-two stories high only about two people opened their door to us out of the whole block. We got wiser as the time went on.'[22]

With perseverance, and key contracts being made, there gradually arose a sense of credibility about these sisters. It was clear that they were concerned to listen to what life was actually like on the estate, without any allegiance to particular agencies on whom the people were dependent. Trust began to be established and experience shared. For the sisters it was a novel revelation of what life could be like, and completely divorced from their own experience. The effect was to strengthen their determination not just to be a visiting presence, but to become fully involved by moving to live on the estate. 'We were meeting people and

---

20   [Of the original three sisters only one is left. The other two work in a major urban housing scheme in Dublin. During the course of my time with the Community there were four sisters, three Irish and one French; three lay women were living with them, of these, one taught full time in a local school, while the other two were full time volunteers with the Community.]

21   Fieldworker A.

22   *Ibid.*

hearing their stories of alienation from society generally, their feelings of being forgotten. It was difficult for us to go back to our communities in the evening and just leave them.' The sisters realised how widespread was their ignorance. 'We felt we had to move in to really understand the hopes and fears and isolation of these people.'[23]

The ten months which passed between the time when they had initially encountered the estate and the time when they moved in were profitably spent in gaining real access and acceptance amongst the people, such that when they arrived, they came as individuals already known and with a degree of acceptance uncommon amongst most new arrivals.

An important dimension in this acceptance by the people was a ready willingness to listen, and indeed to draw out the life experience of the individuals on the estate. This very process of listening, deep uninterrupted listening, is both an affirming of the worth of an individual and the opportunity for joys and sorrows of experience to be put together again, re-experienced in a way that can creatively encourage self-esteem and the growth of self-confidence. Such involvement is one which necessitates a long-term commitment, both to a presence among the people, and also to a patient openness to hear what is emerging from them. 'As we meet people the first thing always is to listen to their stories, their lives, and find the sparks of hope that are there, and build on them. It isn't easy, you have to listen carefully, and it's a long slow process.'[24]

Another member of the Community spoke of the importance of creatively wasting time with people. Going to visit individuals being in their homes, and just sharing something of their life. This is the way for the patient building of trust and of real relationships. It contrasts sharply with the busy professional competence of many of the officials with whom the people are involved. 'Slowly, slowly slowly, trust is built up with people. Those you bump into regularly on the walkways, and chatting about nothing, gradually trust develops.'[25]

This principle of slow attentive listening to build up trust, and ordinary everyday contact underlies the Community practice of visiting homes. Often the Community will visit new arrivals if they hear of them via contacts in the housing office, or from one of the social workers, or

---

23   *Ibid.*
24   *Ibid.*
25   Fieldworker C.

from neighbours. Any who are known to be ill or bereaved are visited, and the families of children who play pool or attend the bible class which the Community run. At a meeting to show experiences and evaluate the visiting policy one sister recounted her experience of meeting a man at Christmas. 'He said I don't want to know anything of Christ, and I don't want the greetings of your Community, but you are welcome.' This sister felt the man's hurt and continued to pray for him. 'Last week I went back to see him and the circumstances were totally different, and he was really open and saying he didn't think he was a Christian but, now his circumstances have changed, he's now employed.'[26]

This practical willingness to give hospitality, even if there is a sense of alienation from God and the church is a notable feature of life on the estate. In discussion the group emphasised the importance of being open to receive from the people; it was not just that the Community was coming to bring something to the people. 'It's important to let the people have the joy of giving to us occasionally.'[27]

The discussion focused upon what it was thought individuals were taking with them when they visited. A variety of suggestions were made: 'friendship, interest, concern; practical help sometimes, mucking in with whatever is happening; support in general; a lot of building up of trust and relationships; sometimes information, introducing someone or something. The leader of the Community announced her intention ultimately as being 'to proclaim the good news whenever the opportunity arises. That may take ages and ages but that's my aim.'[28] However, for another member of the core Community this provided some difficulties. For her there were 'various steps to go through to that. Material needs, emotional needs, the worth and value of the person. I don't believe you can just walk in and say come to Jesus.'

These contrasting views raised issues about implicit and explicit proclamation. For the leader explicit proclamation was important while for another of the Community the very reputation of the Community was both an implicit proclamation and also the possible entry for sharing in a deeper way. 'People know that those in this Community are people who

---

26   Fieldworker B.
27   Fieldworker D.
28   Fieldworker A.

love God and that is the background from which we approach people.'[29] It was revealing to trace the development of the leader of the Community's ideas in a movement within the meeting from stating the importance of being evangelised by the people through emphasising the need to proclaim Christ to the people, and back to the sense of Christ being proclaimed to her by the people. Perhaps this is a fuller understanding of the notion of evangelisation which – as the word of God is said to be – may be understood as a two-edged sword, and thus a process of reciprocity – an interactive process not a one way movement. Here we encounter once more Gadamer's insight that conversation is a process of coming to an understanding which involves the openness of both participants. Perhaps conversation might thus become a model for future evangelisation.[30]

The leader of the Community informed me that it was her practice to endeavour to work in with the local churches in terms of alerting them to those who might welcome a visit for one reason or another, whether sick or wanting the baptism of a child or some such formal church involvement. Such occasions are not infrequent, when mediated through the Community. Although it is unlikely that such a contact would be established without the Community's assistance.

Seeds of hope upon which to build

When questioned about the basic aim of the Community and how it has changed over the years, the leader of the Community emphasised a certain continuity, the essence of their aim has always been to live community themselves and to assist building up the wider community. 'We believe it's important to somehow gather people together and have them involved in community building, networking groups. Its very difficult.'[31]

---

29   Fieldworker C.
30   'It belongs to every true conversation that each person opens himself to the other, truly accepts his point of view as valid and transposes himself into the other to such an extent that he understands not the particular individual but what he says. What is to be grasped is the substantive rightness of his opinion, so that we can be at one with each other on the subject.' Gadamer H., *Truth and Method, op. cit.* p. 385.
31   Fieldworker A.

68

One of the most insidious features of life on the margins, is the inevitable creation of dependency on exterior forces, agencies, professionals of one form or another. The sisters became aware of this reality when they moved into the area and have asserted the importance of assisting individuals to grow in their own self-esteem and gradually shake off this dependent feature of their lives. Again, this is a process which requires time energy and patience. Yet this firm belief that individuals have within them the seeds for possible growth is what sustains the Community and also determined its appellation. It also stands as an article of faith for their commitment to the incarnate Christ present within the people. 'That's one of the reasons why we call ourselves the Hope Community, that you still believe in people no matter how much of a mess they have made of their lives or hopeless their situation is.' Indeed 'They still are made in the image of God. They have a contribution to make to their own becoming and to the human community, and they deserve respect.'[32] This conviction that the *imago Dei* is an ineradicable characteristic of marginalised people encourages individuals to share their own life experience, and to trace something of their own relationship with God. During the course of my time in Heath Town I listened to many stories told by individuals in their own inimitable style. The first is a West Indian in his late thirties. Exploits in his youth brought him into confrontation with the police, for whom he retains little respect. I recount it, as he told it, not to exemplify a common theme, since each individual story is unique, but rather to share an example of how it may seem that the presence of God reappears as a thread through a life. Also, the attitudes expressed towards contemporary church life seem to give an indication of the alienation that may be felt, even by those with some established links with church. For him, this took the form of a family connection with the Pentecostal church.

> I have 2 sisters and 5 brothers, I've lived in Heath Town since I was 20. When I was a little boy I used to go to church and coming from a black church, they used to send a van for us every Sunday to make sure we went. While I was there they used to do a lot of clapping, dancing, that sort of stuff, and it was all right. When I was 9 we moved to a very rough area, most of the people were in and out of prison. That's where I grew up, so while I was there I learned to fight and steal and all other things like that. Not long after moving there. I didn't want to go to

---

32   *Ibid.*

church any more because the other kids around didn't have to go to church, they played on the streets all Sunday or went fishing. After a time when I got older, God went out of my life, and it was all pubs and clubs. Five years back God came into my life. I was going through a bad patch. I had fallen madly in love with this lady, she was my world, she meant everything to me, she was my heaven. It turned sour. She told me she had fallen for someone else and I was heartbroken. I was a pitiful man. I had given her my love, my affection, made her laugh; the pain I felt was unbearable. I was all the time angry, hurt and in tears – basically just gutted – my inside felt as if it was being torn out. Love had brought me to this. I would never love again. I began to turn in upon myself. One day I went to church with a neighbour of mine who had asked me to go previously, and guess what they were all singing and clapping and dancing, just like what they used to do when I went to church as a little kid. I listened to the service, they talked about God's love and how he loves everybody. While I was sitting there I was very much aware of the fact that it was touching me, and I wanted to ask God if he loved me and so I asked him. God came into my life again, and he's been there ever since with my ups and downs. Gradually, through my grief I was able to pray not for myself but for other people who were going through similar circumstances hurts and loss and grief.[33]

The reality of a deeper compassion for others being felt and expressed because of an individual's own personal suffering is a feature which recurs in individual lives. It finds expression in many ordinary acts of generosity, particularly towards those in acute distress. With this particular man, his compassion also finds expression in the time he gives to working as a volunteer with the Samaritans.

The following story is told by a young white man who has lived all his life in Heath Town. He moved onto the estate with his parents when it was built, and has remained ever since, although changing flats at various times. His situation is different from his black contemporary recorded above. He has had previous employment, indeed on one occasion a well-paid job. However, he has been unemployed for a number of years now. The only regular activity he has is on an annual basis when he helps with the children's Summer play scheme on the estate. He has a natural aptitude for relating to children, but a police record for debt, inhibits his employment in this area.

I've lived in Heath Town all my life, at the moment I'm unemployed. I'm one of 6 children. I've 2 brothers and 3 sisters. I live in one of these great big high rise

---

33   Resident T.

blocks, with my dog and my brother. My father died 5 years ago, and my mother's still alive; she lives near me, but I don't see her much. I'm a Catholic by baptism but I don't go to church much. I'm a member of the Hope Community. I consider myself lucky enough to have many friends in and around the estate. I don't think I've got any enemies. I like to play football a lot because it keeps me fit and I make lots of new friends playing, and also because I like to think I'm young but I'm getting a bit old now. I get enjoyment out of teaching children how to play football, and anything really, and I spent a year as a youth worker not long back, being involved with children from deprived areas similar to Heath Town, and I enjoyed it, and I built up a great rapport with the children. Many of them were violent at first but I sorted that out. I help at the local playscheme too every year.

I consider myself among the poorest on the estate. I don't have a television. In my flat I've only got basics, I ain't got no electric. I do get a lot of people who visit me. I don't turn anyone who visits me away, mostly people with problems, mental problems, psychological problems, people who need healing really I guess.[34]

Seeds of hope upon which to build are not confined to the lives of those whose natural habitat is on the margins, they are also found in the stories of those who came to join the Community from other very different spheres of life. By comparison and contrast the following are the stories of how two of the fieldworkers came to be involved on the estate. Like the residents, their stories involve something of the ongoing search for God, but perhaps experienced and certainly expressed in a very different cultural form. The first fieldworker is a young lay woman in her late twenties. From the beginning of the sisters moving to Heath Town, they attracted the commitment of young lay people, mostly women, who would come and spend from three months to two years with the Community helping as volunteers.[35] From observation, the commitment of these lay people mostly in their late twenties or thirties was remarkable and vital to the ongoing life of the Community. The reasons that led them to Heath Town seemed many and varied, but one element was an ongoing search for a living faith with some direct connection with the poor. This was a common element across all stories.

---

34   Resident M.
35   During the period of my research four members passed through the Community in this way, and I also encountered past members.

It was a change in direction in life I guess, but part of a continuous search. Being brought up in a third world country and with parents making us consciously aware of deprived people, I was searching for what I was fulfilled in. I did a lot of work with homeless people and found that I was enjoying this more than the teaching and secretarial work that I earned my living by. I felt much nearer to God, the God whom I was seeking, looking for, when I was with these people who were homeless – people who were in the dirt in a sense. Christianity I felt was more than going to Church on Sundays, singing songs and having a wonderful time, something to do with practical living out of it. The whole thing of Jesus' life, working with those who were poor, also speaking out on justice etc. I was looking for this Christianity put into practice, not just words, not empty, Christianity in action. After 3 visits to the Hope Community I decided to stay, initially for 6 months. But I decided that 6 months was no time at all. It zoomed past for me. I knew I needed more time. Somehow it seemed like a secret that was going to unfold, and I didn't know what this secret was. I wanted to stay with it all. It's very slow for me, just living here and being part of life here not only in Community but on the estate has meant all kinds of things emerging that wouldn't have done if I'd left earlier.[36]

The second fieldworker is one of the sisters. Only the leader of the Community remains from the original three who began the Community on the estate.[37] This newcomer, the oldest sister in the Community's brief history, has had a wide experience of service in different parts of the world. Having retired from teaching she became involved with inner city work in other parts of Britain, and came to Heath Town initially on a very temporary basis. Indeed she expressed considerable reluctance when it was first suggested to her that she might join the Community, even for a brief period. However, when confronted with life on the estate, her attitude soon changed.

Initially I was not too keen on coming, selfish thing really. I had been in Liverpool for a year, and I liked it, but it's not a team there like here. I was sent to replace temporarily A who was due to go to the USA for 3 weeks, and I was supposed to be here just for that time. A's trip was postponed and I stayed on, waiting for the trip. Gradually I slotted in. Finally I said I'd stay as long as I was able. I said I'd give it a year's try, in case I couldn't take it.[38]

---

36   Fieldworker C.
37   The other two were moved to a not dissimilar situation in inner city Dublin.
38   Fieldworker D.

Seeds of hope are apparent within all those involved with the Community, the marginalised and those who work with them. In this way the Community itself becomes a seed of hope for the estate and indeed the area in which the estate is situated. As a stone thrown into a pool, the rippling effect of widening circles has an ongoing exterior motion. This is portrayed by the leader of the Community in the following terms, 'a series of concentric circles. The central nucleus are the Sisters. The inner circle are others who have committed themselves to living with us for various lengths of time. And there are outer circles of neighbours and friends'[39]

The Community Programme

In order to facilitate real listening and enable the people to come together with the Community, a programme for the normal events of the week is made known.[40] For a number of years the Community operated a policy of keeping an Open House for three days a week. However, limitations on personnel resulted eventually in the cessation of this policy as it ceased to be a viable possibility. Also with the introduction of a drop-in centre for those with psychiatric problems, this meant that a major need was being partially met by the statutory agencies. It was felt that the energies of Community members might be better distributed in other ways: in visiting, or involvement with the many and varied organisations which have sprung up on the estate in recent years.

The principle elements of the weekly programme are events designed to allow some sharing of individual and group experience of God, and encourage deepening relationship among the people and with God. Thus on Tuesdays there is a weekly meeting to look at Scripture which is followed by a shared prayer meeting. Both of these meetings

---

39   Walsh M., *Here's Hoping!*, Sheffield, Urban Theology Unite, 1991. p. 4-5.
40   One of the ways this is publicised is on the back of the Hope Community Christmas and Easter Cards, which are distributed to every dwelling on the estate twice a year, e.g. Tuesday evening – Scripture and Prayer; Wednesday evening – Creative evening; Thursday evening – Faith Alive; Friday evening – Video.

have developed over the years. They are evaluated on an occasional basis by members of the Community, as they endeavour to meet the desires of those who attend. In one such evaluation meeting, emphasis was laid on the way in which the prayer meetings had been developed over time. 'A depth of prayer is appearing and people are asking for more scripture.'[41] There was an expressed feeling amongst some of those present that they would like to incorporate new initiatives from the people in the ongoing evolution of the scripture and prayer meetings. In this the concern was both to be relevant to the lives of the people, and also to allow the focus and format of the meetings to be determined by the people. A proposal was made to ask the people for suggestions: 'I'd really like to consult the people.'[42] The oldest sister present, who herself had a wide range of experience, raised a pertinent point with regard to the lack of experience of those who would be consulted. Her concern was to enable the possibility of widening the vision of the people by presenting them with possibilities outside their previous experience. 'The expressed needs are limited by experience – I think we should still offer variety as otherwise they may not encounter possibilities. We don't need to limit ourselves by the expressions of the people.'[43]

This raises the question what or who has the authority to structure the possibilities of discourse? One fieldworker was concerned about imposing alien ideas and language upon the people. Unsure already of what she was involved in, she sought greater clarity and relevance in any proposed changes, with regard to the real lives of individuals on the estate. 'I wonder as we seem to impose all this God language what are we doing. This week I'm on prayer and there's no real come-back, well some sharing, but you don't really know how the people have received it.'[44] Another said, 'Perhaps we're still coming from God to the people rather than starting from where the people really are.'[45] Another expressed her key concern 'Perhaps we don't really listen to people where they are. ... This

---

41   Fieldworker B.
42   Fieldworker B.
43   Fieldworker D.
44   Fieldworker C.
45   Fieldworker C.

whole prayer and scripture thing keeps coming up – over these last few months perhaps even from the beginning. What are we trying to do?'[46]

The tensions here and indeed throughout the meeting are those between a view which would see the time as one in which the people who attended received something from those who ran the meeting. Another view was one which predominantly emphasised an attitude of the meeting being determined by what the people themselves actually wanted. A similar dichotomy emerged in consideration of the prayer meetings whether they should be particularly directed to allowing those present to experience different types of prayer. Or whether again those who attended should set the agenda for this.

One example of the difficulties encountered was a prayer meeting led by one of the lay women who had decided on the theme of discipleship, her aim was a simple one, to use three passages from Luke's Gospel, have them read by different individuals who could read, for the benefit of all, and particularly those who couldn't read. This was to be followed by a time for quiet reflection and prayer, so there would be some silence, a little sharing and some singing, as one of the fieldworkers present could play the guitar.

She started by endeavouring to set a quiet atmosphere, 'I'm going to play you a little music just to help you centre and quieten down.'[47] She proceeded to do so, and a gentle calm settled over the room. Afterwards she said – 'I'd like to read or rather ask some people to read a few passages about discipleship and then we'll spend some time thinking about them.'[48] At this point one of the residents asked if he might read the first one. He proceeded to do so, however, his inability to pronounce some of the words led the fieldworker to take over, and read the passage through to the end. There was then a pause for silence. Into this silence the same resident – a man in his late thirties, with a history of psychiatric problems – began to speak. His words were somewhat incoherent as he was obviously upset.

What was most impressive throughout the whole time was that, despite the amusement of some present, and there were more than a dozen people, all tried very hard and successfully not to show it, and more than

---

46   Fieldworker C.
47   Fieldworker C.
48   *Ibid.*

that there was a real sense of support and positive acceptance of all that X. might say. It was recognised that something had happened particularly to disturb him. Indeed, later it emerged that earlier in the day he had been registered as a disabled person, and he found this very hard to accept. The atmosphere of acceptance within the group which was supportive of this individual is a common feature of such meetings. There is a lack of judgmentalism that facilitates the expression of the most simple forms of prayer. The very willingness of the fieldworker, on this occasion, to allow this resident seemingly to disrupt her planned programme dispelled any possibility of a conflictual situation emerging. Thus the discourse as here illustrated is accepting of a wide range of experience.

Common elements of all the meetings include: an atmosphere of acceptance which allowed any present to participate; a simple articulation of need, or distress, or concern; a willingness on the part of the one leading the meeting to allow space for others to contribute and if necessary determine the progression of the meeting. On many occasions silence played an important part. Music was also a common feature. The setting on most occasions was the same – a large circle of chairs, dim lighting and a candle burning in the centre of the circle.[49] On each occasion there was a tangible sense of the involvement of the people with the prayer evoking the mystery of Emmanuel. The discourse is inclusive of the contributions of all.

Certainly, it would appear to be true that the more simple the prayer, the easier in many ways it is for the people to enter into it. The more wordy and abstract it becomes, the more difficult it is for individuals to feel drawn into it. It would be difficult to overestimate the vital contribution of silence here. Indeed, all whom I interviewed, both fieldworkers and residents, unanimously emphasised the need they experienced for a degree of silence amidst whatever else was happening in the prayer time. 'I find silence in prayer definitely helpful. It's very important to me. It

---

49   This use of symbol, image, memory is both simple and powerful. Miles in her work endeavours to explore a somewhat similar theme. She indicates the importance of understanding the personal interaction with image or symbol. Here it might be helpful to bear in mind Coleridge's maxim with regard to the consubstantiality of symbol and meaning, for it is the realisation that through symbolism and sacramental vision, that humanity establishes its most vital contact with the realities of life. Miles M., *Image as Insight: Visual understanding in Western Christianity and Secular Culture*, Boston, Beacon Press, 1985.

helps you to think about reading or something like that, and reflect back on your daily life and that, it's very important in prayer.'[50] And from one of the fieldworkers, 'The coming before God in that silence is just a relief in a sense that someone has it all in his hands. I guess it's knowing how to pray the silence, that I find hard.'[51] And from a group of residents just the one telling comment. 'We like the silent times.'

Finally two comments indicating the variety of response to prayer, at both a personal and communal level. Though these two residents are more articulate than some others, the expression of involvement in prayer is far more widespread among residents above and beyond those who might frequent the regular Community meetings. 'At the moment, I'm not a very prayerful person. Sometimes I do, sometimes I can't be bothered. But I figure that God knows me and understands me and knows there's times when I don't feel like praying – without falling out.' He went on to say 'I also think prayer is also by your actions not just talk; your whole life is prayer. If you're living a good strong Christian life, that is a prayer to God. Sometimes I can do it and sometimes I can't so when I can I do.'[52]

The following is a comment from a very reflective individual who spent some time thinking about the question I had asked, namely what prayer meant for him, and how he viewed prayer with the Community. He is a man whom the Community have seen grow in self-confidence over the years, and willingly undertake a leading role in meetings or celebrations if called upon. 'Prayer for me means talking to God, even though I'm not visibly praying. It's changed my life. I believe what you pray for, you may not get it, but the fact that you're praying for it, that's faith, that's acknowledgement that God exists.' Then he reflected on praying with the Community 'This brings us closer together. If someone prays for me it strengthens me, helps me and others too. With Community prayer it brings me closer to the people around me gives me a sort of bond there.'[53]

One of the fieldworkers had considerable misgivings, with regard to the prayer meetings, about any kind of imposition upon the people of an

---

50   Resident M.
51   Fieldworker C.
52   Resident T.
53   Resident M.

agenda which came from the Community. 'Maybe we need to involve the people more in the leading of it. And it doesn't matter if it's messy – who wants neat prayers? I'm wanting things to flow smoothly but maybe that's not what prayer is about – maybe it is messy.'[54]

The model of listening, deep listening, is one that this fieldworker appears to espouse. However, the practical difficulties involved, and the still underlying ethos of something to be taught by someone to another, is one that is fundamental to formation within the Church, and appears to have a significant resonance within the Community. The issue of what emerges from the people and what is essentially presented by the core group is one which recurs, and finds a significant expression also in the opinions of those who work alongside the Hope Community either as residents who have chosen to live on the estate or as clergy involved in ongoing ecumenical contact.

On Thursday nights there was a meeting entitled 'Faith Alive'. Here, it might begin around scripture, but discussion focuses around a chosen theme. These might range from difficulties on the estate to problems of the third world. Some nights there could be very limp discussions reflecting the lethargy of the participants; while on other occasions the very vibrancy of the exchange was evident to all who visited. One such occasion was a meeting which began by looking at life on the estate particularly the lack of medical provision; the conversation moved on to consider the problem of unemployment and social benefits as experienced by residents on the estate; where individuals would like to be in five years time and into the problem of racism on in estate. Participants appeared to become more energised through the course of the conversation, and all present felt able to voice any opinion they felt inclined. The following views emerged in another Faith Alive meeting, when the people present were asked what they thought about God. 'He's definitely not a copper.'[55] 'Not racist'[56] 'He comes to us'[57] 'He's not stuck out from us.'[58] 'He's not poor,'[59] 'She's rich in love'[60] 'He guides us.'[61] 'He's ready to roll

54   Fieldworker C.
55   Resident W.
56   Resident P.
57   Resident S.
58   Resident R.
59   Resident K.
60   Resident E.

up his sleeves.'[62] 'I'm not sure there is one.'[63] 'He's unwaged.'[64] 'Why does he have to be he?'[65] 'Not a lot makes sense without God.'[66] 'God means existence for me. If I didn't have God in my life I'd probably have been dead a long time ago.'[67] There is the sense of a freedom of access to this God who is not demanding of formal church commitment. Also, there is an interesting ambivalence with regard to the gender of God which gives grass roots authenticity to the ongoing debate within more academic circles of the Christian community. In later interviews with individuals I asked for some general views about God, and the following are some of the replies which I received. The first is from a young black man in his mid thirties.

> There's theories that people see God as something like their father, in that case I would say God was a rough mean old sod, cos that's what my father was like, but I know that God's not quite like my father. He's strong, not wishy washy. One thing I like about God is his loyalty, if he says something he'll do it. I see him as a warm Lord, sounds good that doesn't it, but I like it. Sometimes he must be quite grumpy too. He's also full of love, and passion. I should say too that he's a God that's in a lot of pain.[68]

The common humanity of this picture of God is poignantly conveyed in the above remarks. Though the family relational bond for this man has lacked authentic affective depth, yet this has not resulted in the repudiation of God. Rather, it has promoted the search for other more creative and resonant images wherein to conceive of God. Thus a 'warm Lord', the sense of comfort, well-being, and affection become almost palpable in this term; combined with the reverence that 'Lord' implies. Still the humour and humanity is paramount in the anthropomorphism that sometimes God might be grumpy. While the consciousness of the pain of God

---

61   Resident T.
62   Resident X.
63   Resident H.
64   Resident L.
65   Resident Y.
66   Resident G.
67   Resident N.
68   Resident T.

was linked by this resident with the pain in the world, and an expressed certainty that in some way God was intimately involved in this reality.[69]

Another resident in relating something of the story of his life, emphasised the importance for him of faith. Though his material circumstances are very poor, his outlook on life is very simple. 'My faith is the most important possession I've got. I ain't got many possessions but I'd give anything else away, but my faith I'd keep. I trust in God in all I do and hope. I'm not just saying that, I really do.'[70]

The divinity of Christ is a phrase which means very little on the margins. Theological terminology appears abstruse and alienating there, an exclusive esoteric in-language, associated with ecclesiastical structures and sub cultures. Yet surprisingly, there appears a more orthodox Chalcedonian perception underlying much of what individuals may relate concerning their understanding of Christ and the second person of the Trinity. Never having heard of the definition of the early fathers there can appear a resonant appreciation of the reality of consubstantiality which evades many a more well-educated contemporary. A sense that Christ is at the same time involved in daily life, and this not just as another official representative defining lives, nor himself subject to such disempowering procedures, but rather intimate and yet transcending pragmatic constraints. Divinity of its very nature seems to have a human face on the margins. Or in the words of one member of the wider community, 'Jesus was a most extraordinary guy. He was really human. I just wish I could help others to see something of the excitement of how Jesus really is.'[71]

---

69 When asked what he meant by God being in pain this resident replied, 'Think about it, if you had 5 or 6 kids and you watched them play, suddenly you saw them start to fight, it would cut you up. Well, God's supposed to be all kind and that, he must be in a lot of pain seeing people kill one another. I reckon he's going through the suffering with us.' *Ibid.*

70 Resident M.

71 Resident G.

Celebrating the reality of God in life

Very few of the people on the estate go to church. Indeed as has become evident, there appears to be a considerable amount of alienation from the church. Yet there is evident a desire to pray and to come together to celebrate the recognition of God in their lives. This led to the formulation of local people's liturgies on the estate. They happen about once every two months and are planned and prepared by the local people in conjunction with the Hope Community. They take place in the local community centre on a Saturday afternoon. This community ground is a very important venue for the celebrations.

The celebrations have now become a regular feature on life on the estate. Individuals attend who perhaps rarely if ever come to the Community flats, but who feel they want to be part of such a gathering. Indeed, some of the local residents describe the celebrations as their church. A notable feature of these occasions is the great 'freedom' of those not accustomed by a tradition of liturgical involvement into certain forms and appropriate responses. This freedom is not just a significant contribution to all that occurs, but it adds a certain atmosphere of anticipation since no one is quite sure what might happen next. Although celebrations are well prepared, there is an irrepressible spontaneity of response amongst the people which may undermine any restrictive formalism. In this way, the leader of the Community considers the people of the estate have a lot to teach the institutional church about possible forms of worship which are more directly participative. 'I'm sure the people here have a lot to contribute to the renewal of the Church and they're so free you know, because they haven't been brought up in the tradition and all of that.'[72] Over the years the residents of the estate have grown in confidence also in their knowledge of the scriptures and of hymns and songs which might be appropriate to different themes. Individuals have felt more able to contribute either with a prayer or choosing slides to illustrate a theme or drama to draw out the reality of a Gospel story or a local issue.

A specific example would be the celebration which took place one February. It had required extensive preparation. A number of meetings were held with local people contributing ideas. Gradually the following

---

72   *Ibid.*

points emerged as key features of this particular celebration: the theme was peace, forgiveness, understanding, and the peace of Christ. A series of preparatory meetings took place first with a larger group and then a smaller steering group. It was the practice of the Community to have one member of the core group involved with the steering group meetings to work out a possible programme, they would present this at one of the Faith Alive meetings to the wider group, for comment. If it was acceptable with whatever modifications were thought necessary then the task of allocating responsibility would begin.

First there was to be a welcome extended to all by a local resident, followed by a word of scripture – John 14: 27 read by another resident. Following this, the idea was to distribute badges of peace – however, there was a 'technical hitch' – no badges. A hymn was then sung by all the assembled, followed by a slide presentation on the plan and harmony in all created things accompanied by the reading of Psalm 104. There followed a talk by a Jesuit, the matter for which had been suggested by residents at the local planning meetings. These included world conflicts, famine in Africa, isolation and brokenness within our own local community, our need for friendship and support, the ignorance which leads to a lack of understanding and appreciation and which sometimes results in prejudice, aggression, even war. It was unusual to have an outside speaker on these occasions, but there was a sense that the people had helped to set the agenda for the talk. This was followed by a rendering of the hymn Amazing Grace by another local resident. The scripture passage Mark 10: 46-52 concerning the healing of the blind man of Jericho was read and dramatised. There followed another hymn by the assembled gathering, and this was to have been followed by various personal testimonies, where individuals contributed whatever they wanted to with regard to life on the estate. However, these were also subject to a technical hitch – the individuals concerned did not turn up. Finally, one resident talked about our need for physical, mental and emotional healing, forgiveness and wholeness, at a personal level and in our broken world. There followed a prayer of anointing and one local resident anointed any who wished to come forward. The event concluded with a sharing of the peace of Christ and tea and sandwiches.

Perhaps the most 'miraculous' feature of the event was that it took place at all considering the numbers of 'drop out' due to the flu etc. Still there were enough local members to step into the breach and apart from the badges and the testimonies, all the features outlined above were present. There was a very strong undercurrent of support most notable in that, very shy, generally inarticulate individuals made a contribution in public to share something of themselves and their ideas, their hopes and their fears with regard to peace. The local resident who welcomed everyone, had obtained a new outfit for the occasion, and just before she started she muttered to me, 'me stomach's turning over I'm dead nervous'[73] And the resident who introduced the anointing, in a very thoughtful manner said 'I need healing and we invite any of you who would like to come and be anointed with a little oil and our prayer will be for heal ing,'[74] There were also those who shared without words – the young single parent who anointed all who went forward, and did so with real reverence for individuals, while her niece – also a single parent – held the oil for her. Another who contributed without words was the man who played Jesus in the drama of whom it was remarked, 'I've never thought of Jesus as limping, with a fag behind his ear and a flat cap – it gives a whole different slant to things.'[75]

There was an ongoing dynamic through the proceedings, a move from being welcomed to feeling at home.[76] Listening to scripture moved into the visual images of the slides, and the hall was also decorated with the artistic contributions of some of the residents. The theme was drawn together by the Jesuit's contrasting of the peace of the world and the peace of Christ, which led into the notion of peace requiring our interior need for healing; leading ultimately into a powerful and reverential administration of a 'sacrament'. Certainly there was a powerful quality of silence. Finally it seemed like a natural leading into the sharing of tea, and though it was easy to see on the day when the celebration began, it was not easy to see where it ended.

Relationships were 'good', old and young combined to be at home and to 'celebrate'. There was little particular tension and conflict at the time, the frustrations and anxieties had come before. The local people

---

73   Resident J.
74   Resident M.
75   Fieldworker B.
76   It is always important to provide ash trays as once the local people begin to feel comfortable and at home in the environment, they like to smoke.

were nervous, but required little prompting. The presence of the sisters was not in an organising capacity. My intuitive sense was that peace meant a little more to the people present at the end of a moving occasion. There was very positive feedback from many individuals who had attended with regard to their appreciation of the event. There was a good sense of participation by the people, and a qualitative sense of 'spirit'. It was certainly a sense of a moving experience for those who were involved and something of a celebration of God amidst the people. 'The people themselves over the years have become more self-confident, and so are more willing to come forward to lead parts of it. We try not to depend too much on particular individuals.' The Community leader saw her aim as helping individuals grow in confidence. 'It's a question of waiting for people until they're ready to do their bit.'[77] There had been a serious attempt by the fieldworkers to wean themselves and the people away from clergy presiding in anyway at the celebrations. The sacred principle espoused in theory, and endeavoured for in practice is that the celebrations should be from the people, by the people, for the people.

This seems to be an attempt to guarantee the ideas and fragile self-confidence of the people. On this point there is ongoing tension within the Community. The leader sees the need to contribute the gifts and skills which lie within the Community. 'I think we have bent over backwards and perhaps too much so to make it the people's liturgy and standing back from it ourselves. We have a responsibility and a duty to share our gifts and accumulated knowledge over the years.' She continued 'I'm a lot more ready to put at people's disposal at least some suggestions, some resources from which people may draw. Now I know some other members of my Community wouldn't agree with that.'[78]

Other members of the Community insist that taking the leader's stance would inevitably lead to the celebration becoming the Community's liturgy and not the liturgy of the people. For the leader there is the frustration of agonising over the ideas arising from the residents when 'there is often so little in them'[79], for her the matter is primarily one of finding the right balance between the views of Community and residents. Here she maintains that the Community are also part of the proceedings,

---

77   Fieldworker A.
78   *Ibid.*
79   *Ibid.*

and that their contribution has equal validity with that of any other resident. Paradoxically she sees the very reticence of the Community as a
perverse exercise of power. 'You can be in a terrific position of power
because you can be planning the liturgy and they know you have the
ideas and are holding back. Then we are putting them into a great position of powerlessness.'[80]

One of the avowed aims of the fieldworkers is to try to bridge the
gap between the institutional church and the lives and experiences of the
people. In order to facilitate the accomplishment of this aim they make a
point of inviting local clergy to the celebrations, not as any principal ac-
tors in what occurs but rather to participate as a member of the 'congregation'. The leader explained, 'We invite a lot of our clergy friends to
attend, and we make sure the students who come here on placement in the
Summer come back for celebrations.' She sees the celebration as having
a two-fold purpose: 'celebrating that God is amongst the people, and it's
an occasion for the church to be evangelised. It's a way of ministering to
the clergy; they're not coming to lead, but to receive.'[81]

The response to this invitation is variable. Of the five celebrations
that I attended, generally only one local Anglican clergyman was present.
The principle of a reciprocal effect in terms of the institutional church
learning from the people's liturgy is an important one. Yet one of the
local clergy who is supportive of the Community's work has very ambiguous feelings about attending a celebration. 'I wouldn't know how to
fit in. I'd feel like I was a voyeur. If liturgy is actually coming up from
below. To participate but not be involved in it as the one formulating it.
I would find it odd.'[82]

For the fieldworkers the lack of clerical participation in the celebrations has had profound repercussions for their own deeper involvement in
the events which take place. One spoke of her own experience of the
particular celebration outlined above. The most poignant moment for her
was the anointing of people by a woman who lived on the estate. 'It was
a most moving time for me. If the person doing the anointing had been a
priest I would not have been moved in the slightest.' Her knowledge of
the women made the difference. 'I know too that she didn't study for five

---

80   *Ibid.*
81   *Ibid.*
82   Clergyman V.

years in theology. It just touched me very deeply.' The effort for her was profoundly moving 'Her anointing me was so deep and real for me, like God through her anointing me. That for me is what church is about. And watching a stream of people go up to be anointed.'[83]

Again there is the realised experience of a sense of God being communicated to the fieldworkers by the people. This was made evident within the discussion concerning visiting, there was further ramification in the prayer meetings discussed, and here when the local community gathers for the celebrations, once more the same feature recurs. Indeed, this appears as a most profound dimension to the involvement of the Community with the people, that the effect of their lives and presence is a reciprocal one. The presence of God is perceived within the life of the people and shared in reciprocity by interaction with the Community. Thus the very experience of the people brings life-giving possibilities to the discourse.

---

83   Fieldworker C.

Chapter 4

The Reaction of the Institutional Church

> People who are living in old industrial inner cities and post-war housing estates...
> are important to God, to the Church, and to the Nation, and their needs must be
> met.[1]

> All in the Church, whether they belong to the hierarchy or are cared for by it, are
> called to holiness. ...This holiness of the Church is constantly shown forth in the
> fruits of grace which the Spirit produces in the faithful.[2]

In the previous chapter it was apparent that the involvement of the Hope
Community with the people of the estate necessitated the expense of time
in patient and attentive listening to individual lives. Such listening was
actualised on a pragmatic basis in the continual daily exchange in visiting
and in more formally structured meetings and celebrations. The effects of
this upon the people of the estate appeared to be a growth in self-esteem
and self-confidence and a willingness to share their own insights into the
presence of God both as a personal and communal experience. The reciprocal effect upon the Community is an awareness of receiving through the
people a deepening appreciation of God at work in their lives.

Local clerical involvement

The local churches are involved within this converse in a variety of ways.
There is a monthly ecumenical prayer meeting held at rotating venues,
including the Hope Community. There is the practical outworking of in-

---

1   *Living Faith in the City*, para. 4, London, Publication of General Synod of the
    Church of England, 1990.
2   *Lumen Gentium*, para. 39, in Flannery A., [ed.], *Vatican II: The Conciliar and Post
    Conciliar Documents*, Worcester, Fowler Wright, 1975, pp. 350-440.

volvement with local management committees on the estate and the establishment of a project specifically aimed at reconciliation within the community. Most importantly there is the ongoing pragmatic contact at an individual level where support and encouragement is given. One of the local Anglican clergy who considers his involvement with the Community to be one of ongoing inspiration and enrichment, particularly concerning team ministry and ecumenical engagement. 'One of the most enriching aspects of the experience here is that I've learned so much through the Hope Community and learned a tremendous amount about the corporate approach to urban ministry.'[3] This cleric has a regular pragmatic involvement with the Community at many different levels of its activities, and thus a clearer picture of the Community's interaction with the local community. His own working partnership with the leader of the Community has provided reciprocal support on numerous occasions. His conviction has grown that the only viable approach to urban ministry must be a co-operative ecumenical one. 'To try and paddle your own canoe is ridiculous, and it presents a muddled picture to a world not concerned with the debate about the intricate differences between denominations.'[4]

There is a degree of confusion amongst some of the local clergy who have less contact, with regard to what actually occurs within the Hope Community, and what each individual's commitments might be. This was clearly expressed by one clergyman who stated, 'Basically I would be unable to say what most members of the community are actually doing all the time.'[5] The man's visits to the estate are rare occasions and his first meeting with the Hope Community left him with the impression that the members were there with a broad brief of the promotion of 'good works'. Only later did he realise that there were different dimensions to the community's involvement on the estate. 'Only when I started to meet A. on management committees and that sort of thing that I realised there was a slightly different dimension and impetus to the community life.'[6]

This sense of confusion about how the Community functions, its purpose and aims, was echoed by the local Roman Catholic priest who

---

3   Clergyman U.
4   *Ibid.*
5   Clergyman V.
6   *Ibid.*

frankly acknowledged that, 'I don't really know where they are going.'[7] Initially when the sisters arrived to begin the Hope Community, the priest thought at least one would minister in a traditional way as a local parish sister. This however, was not the aim of the Community, and was considered to be a possible hindrance to the new initiative being undertaken. The lack of involvement with the local parish has been a source of regret to the local priest, who still finds it difficult to understand. He feels that an opportunity has been missed to assist within the mainstream parish. 'The parish was a bit disappointed that one sister hadn't been deputed to liaise with the parish.'[8] However, the parish priest still gives real financial support, even though he continues to wonder about the fruits of the work of the Community. For him this is assessed in the more traditional terms of any possible increase in baptisms, weddings, or people coming back to the church. The unstructured approach of the work of the Community, as compared with the structured forms of the institution, he finds difficult to comprehend and impossible to assess. For his part, the lack of involvement between parish and estate is not a denial of responsibility to serve the people on the estate, but rather an admission of a vast area of involvement far beyond the physical capabilities of the two men at present ministering in this area. The parish is divided into two or three distinct areas, of which the estate is only one part. Because the Hope Community are present, the inference is that the people on the estate are in some way being served by the church.

There is unanimity of support amongst local clergy for the Hope Community. The very presence of the community on the estate is seen as its most valuable contribution. That presence is a contribution not made by any clerical denominational representative. Yet it is an overt and not covert Christian presence. The sisters are identified as part of the institutional church, and all who live with them are accorded similar credentials. 'Just the sheer fact that it is there, that there is an identifiable Christian presence on the estate, living in the same grotty flats is saying something about identification and incarnation. That's the greatest good the community achieves.'[9]

---

7   Clergyman P.
8   *Ibid.*
9   Clergyman V.

Although occasionally the Roman Catholic curate and one of the Anglican clergy make visits to the estate, primarily at the instigation of the Hope Community, other clergy are rarely if ever seen around the shopping precinct or more particularly visiting in a general way. Estate project meetings draw clerical attendance, but this is at the level of middle management and the organization of resources – primarily financial – and personnel. One of the local clergy made the point that, although his church is the nearest to the estate, he has very few members living in that area. Indeed his congregation is drawn from a very wide area across the town. 'There is no close relationship with the estate. I have the desire to minister more to that area but we have not impacted on the estate as much as I would want to.'[10]

This is a local Black Pentecostal Church which is situated on the very boundary of the estate. Here the attitude of the church towards the Hope Community seems handicapped by particular doctrinal issues. These make closer ecumenical co-operation and collaboration more problematic, especially in terms of more realistic involvement with the local people via increased involvement with the Hope Community. However, this doctrinal stance does not detract from the support and encouragement that is verbally accorded to the Hope Community initiative. 'I was brought up to detest Catholics. I've modified my opinion in recent years, but there are still doctrinal difficulties. But it is courageous of those ladies to go and live on the estate.'[11]

By contrast to the above views, a Free Church clergyman was so impressed by the life and work of the Hope Community, that when the time came for him to move from the place where he was living, he specifically requested a flat on the estate in order to share more fully in the work of the Community. He continues to maintain a full-time job, but joins in community events whenever he is able so to do.

Having lived on the estate for two years when interviewed, he was able to confirm that his initial perceptions had been reinforced during that time, as he lived in closer proximity and became more involved. For him, at that particular juncture the Hope Community was 'my number one spiritual home and source of support.[12] He said, 'I've been able to put

---

10   Clergyman V.
11   *Ibid.*
12   *Ibid.*

these initial perceptions to the test. I've called on various members of the Community, and that call has always been answered. I've received the support I was looking for at each particular time.'[13] From his vantage-point on the estate he has been able to view also the interaction between the other residents and the Hope Community. Here he has been impressed by the way in which in particular the sisters have made themselves accessible. 'I hear in the way the sisters are talked about, that the people do not feel that they must do things in a certain way, or attend all their meetings. They have done a good job in trying to break down the barriers of people's perception of them as religious.'[14]

The interaction of the local clergy with the Community is generally a major determining factor in the possible involvement of the members of local congregations. Though some endeavour to give prayerful support on a regular liturgical and informal basis. 'At least once a month I offer mass for the community, so it's on our intention list. The majority of my church I suspect don't know what the Hope Community is or what it's there for.'[15] For this cleric the vision of his ministerial calling was to be of service to a whole community, yet the very mechanics of being a local Anglican representative meant he was encumbered by certain preordained structural responsibilities which often precluded this wider involvement. 'The theory of the establishment is that my pastoral concern is for everybody who lives within the boundaries of this parish all 4,500, regardless of colour, creed or whatever.' The reality is somewhat different. 'What you end up doing is looking after the 100 pious souls who basically make up the congregation.'[16] The support and encouragement which the other Anglican priest and his curate give to the Community has meant that members of their congregation have made real contributions to community events. This has been particularly appreciated on the occasion of local celebrations when those involved in the church music groups have freely given of their time to come and play for the community event. 'We perhaps ran ahead of the congregation, meeting regularly with the

13   Ibid.
14   Ibid.
15   Clergyman V.
16   Ibid.

sisters for prayer once a month. But we've encouraged others to get involved.'[17]

Within the Roman Catholic parish despite any regret that the congregation might have concerning the lack of a parish sister, there has been the traditional support accorded to the sisters. One individual helps with accountancy, while the St Vincent de Paul society, a traditional source of Catholic charitable giving, has contributed generously in material form to help both the sisters and the people of the estate. The local curate considers himself to be the Community chaplain and regularly visits to preside at the Eucharist.

However, it is clear in the comments already cited that the presence of the Hope Community on the estate has raised for the local clergy issues requiring further reflection and consideration of the very nature of the church and parochial ministry. This is particularly acute in consideration of the local Roman Catholic parish. The sisters as religious occupy a traditional position within the church. Yet they are not involved in a traditional ministry. This may pose questions for the local parish, but more particularly for the clergy. For the local curate, the community 'raises questions by being there'. In a very frank discussion he owned to his own frustration, and the limited nature of his own efforts when contrasted with the vast needs within such a large parish. It is intrinsic to the very structure of the present parochial system that one uniform structure is still expected to cope with any and every parochial possibility. 'It's very easy to become depressed, our model is too vast. I'm only one person. I'm not going to change anything by my work. There are no clear answers.'[18]

For this priest the church appeared to be in continual slow transition. He stressed the post-Vatican II emphasis that all have responsibility within the church for the care and nurturing of members. Yet this development paralleled the traditional emphasis on church attendance as the most important ingredient of the faith life of any individual. 'Without people in the pew putting money in the plate the church building wouldn't be there and the church enables us to be community. What we're about is being community. The church building is vital for the

---

17 Clergyman U.
18 Clergyman L.

mass.'[19] Yet it was also clear to this cleric that if the avowed aim of the church was to see a return of numbers to the church, it was also an unrealistic and unattainable aim. Such an untenable position was seen by him as part of the general confusion pervading the church, particularly in the wake of the espousal of the preferential option for the poor. 'It's muddled... The option for the poor is strange for many priests still.'[20] The view of this particular priest finds echoes in the views expressed by other Catholic priests in the diocese. This was vividly revealed in a report looking at the needs and expressed views of local parish priests throughout that area.[21]

The ongoing emphasis within the church upon attendance figures appears to exacerbate such a situation of disillusionment. Although it seems theologically disastrous to equate the church with those who attend, and though it is palpably obvious that the Kingdom of God is not to be equated with institutional churches; still, the actual practice of the church as institution is to continue to operate as though these undeclared assumptions retained some validity. Such a *modus vivendi* maintains the paranoia associated with church attendance figures as signs of success, although the Faith in the City report clearly refuted such an emphasis. 'The church must beware of using numerical attendance as a sole criterion.'[22]

Indeed a focus of the report was to bring to the attention of all in ministry the necessity of reflecting on the manner of Christian presence in urban life. Such sentiments find an echo in the views of one of the local Anglican clergy, who sees the Hope Community as assisting his own re-

---

19   *Ibid.*
20   *Ibid.*
21   Lots accept the church, warts and all, are carried along by faith. But they are conscious of a debate in the church; they read a lot, see the hierarchy, not as serving as they used to be, more trying to dominate. The way the church is being run at the moment puts people off; the leaders can't see themselves as part of the problem. Many here don't agree with the debate on ministry being closed down; many have no objections to women taking ministries. There is a sadness about ecumenism; it's being blocked. We are not growing. The Catholic Church is in need of healing if it is to go forward. Ryan D., *The Catholic Parish: Decline and Development in an English Diocese*, unpublished manuscript, 1991. p. 34.
22   *Faith in the City: A Call for Action by Church and Nation. The Report of the Archbishop of Canterbury's Commission on Urban Priority Areas.* London, Church House, 1985, p. 31.

flection on how to be Christian when living in a very exposed situation on the margins. It also acts as a sign of hope for him that, on behalf of the church, the Community is endeavouring to become involved in a way others might find impossible. The price of this is to be also marginalised within the church. 'I see the Community as trying to work out for the rest of us how to be Christian when they are living in a far more exposed situation than most of us.' Yet there is a cost involved. 'Being an innovative community means slightly 'on the edge', not just marginalised with the marginalised of society, but marginalised within the church.'[23]

From his own standpoint he finds himself ambivalent about increased involvement. His own preference is for a clearly delineated role to be fulfilled. He owns that he does not himself try to 'get alongside' the people of the estate. 'I go in and do things for them, sometimes with them.'[24]

He highlighted another fundamental dilemma which he felt must be shared by the Community, namely how far to determine events in relations to the people on the estate, and how far to let events be determined by the people. This key issue has already been raised in the previous chapter, when looking at the functioning of Community meetings and celebrations. In this case the situation in question is that of local management meetings on the estate. On these committees both the Community and some of the local churches are represented. 'I just want to get in there and run it, because I know I could do it more efficiently. Even though it might be that the other methods that people are using, irritating as they are to me, might have an efficiency in themselves. I find that frustrating.'[25]

The dichotomy between the interests of the people and the best way of serving those interests causes profound ambivalence. For the other local Anglican clergyman there are times of real conflict with the established nature both of the church and society. However, he sees the local bishop as having a crucial role with regard to supporting initiatives outside the normal practice, and his bishop has committed himself to this area. 'At times in urban ministry I feel a greater confrontation. A lot is

---

23   Clergyman V.
24   *Ibid.*
25   *Ibid.*

dependent upon the stance of bishops in particular and I think we're blessed ourselves here.'[26]

Given the institutional allegiance of the Community and the local clergy, there are certain dilemmas which hover, scarcely veiled, over any ecumenical involvement with the marginalised people of the estate. Given the underlying agenda of the institution which requires formal church attendance as the measure of 'success' there is a degree of unacknowledged pressure to ensure the formal commitment of residents of the estate to a particular denomination. This underlies the remarks of the local parish priest recorded above in the stress laid on the numbers of individuals returning to the church, or the sacraments. The prominence given to such tangible and numerical commitment is one which appears inimical to the practice which has been developed by the Community and indeed within the ecumenical initiatives undertaken. Consequently, there has been an avoidance of either acknowledgement of, or discussion about this issue. 'I think we've skirted around this question because it is fraught with difficulty.'[27] For this cleric, clarity appears to lie within the area of enabling individuals to give their own expression of Christian faith. A sharing of the Christian tradition for him does not imply an assimilation of the particular rubrics of a tradition but rather assisting the development of what is most appropriate in the form of Christian expression governed by the circumstances and situation. 'We should be in the business of passing on the tradition to those around us and allowing them to develop the situations which are appropriate for their expression of Christian faith in these places.' For him, it is not about, 'bringing with us the trappings of what is pretty much entrenched middle class culture, in the Anglican Church at least.'[28]

This approach is particularly applicable in consideration of community celebrations. This cleric's attitude towards liturgy is again one, which is seen as more flexible and fluid than the pervading institutional norm. It is his conviction, 'For a service to happen as I'd really like it to happen, groups in the congregation would plan it, and we clergy would be

---

26   *Ibid.*
27   *Ibid.*
28   *Ibid.*

acting much more as a catalyst. We would be told by the people what they wanted us to do.'[29]

For the Free Church clergyman living on the estate, the involvement of the local people in the planning of the Community celebrations is very important. He has been impressed by the way contributions from the people were actively sought and valued without any overt or covert imposition. 'They were genuine participative experiences. It would be quite possible to devise a sham participation. But it would be fairly obvious and would quickly provoke a negative reaction if that was the case.'[30]

Hierarchical mystification and demystification

A focus on church attendance figures effectively acts as a form of defence mechanism circumventing the necessity of addressing other problems. By focusing attention firmly on those within the institutional fold, there is an implicit denial of any need to look further afield. Such an attitude is most clearly illustrated at the more senior levels within the church. It does appear that the further a cleric progresses within the institution the more likely he is to become increasingly removed from the grounded reality of ordinary life.[31]

With regard to the Roman Catholic Archbishop within whose jurisdiction the Hope Community lay, by his own admission, his impressions of the life and work of the Hope Community were 'Vague, I've not actually been there.'[32] He considered that the opinion within the diocese would be 'favourable' towards the Community. He emphasised that students from the local seminary were regularly sent to the Community on placement. He did not consider that work being undertaken in the Com-

---

29   *Ibid.*
30   Clergyman Resident D.
31   Notable exceptions were Dereck Worlock and David Shepherd in Liverpool. 'With Bishop Shepherd, I have bull-dozed in one way or another buildings and authorities to help communities to stay together on grounds other than racist discrimination or religious sectarianism.' From an address delivered by Archbishop Dereck Worlock in Lichfield Cathedral, 4 May 1992.
32   Clergyman M.

munity influenced in any way either ongoing reflection with regard to priorities for ministry within the diocese or his own reflection with regard to the church and the 'option for the poor'.

In an interview with another senior clergyman who has visited the Community and generally approved of what was undertaken there, his opinion was that the Community was somewhat limited in its activities and effect. They were, 'not doing anything else other than being there, helping community development on the estate.'[33] He felt that the work on the estate was without great effect in terms of people attending church, and he acknowledged the importance that is still attached to the numbers of people 'returning to the pews'. Yet at the same time he was able to say that he considered the aim of all Christian outreach is, 'To put people at peace with God.'[34]

He appeared to see no potential conflict between these two aims. Rather he seemed to feel that the latter was perhaps the ideal while the former was geared to the pragmatic situations of daily life. From my own observation, individuals coming to a sense of peace with God was something considered vital to the life of people on the estate, while their attendance at church services was something far less real and possibly in the realm of the ideal. Thus here, there seemed a stark contrast between the everyday practical reality for clerical members of the institution and that of the marginalised people on the estate.

The Anglican Bishop is both appreciative and supportive of the community's work. His involvement has been predominantly at the level of encountering the leader of the community at various meetings, although he has also visited the community on a few occasions. He gives real encouragement to the involvement of the local Anglican clergy with the initiative, and expects to hear of the developing relationship in any report from the local parish. However, he freely admitted that the presence of the Community within his area had not led to a dramatic change in his own life style and practice. For him there is a clear distinction between those who live in an area amongst marginalised people and those who do not. The traditional model had seen mission as primarily moving into an area from an exterior base. In contrast, the very presence of the Hope Community upon the estate is seen as the most vital contribution to

---

33   Clergyman A.
34   *Ibid.*

any mission activity. By implication, he saw the role of Bishop as inevitably drawing away from any form of direct involvement and solidarity. 'I'm not incarnated in amongst the poor. There is a qualitative difference being in and out of such an incarnational enterprise. Bishops become caught up with strategic directions, management etc.'[35] Consideration of the future was for him the difficult path of trying to encourage new initiatives that were emerging, while at the same time realistically acknowledging that those who engaged in such initiatives would always be in the minority. However, he saw the vital role of the church as being to give real encouragement and support to those so engaged. 'It's easy to talk about the poor, but to walk alongside that's different. The Church needs to offer prayer, support and encouragement to those who can do so. The Hope Community continues to keep the poor on the agenda for me, which is so important.'[36]

The relationship of the local churches and the hierarchies to the Hope Community is for the religious sisters involved only one part of their involvement with the Church. Another vital area is the commitment they have to their own order. Accordingly, the sisters were asked what kind of support they received from their own religious congregation. Answers stressed the general sense of good will that accrued to the community throughout the Province, but raised questions particularly concerning the lack of involvement of other sisters in the Province. The Community leader expressed her own sense of isolation within this. 'There's a lot of good will to support what we're doing. But there's a lot of fear and most don't understand. Why aren't other I.J's coming here, when it is so much in keeping with our original charism?'[37]

The perceived reality in the congregation is that the work of the Community in Heath Town is one among a number of projects with which the congregation is involved. Indeed in a written response from the then Provincial of the congregation, a similar point was emphasised. 'The ministry of the Hope Community in Heath Town is one of a number of our ministries in poorer areas which emerged as a direct response to the priority we too for the poor.'[38]

---

35   Clergyman O.
36   *Ibid.*
37   Fieldworker A.
38   Provincial Letter.

It is the opinion of one of the sisters that the way in which information about the Hope Community reaches members of the Province is really by personal contact. One sister saw that there is deep grass roots support for the work itself.'[39] The Provincial, however, laid stress on the demanding nature of this particular apostolate. 'These projects in the inner city areas are always a priority for us. At the same time we are also very careful to choose people who can cope with the demands of the various ministries involved.'[40] It did appear that those sisters who had actually visited were those who gave the strongest support to the Community's efforts, for they had a better understanding of the real context.

The problem of publicity

One of the criticisms levelled against the Hope Community is that of accruing too much publicity. Behind this charge appears to be the fear that as the Community becomes better known this will detract from the work on the estate, and disrupt that work. In addition there was the fear of a form of publicity that might alienate the Community from the local residents by laying stress upon the sacrificial nature of the involvement of the Community with the people, rather than the emphasis that members of the Community give to what they have learned from the people during their time on the estate. One cleric expressed his concern in the following terms. 'At one level you need publicity to be effective as a sign of the kingdom. Danger could come in that it becomes something which almost destroys the Community by separating you off from the estate as those heroic women – that could be very damaging.'[41] Another cleric feared that the Community might become too insular since the focus of their concern was precisely those who lived on the Heath Town estate.

---

39   Fieldworker D. It is perhaps pertinent to note that this sister is actually 67 herself and most concerned to remain involved and part of the community as long as she is physically able so to do.

40   Provincial Letter.

41   Clergyman V.

The concern about becoming part of the public domain is one which some of the Community share with members of the local clergy. There exists a degree of fear that if the Community becomes too well known then the invasion of visitors might begin to have a disruptive and even damaging effect on the life and work of the Community. 'Maybe it would be better if nobody else knew that this place existed. If there was not all the publicity. If people know they want to find out more, then they come, then they change things.[42]

Another vital consideration for this member of the Community was the stress engendered by constant visits from those who wished to know more about the life and work of the Hope Community. The policy of the Community as espoused by the leader is to enable anyone who wishes, to come and learn from the Community's life and work. Consequently, individuals may come for varying amounts of time all through the year, although the summer months tend to be the most busy. Visitors are shown around the estate and introduced to residents. They engage in the Community activities and participate as fully as possible in the life and work. However, this brings added pressure and anxiety upon the members of the Community. 'It's hard, because you don't actually know sometimes the person you are taking around to introduce to residents. There's a tension in thinking are they going to say something really stupid here and are you going to be left having to deal with the mess?'[43] Another fieldworker shared this concern 'We have to be careful. We can forget the respect due to people on the estate, and if we don't respect them, then we should not be here.'[44] For this member an ideal situation would be if residents from the estate were the ones who showed any visitors around, and shared something of their own lives.

One particular incident of a television programme, which included a brief reference to the life and work of the Hope Community and involved filming on the estate, had crystallised the problem of publicity for this woman. 'I thought how do people see the public image that is portrayed out there. We can make 'the poor' sound too much like something with

---

42   Fieldworker E.
43   Fieldworker B.
44   Fieldworker C.

icing sugar, sweet and nice. Whereas it's not like that here; it's mucky, it's manure-like sometimes.'[45]

The actual practice of publicity predominantly involves the Community leader. On numbers of occasions she has gone to give talks to local groups or conferences, or radio or television interviews sharing something of life on the estate. Other members of the Community have been content to leave such a public profile to her and consequently the Community has come to be associated almost exclusively with the leader, who is seen as the lynch pin of all activities in the Community, indeed of the very survival of the community itself. 'A fair amount of community stability seems to devolve on A. If A. was to decide to go or her order to tell her to go and do something else, would the Hope Community succeed in maintaining its life without her?'[46] This is a situation which the leader of the Community is both cognisant of and concerned about. For her it induces also a feeling of loneliness and potential alienation. Her own concern about publicity is that very often what the Community is trying to do is not adequately apprehended by those outside, while within the Community most major initiatives are inspired and sustained by herself. In such a situation the potential for demagogic activity is great. She appreciates the dangers within the situation for building her own empire, and acknowledges the need for ongoing discernment. 'If I'm working to free people from dependency and yet here I am in a position where people are so dependent on me, it's a contradiction. The fear of building a kingdom around myself is always with me.'[47]

The exterior perception of the Community is that A. alone has the power and initiative to carry through any novel practices. For her own part, A. avows that she would welcome others within the Community taking more initiative and indeed more responsibility. 'I believe there is within the Community plenty of opportunity for individuals to be involved and to take responsibility at all levels. The aim is for us all to take responsibility, for us to recognise the gifts within the group.'[48] The hope of one of the local clergy is similar. He hopes that the Community would both continue and develop in its manner of presence in the locality as a

---

45   *Ibid.*
46   Clergyman V.
47   Fieldworker A.
48   *Ibid.*

witness both to the residents of the estate and to the church. Indeed, that it will continue to be church for the people of the estate, until such time as a more effective way can be found to establish a vibrant relationship with the institution. For this to be possible, he considers it essential that the Community concentrates more on its presence among the people, than on the many and varied activities in which it might become involved. He feels there is a 'danger of doing', and that this might undermine the very purpose of the Community's presence. 'We justify ourselves so often by work, instead of saying the purpose of the Hope Community is to live and to show Christian living in the middle of the estate, where Christian living is not thought about, or considered absurd.'[49]

This cleric raises a dilemma. He would espouse an ecumenical collective acknowledgement of, and support for, the life and work of the Community. At the same time he would consider it vital to protect both the anonymity and the pragmatic interaction of the Community with the local people. How to ensure adequate assistance and support while at the same time respecting the vulnerable nature of the local context is a problem as yet unresolved.'[50]

A focus for local reconciliation

One way in which the local community is involved with the Community is through a local initiative involving the Churches and the Community endeavouring to promote reconciliation within the area. Following a police attempt to crack down on the drug problem in Heath Town there was a major public disturbance, and the coverage in local press and media made visible the degree of hurt which was festering within the estate. Living in the midst of the estate, the Community was receptive to the

---

49   *Ibid.*
50   *Ibid.*

confidences and confusion of the residents.[51] 'The Hope Community were in a position to hear and feel the hurt of the community, and they naturally found themselves as a buffer between the police and those who were hurting.'[52]

Out of this situation the BREACH[53] project was born. There was a concern amongst the local churches in conjunction with the Hope Community to rebuild relationships within the local community. It was felt that the issue of reconciliation was at the very heart of the restoration of right relationships and addressed the issues of justice and full participation in the community by all individuals. The purpose of the BREACH venture is to bring reconciliation to each and all in the community of Heath Town and to assist in the empowerment of local people.

A service was held to mark the appointment of two fieldworkers. However, though the aim of the project was reconciliation and empowerment, the very format of the service was such as to emphasise the alienation and powerlessness of the local community. This was particularly apparent in consideration of the language of the service. Language is the most common form of communication, the 'ordinary' means of discourse, yet it may also alienate and divide, increase isolation and frustration. It may be used to satisfy the desires of the articulate and yet never touch the aspirations of the inarticulate. It may be used to preach at God, rather than be the simple plea for openness to the word of God.

The order of service included many prayers with congregational participation – for those members of the congregation who could read. All the prayers, passages of scripture, and hymns had been thoughtfully chosen for the occasion. Yet the lack of silence – in which all could participate – and the very virtuosity of some of the prayers were of a genre far removed from the group from Heath Town who had come to the service. The prayer of confession certainly expressed what many of those present felt. 'We confess that we have failed to share the good we have been given, have made the wrong choices and taken away others' powers

---

51   In listening to the hurt of the local residents, key issues began to emerge. These included – a history of rejection on the ground, the lack of support for mental health patients sent into the community, poor relationships with the local police, and economic and social injustice at many different levels.

52   Clergyman U.

53   Literally BREACH refers to standing in the breach across a divide. This seemed to the management committee of the project the most appropriate name.

to choose, have built barriers, called names.' It confirmed, 'We have not loved you, Lord, whole-heartedly, nor our neighbours as ourselves. We have failed to recognise and receive what you offer to us in the gifts and ministries of each other.'[54] Yet the 'Oh dear.... Bloody hell' of Z. – from an elderly gentleman who was recovering from a stroke, was frustrated by his inability to say more, but wanting to make his own contribution towards reconciliation – expressed perhaps more eloquently to God the reality of our human condition. It may be that the very framework of our 'so many words' is but a defence against our own inadequacy and vulnerability before God and other people. In the presence of the marginalised it is difficult to evade such unpalatable insight.

The focus of the BREACH project has been to try to identify what issues are considered by local people to be important and identify potential local leaders. The two BREACH workers have focused their attention on contacts with key groups and workers, not as professionals talking to other professionals[55] but as local people involved with other local people. 'So much potential is all but knocked out of them, hope is also knocked out of them.'[56] The aim of the project is to harness such potential before it is snuffed out. Thus the workers affirm individuals and groups in their concerns and endeavour to act as co-ordinating personnel to bring people together, and then fade into the background. Accordingly, the role of the workers is essentially one of facilitating, listening and drawing out issues that are raised for the benefit of all in the locality. In this process they are seen as promoting a deep form of reconciliation both within the local area, and between the local residents and various official bodies with whom the people come into daily contact.

---

54 From the order of service to mark the inauguration of the BREACH venture, 23 January 1991.
55 Here I am indebted to Austin Smith's insight that no one uses the term professional except professionals, for ordinary people the term is a major snub.
56 Clergyman U.

Gender specific issues

An important aspect of the life of the institutional church with which the Community has become involved is the formation of personnel for religious life. In this connection, one novice director regularly sends novices to the Hope Community on an experimental basis.[57] In reflecting on the experience he has had with various novices, and his own experience in visiting the Community, he raised the interesting point that perhaps in some way the form of Community living and apostolate might be something more easily approached by religious women than by men. His reasoning here was that most religious men were in training to be priests with a specific active role envisaged. This role prescinded from the kind of participation which might involve a form of activity seen as more passive and less structured then those traditionally associated with priesthood. 'I got the impression there was an enormous amount of sitting around drinking cups of tea, rather than getting on and doing things.'[58] To this novice director the time spent on such an apostolate was not something which men found either easy or conducive. 'It comes hard to men. Just being there to allow people to be themselves and come and talk, and be ready for whatever is offered.'[59]

Paradoxically this openness to just being with the people and listening to their lives and all that this contained was a consideration that the novice director felt it was very important the novices should experience. It was noteworthy that most novices both felt that something important was taking place within the Hope Community and maintained a link after they had left. Indeed they frequently returned and would take others from the noviceship to events such as the Community celebrations. For the novice director the important of this ministry amongst the people and the emphasis that it appeared to give to a particular ministry by women had further ramifications with regard to the development of the social apostolate amongst the Jesuits. 'I would wonder whether some groups of women religious, are much more able for this. There seems to be some-

---

57 An 'experiment' in these terms refers to a placement commitment which forms part of the formation programme of the Society of Jesus.
58 Novice Master I.
59 *Ibid.*

thing fairly normal about a group of women sitting chatting to people over cups of tea and making contacts.'[60] He continued, 'perhaps it might be best for us simply to accept that women religious are able to do this much better so let them get on with it.'

The most important feature of the Community life as far as the novice director was concerned was being available to the people. It was he felt a lesson that could be learned by the Jesuits if they decided to engage in a similar apostolate. Yet a particular problem still remained for them, namely what they were to do as priests. Priesthood thus acquired a major dynamic in ministry which if disavowed by the priests themselves would be open to question by the people, some of whom might well be inured in a traditional way of relating to priests. Priesthood also carried with it the inevitable involvement with structure and the institution which to a degree the sisters managed to escape. 'The sisters are members of the institution but not working in a way that is part of the institutionalised setup. They are not parish sisters.'[61] Without entering into the major debate on the nature of priesthood, it does appear that the issue has a certain bearing on the possibilities of men being involved in a ministry similar to that of the Hope Community. An important feature of this kind of ministry appears to be the notable lack of structure involved. Indeed it might be seen as a ministry that precedes structure. A problem might then result if at some future point attempts were made to impose a structure, with all the consequent problems that structures are subject to.

The importance of the mission of women, as identified by the novice director, has a singular form of outreach in the engagement with women on the estate, many of whom are single parents. A women's group was established to bring together the single parents for meetings on issues of current concern to them, which might range from Easter cooking, through the possibilities of further education, to discussing the problems of estate management which directly relate to them. Trips have been organised to more distant shopping areas, leisure complexes, and other women's groups, always with adequate child-care provision. The Community minibus has been a vital resource for any such journeys. The group was under the direction of the oldest sister and one of the young lay women who had established particularly good relations with her contemporaries

---

60   *Ibid.*
61   *Ibid.*

on the estate. For the sister there is a vehement attitude towards the abuse which she feels these women suffer in often very volatile and certainly potentially explosive relationships with their temporary or permanent partners. 'I feel the women are used and abused. They don't know their own potential.' Her own personal belief was that, 'Women and men are equal in the eyes of God, so why should they be existing almost like slaves, grateful for any attention from the greatest blackguard on the estate. They have lots of potential in themselves.'[62]

For this sister the most important feature of her work with the women's group was helping to facilitate, very gradually, a growing sense of self-worth on the part of individual women. This sense of self-esteem was linked to a recognition of latent ability, and as the women worked together they began to realise something of their own gifts and talents, which might be utilised both individually and in a communal way to assist other women. Such a growth in self-awareness and self-confidence was the only way in which this sister could conceive of a change of attitude from one of servile fear towards their male partners to one of equality and potential rapport. The consequent effect on the lives of their children could be potentially transformative. 'I think if the women could reach a better awareness of their own value, they would look at their families differently.'[63]

Of particular concern to this sister was the way in which boys within such families were handled. The laxity of any discipline meant that they rapidly achieved a state beyond the control of their mothers in their endeavours to emulate the father figure of the household, who might or might not be their natural father. 'They disobey their mothers from an early age. They take it as their right that they should have more consideration than girls and easily abuse their mothers. So they grow up into the same type of man as the one who fathered them.'[64]

Another member of the community was particularly aware of the latent aggression which she experienced amongst the young boys on the estate. A product of their own deficient rearing and lack of self-discipline, such aggression was poised below the surface, ready to erupt into violence at the least provocation. 'There's a volcano of anger. The

---

62   Fieldworker D.
63   *Ibid.*
64   *Ibid.*

children are like sponges, they pick up the anger and frustration of their adults and store it all at a subconscious level.' She had experience of the efforts of this anger. 'It comes out at the slightest hint of challenge or opposition to their viewpoints and they sometimes go berserk.'[65]

For the oldest sister, starting the women's group was an attempt to enable the gradual growth of self-confidence and self-assurance amongst the women in order that they might eventually be able to take control of their own destiny. In this fashion there might be the hope that they could provide a greater degree of security for the children. Indeed, she felt that because the women formed a substantial group on the estate, if they could begin to grow in confidence and support one another, they could have significant effect if they participated in the organisations on the estate. 'I know it wouldn't happen that all would be involved, but if enough were, it could make a real change.'[66] For the young lay woman in the community, her relationships with the women on the estate has involved sharing at some real depth. 'I've spent a lot of time with them. Over the months I've built up relationship with a handful of women where trust has grown. Where they have opened up a lot to me and vice versa. We've shared a lot.'[67]

Coming from the south of England with a pronounced accent, this young laywoman, has found it difficult to be accepted across the cultural gulf of class relationships. What has sustained her connection with the people is the reality that she is part of the Hope Community, linked with the sisters and benefiting from the credibility which the Community has established with the people over the years. 'There is an immediate sense of "She's OK, she's part of the Community". Over the years the Community have built up their street cred.'[68] The nature of her involvement with the women of the estate is often on the very practical level of taking food to homes or helping to decorate, 'getting my hands dirty.'[69] In this way trust has been established, and for this fieldworker both recognition of the precarious nature of the life of the women and an admiration for the way in which the women manage to sustain life for themselves and

65   Fieldworker E.
66   Fieldworker D.
67   Fieldworker C.
68   *Ibid.*
69   *Ibid.*

their families. 'And they've given a hell of a lot to me in so many ways.'[70]

Within the women's groups the members are predominantly white, and the Hope Community's contact with the black community has been very slow to develop over the years. There are some key members of the black community on the estate who have good relationships with the Community, but from a wider vantage point, given the proportion of black people living on the estate, they are disproportionately represented in any Hope Community activity.

When I raised this issue with the black worker of the BREACH project, his answer was illuminating in terms of the historical and cultural gulf which needed to be overcome for there to be real contact between the Hope Community and the black community. He stressed that the black community was so marginalised within society that in general members would only react to something which appears to have a clear meaning or use for them. Thus if the Hope Community were offering a specific service which was relevant to the black community's needs then more people would be involved. Thus the actual colour issue, i.e., that all the Hope Community members were white, would not be so central a factor as whether what was provided by the Community had any relevance to black people. This had particular importance with regard to the involvement of black women in the women's group. It was important that what was taking place was seen as having specific relevance to needs within the black community. In order for this to be addressed, he suggested there might need to be some further consideration about the format of the group. 'Are we wanting black people to come to what is already set up, or whether we want to go ahead and do something with and for black people?'[71]

A key issue also in relating to the wider black community was the fact that all the community were women. For black men this might well prove a problem to establishing any meaningful interaction. 'Black men wouldn't see you as being much use to them. Growing up as a black man, to actually confide in a woman is not the normal thing, to relate and share on that level. It is only beginning to occur in this late generation'[72] The

---

70   *Ibid.*
71   BREACH Worker F.
72   *Ibid.*

presence of Roman Catholic religious sisters could also pose a problem for the black community few of whom were of the same denominational persuasion. On the part of this black BREACH worker, there was also the consideration of how he could more effectively integrate his work with the Hope Community. He considered that it was an opportunity for a reciprocal process of understanding. 'I think it is also an opportunity for some of the black community to learn also what you have to bring being women and Roman Catholics.'[73] Emphasis was given by this man to the very real positive reputation that the Hope Community has amongst the Black community. Yet he stressed that this good reputation is again general rather than specific. Thus the very presence of the Community on the estate, though valued, is not necessarily considered 'enough' in itself without more tangible successful results of such involvement.

Such a view stands in stark contrast to the opinions of local white clergy cited above, who stressed the importance of the presence of the Community as being in itself of importance over and above anything which they might be engaged in. This is indicative of the differing priorities given to the involvement and activity of the Hope Community by the various affiliating bodies to which they are or wish to be committed. It also illustrates the pressure upon the community from conflicting expectations and the ongoing need for reflection on their varied involvements and sensitivity to the differing needs of individuals and groups upon the estate.

Community views of the Churches

The as yet unconsidered element in this conversation is the spectrum of understanding evinced by members of the Hope Community themselves with regard to their involvement with the local churches and their views of the institution from the perspective of their life on the estate. A general question was posed to members of the Community about their involvement with the institutional church and a supplementary question as to whether their ideas about church had changed during their time of involvement with the Community.

---

73   BREACH worker F.

For one sister, her own sense of church and its relevance for herself had not changed at all, yet she stressed that the institution seemed irrelevant for the people of the estate. 'It's relevance to me is the same as it always was. I was brought up in it, I'm part of it, in a community of sisters. But it has little or no relevance to the people here as such. God has relevance but not the church.'[74]

For one of the young lay women, her relationship with the church had deteriorated during her time with the Community, but this appeared to have more to do with the lack of vibrancy of the liturgy at the local parish, than with any particular reflection with regard to her life on the estate. Such a sense of alienation from the ritual of the Church finds an echo in the lives of the local people as already indicated. Indeed, the very resonance of this opinion with the life of residents on the estate gives this young lay woman a greater feel for the forms and symbols of prayer which have meaning for the people of the estate.

For another of the young lay women there is more of a sense of frustration than alienation. Rather than causing her to lose touch with the institution, it would appear that her time on the estate has caused her to wrestle more directly with key issues. These appear to centre for her on the inability of the church to use the gifts and talents of those who attend. Moreover she see the reason for this as being the fear of the church that such potential incorporation into the life of the church might lead to a situation beyond the control of its governing authorities. By contrast the activities of the Hope Community on the estate, in particular the regular meetings for prayer and scripture sharing and the Community celebrations, actually do endeavour to incorporate contributions from the people. 'The church institution as far as I'm concerned is a pain. It seems to want always to control – mostly out of fear and I think that is its downfall, because there's a lot of potential within people but this is not allowed to show.' By contrast 'here in this place evangelisation takes place through people who aren't tied to regulations. The same God is operative, but here things are people-directed.' Consequently, 'it's easier for people to be involved here than going to some church where they don't know the rules and regulations.'[75]

---

74   Fieldworker B.
75   Fieldworker E.

For this lay woman, the contrast between what occurs within the institutional church and what she experiences upon the estate has caused her to rethink her whole understanding of church attendance. In her process of reflection she had come to a stage where the most helpful thing for her own faith was not to attend the local Anglican church, which would have been the place of her denominational allegiance. She continued to attend the weekly mass in the Community chapel. Apart from this she had come to give increasing value to the Community celebrations and to feel that these were earthed in the lives of the people of the estate in a way unlike any formal church liturgy that she had ever attended. What has caused her to abandon – at least temporarily – formal church attendance is the direct result of her experience in living and working on the estate. She does not see this as an irretrievable step, but rather part of her own journey in faith. 'How do I view church? That's a big one, cos I'm in the middle of that muddle.' She continued, 'I think in a way church for me is the celebrations here which have spoken to me in a different way from any church service I've been to.' For her 'the institutional church is still so middle class it makes me angry. It's so apart from the people.' Her life has been changed since coming to the estate. 'Living here has changed me. I just love the way the liturgy here comes from the people and is an 'altogether thing' not an imposed thing.'[76]

For the oldest of the sisters, her view of her relationship with the institutional church has changed over the years, and she associates this with the coming to maturity of her own understanding. She find herself aware of the human reality of the church which includes individuals such as the local clergy with the pressures that they too are subject to. What concerns her most is that the church should take a stand with those who are unable and ill equipped in contemporary society. She would welcome more involvement of those from the institution on the estate, but recognises that the form of organisation acceptable to the institution would be a far too intrusive presence for those on the estate. 'I'd like to see it more involved here but how? People don't want to be organised.'[77]

The Community leader would describe herself, as a conservative Catholic with regard to her relationship with the church. The liturgy of the mass is important for her, though very often her involvement in af-

---

76   Fieldworker C.
77   Fieldworker E.

fairs on and off the estate prevent her from regular attendance. She affirms the tradition of the church and acknowledges the need for an external authority. 'I believe firmly in an outside authority or you pick and choose what suits you.'[78] For her too the very nature of her commitment to religious life in the evangelical counsels is both a consecration to God through the Church and to the people of the estate. Thus she would re-envisage the vows through a dominant dynamic of availability. This she sees as the key to who the sisters are and the reason why they live on the estate. For her there is no question of devaluing the traditional call to celibacy. It is a subject which is viewed as an anachronism by the people of the estate, yet perennially occurs as a topic in discussion. In the midst of often very broken relationships, and with an ethos that insists there cannot be human fulfilment without an intimate sexual relationship, the presence of a community of celibate women who appear to be normal poses questions concerning the nature of loving relationships. 'Relationships are so broken, no stability, and yet it is felt that you can't be human unless you have a sexual relationship. But here we are and we seem to be normal and celibate. It raises terrific questions regarding love and what it is.'[79]

With regard to the vow of poverty, again she tied it to her understanding of being available not tied in to certain material securities, but the adoption of a simple lifestyle. In this way also she felt there was the opportunity for sharing with the local people, who have no choice but to live simply, and the chance to reflect on what were the priority factors in life. 'The people here have the opportunity to live a simply lifestyle, but in the main they are angry at being deprived of so much. Because of the example of our lives this could present the opportunity to look at what is important in life, what they value in life.'[80] Obedience was seen by this sister as primarily rooted in understanding the will of God, and finding something of this through pragmatic realities. 'Obedience is for me the will of God, understanding what God wants, where he is, in our day, through people and events.'[81]

---

78   Fieldworker A.
79   *Ibid.*
80   *Ibid.*
81   *Ibid.*

It has become apparent within this chapter that the Hope Community's relationship with Christian churches involves no stable equilibrium of approach. At a local level there is a predominant dynamic of support, although the commitment within that in practical terms is variable. At a diocesan level the divergence is more marked, there is both a favourable attitude towards the community coexisting with what appears to be both ignorance and low prioritising of their endeavours. A similar contrast appears to exist within the religious congregation to which the sisters belong. Grass roots goodwill appears to predominate, while the attitude of the hierarchy appears more guarded. The ecumenical support at local and diocesan level appears impressive while not denying denominational allegiances.

The experience of the Hope Community members with regard to the institutional church has been variable but, not static. If it is the case that the very form of their ministry is one predominantly feminine and both alien and incomprehensible to the present male clerical modus operandi, confrontation with the institution may be inevitable. Yet the avowed recent declarations of the churches concerning the involvement of women would appear to mitigate such a conflictual necessity. There appears to be the emergence of both potential and actual theological and ecclesiological cognitive dissonance on the part of the institution. This is the subject of further exploration in the following chapter.

Chapter 5

Disabling Dissonances

I don't' know if I could live with the poor
if I didn't find God in their rags,
if God was not there like a fire,
burning my egoism slowly.[1]

A lot of people feel they have to jump the hurdles to fit into any congregation. They must do the changing and must present themselves as in need. They have to look down on where they are at, at this moment in time, and this is in order to feel that they might be accepted in that church family – that's a terrible thing really.[2]

The Church is the community of people that Christ calls not only to live justly with each other and with the world, but to do so in a way that acknowledges him explicitly as the Lord. In this community the poor and deprived have a place of privilege. This privilege obviously does not consist of power or wealth. It is rather the special love that Christ has for those who are marginalised. This love is special in the sense that the universal love of God cannot tolerate the exclusion of anyone, and so has particular regard for those who tend to be excluded by the rest of us.[3]

The inclusive love of God challenges the exclusive nature of the systems and institutions within society. Though the Church, in a sense, embodies a guarantee that God's love will ultimately triumph, here and now this dramatic conflict is being acted out within it. The picture emerging from previous chapters regarding life on the margins is one of individuals caught in a position of excluded marginality. This is implemented and sustained under social and economic conditions, reinforced by cultural upheaval and accommodated by the church. It leads ultimately to an exterior devaluation of their dignity within society and an interior sense of

---

1   Casaldaliga Bishop, cited in Gonzalez-Faus J., 'We proclaim a crucified Messiah', in Duquoc C. and Floristan C. [eds.], *Where is God? : A Cry of Human Distress*, [Concilium], London, SCM, 1992, pp. 82-93.
2   Clergyman, Resident D.
3   Hamilton T., *solidarity: The Missing Link in Irish Society*, Dublin, Jesuit Centre for Faith and Justice, 1991, p. 61.

worthlessness. Such individuals have become as the flotsam and jetsam of a society which no longer requires their existence but merely tolerates their presence. The very life and work of such as the Hope Community, with the alternative priorities to which they endeavour to give witness, is a potential challenge both to the prevailing ethos of such a society, and to the accommodationist stance of the church within it.

Meanwhile dramatic moves within the cultural sphere appeared to be moving toward a form of metanoia particularly focused in terms of post-modernism. There did appear to be a strange combination of playfulness and violence in this post-modern world. The playfulness expanded across a colourful kaleidoscope of pastiche while the violence, partially pro-voked by increased social polarisation, acquiesced in the impetus toward the utilitarian status of individuals. The inextricable interwoveness of life ensured that postmodernism could not simply be what existed after mod-ernity but rather the state of being entangled in modernity, perhaps as something from which we could not escape but in which we no longer had any faith.[4] There is a problem in endeavouring to make any state-ment with regard to postmodernism. This in-built linguistic problematic, resulting in a degree of incoherence, would seem to be one of the most distinctive attributes of postmodernism, indeed arguably its defining fea-ture. Such incoherence linked with the sense of existential insecurity [it is contended], gives the potential both for a reappraisal of, and an enter-ing into solidarity with, those in a marginal existence within our inner cities. However, there is also an insidious potential for exploitation here. For the 'marginal' within post-modern thought has ceased to be periph-eral but rather has moved to a novel intellectually applauded position, thereby often acquiring the subservient role of a pawn utilised to score some particular subversive point. According to Yudice, 'Contemporary post-structuralist thought has apotheistically reclaimed 'marginality' as a liberating force.'[5] Thus those who have had the status of marginality

---

4   This tragic demise of faith is depicted by Hebdige in a chaotic image as modernity without the hopes and dreams which made modernity possible. 'It is a hydra-headed decentred condition in which we are dragged along from pillar to post across a succession of reflection surfaces drawn by the call of the wild signifier.' Hebdige D., *Hiding in the Light: On Images and Things*, London, Routledge, 1988, p. 195.

5   Yudice G., 'Marginality and the Ethics of Survival', in Ross A., *Universal Aban-don: The Politics of Postmodernism*, Edinburgh, Edinburgh University Press, 1989, pp. 214-236.

thrust upon them, by exclusion from mainstream society, suffer the further indignity of the exploitation of their position in order to further the
purposes of novel social and economic injustice. No longer accorded the
respect of individual identification, those on the margins are considered
en masse as a potential pressure group to be utilised for the acquisition of
power. However to be a person is to have an intrinsic value, and not
merely to be important as a source of potential power for another. It follows therefore as an article of faith that no human being may be used
merely as a means by somebody else. If there is indeed a process of reciprocity whereby Christ is encountered in people on the margins and proclaimed to them, it becomes more apparent that there is a degree of ambiguity as to what evangelisation might mean. The response to such ambiguity may mean a waiting in powerlessness with ongoing reflection on
the experience and patient discernment of future activity. Alternatively, a
response may involve the evasion of such seeming passivity by the advo-
cacy of more immediately active policies.

Power and powerlessness, activism and non-activism were central to
a document from the Roman Catholic Bishops Conference of England
and Wales, *From Charity to Empowerment.* The avowed aim of the
document was to initiate a discussion about power, and it endeavoured to
raise some of the complex issues involved. 'We choose power as the
centre-piece of our reflection because difficulties about power can come
between the Church and the poor in a variety of ways.' Indeed the document reflected 'As Christians we are often ambivalent about power, and
we sometime find ourselves approving of power in the hands of authorities while disapproving of it in the hands of ordinary people.'[6] Conflicting power situations continue to be a feature of the interaction between
the institutional church and the poor – the power of the former and the
powerlessness of the latter. The definition produced by the Bishops
sought to avoid this, but despite their best efforts, the honest admission
that there may indeed never be the equitable distribution of power that is
the goal, appeared to denote the underlying tone and theme. There is almost a sense of resignation that the poor will never be able to shape their
own destiny in a way that is accessible to others. 'Positively empower-

---

6   Committee for Community Relations Catholic Bishops Conference of England and
     Wales *Charity to Empowerment: The Church's Mission Alongside Poor and Margi-
     nalised People,* London, 1992.

ment is based on solidarity and mutual respect and strives for an equality of relationship which it may never fully achieve.'[7]

It is possible that the failure to achieve this relationship may be partially caused by the approach to the marginalised still coming from the realism of a benevolent paternalistic philanthropy. Difficulties arise also in working with those who are unable to enter into this kind of educative process, but who nonetheless have something to contribute by the very uniqueness of themselves, their lives, and their understanding, even if they are formally inarticulate.

It may be that the only decisive counter-force to the social, economic and cultural pressures of our time is the power of communities proposing alternative priorities for living. In a world characterised by the proliferation of images and so many forces vying for our attention, even the struggle together to know what deserves our attention is an important communitarian form. For our lives are defined by that to which we give most serious attention.

Traditionally it is the church who has given the lead with regard to communitarian forms, always upholding the family as the basic unit of society. Hauerwas in *Resident Aliens*[8] argues that the church, as those called out by God, embodies a social alternative that the world cannot on its own terms know. His assertion is that theology since the Enlightenment has tended to ask the wrong question – how do we make the gospel credible to the modern world? – and by so doing has allowed the said world to determine the corollary questions and thereby limit the answers. From this arose an apologetics based on the political assumption that Christians are committed to transforming our ecclesial claims into intellectual assumptions that will enable us to be faithful to Christ, while still participating in the political structures of a world that does not yet know Christ. However, it is Hauerwas' assertion that in the life, death and resurrection of Christ, all human history must be reviewed. So the theological task now, unlike previous centuries is to make the world credible to the gospel – an important inversion.

The Christian faith for Hauerwas is the invitation to be part of what he terms an 'alien people', a group who base their entire *Lebens-*

---

7   *Ibid.*
8   Hauerwas S. and Williman W., *Resident Aliens*, Nashville, Abingdon Press, 1989, p. 20ff.

geschichte on the reality of their faith in Christ. Christianity is asserted to be mostly a matter of politics but politics as defined by the gospel, and thus a countercultural phenomenon. Accordingly the challenge of Jesus is the political dilemma of how to be faithful to a strange community which is shaped by a story of how God is with us. Thus there is the constant reiteration through Hauerwas' work of this call for the church to renew itself as the distinctive community that it was called to be, and in which it will enable others by its witness.

For Hauerwas the church is the one comprehensive community: the one political entity in our culture that is global, transnational, transcultural. Thus the church does not have a social strategy, the church is a social strategy. With increasing urgency he reminds his readers of the need for a faithful community rather than an efficient organisation. Yet this is seen as requiring a lifelong call to conversion a long process of being engrafted into a new people. Thus might the church become a countercultural social structure, which seeks to influence the world by being church, being something the world cannot be, lacking as it does faith and vision. The most credible witness of the church is a living breathing visible community of faith. Here the church needs leaders who can help to form such vision and pragmatic reality, and it is in the formation of ministers, and indeed in the theological rationale for ministry, that Hauerwas sounds a clarion call for change. 'What pastors and laity need is a theological rationale for ministry which is so cosmic, eschatological and therefore countercultural that they are enabled to keep at Christian ministry in a world determined to live as if God were dead.' Indeed, he goes on to say 'Anything less misreads both the scandal of the gospel, and the corruption of our culture.'[9]

The gospel is so demanding that there must be the expectation that we will need to suffer and sacrifice for it. This is no masochistic vision, but a calm perception of reality. However, today's church suffers from an over-surfeit of suffocating niceness and domesticated metaphor. It has lost its vitality and vibrant engagement with pragmatic reality. Hauerwas raises the question – how do we help people to survive as Christians? There is a sense in which our world recognises the challenging nature of the Christian faith and subverts it either by ignoring Christians or by giving them the freedom to be religious within the private domain. The

---

9   *Ibid.* p. 145.

challenge facing the church is political, social, and ecclesial – the formation of a visible body of people who know the cost of discipleship and are willing to pay it.

The fundamental endeavour of Christian social action, Hauerwas argues, is to create a community that makes it possible for people to live by the truth rather than to exist by what is false. Our materialism and self-deceit are ways we appropriate for trying to deal with our insecurity. Most of our social activism is formed on the presumption that God is superfluous to the formation of a world of peace with justice. Yet the moment that life is formed on the presumption that we are not participants in God's continuing history of creation and redemption, we are acting on unbelief rather than faith. Therefore Christian politics has come to mean Christian social activism. Hauerwas argues that the political task of Christians is to be the church rather than to transform the world. He argues that the church gives us the interpretative skills whereby we come to see the world for what it is. 'Much of what passes for Christian social concern today, of the left or right is the social concern of a Church that seems to have despaired of being Church – led into ersatz Christian ethical activity.'[10] Within such a society, it is important for our purposes to consider the particular position of the Roman Catholic Church. Here according to one authority, the potential for challenging the prevailing ethos is available particularly in the lives and work of its clergy and religious. The value it sets upon the life-long commitment of its priesthood and religions 'has enabled them and could still enable them, to stand as a sign of contradiction to the pretensions both of the state and of the forces of cupidity that the state has unleashed.'[11] However, it has become clear from both Archer[12] and Boyle's work, that in the desire for respectability the Roman Catholic Church in Britain has adopted a middle class oriented, élitist and secularised mode of being. Such criticism finds its corollary in Milbank's[13] criticism of the two opposite wings of the international Roman Catholic scene: the theological conservatives and the

---

10   *Ibid.* p. 80.
11   Boyle, N., 'Understanding Thatcherism', *New Blackfriars*, Vol 69, No. 818, July/August, 1988, pp. 307-324.
12   See Chapter 2.
13   Milbank J., *Theology and Social Theory: Beyond Secular Reason*, Blackwell, Oxford, 1990.

third world liberation theologians for being the bearers of secularisation in their respective fights for democracy and equality. For him, political and liberation theology has moved beyond the position where reflection and evaluation are possible, because of their association of Marxism with a Christian coming-to-terms with Enlightenment freedom, they are therefore inevitably wedded to a positive evaluation of the secular.

Williams supports Milbank's critique of liberation theology. His conviction is that liberation theology is insufficiently political in that it has given up on the traditional political practices. He sees it as caught in a trap of projecting the only way forward in terms of some cataclysmic social change. For some liberation theologians this would appear to be the only possible condition for real social justice. Such liberation theologians have no perception of creative social change emerging within their present political processes. However, he also clearly states the difficulty of making any helpful generalisations about liberation theology in terms of applying practice in any pandemic manner. 'Increasingly, it has become impossible to generalise usefully about liberation theology as a project that makes Christian language and practice instrumental to a programme whose norms come from elsewhere.'[14]

However, the work of Rowland and Corner[15] provides an ameliorating codicil to the above view. Here it is asserted that liberation theology cannot be properly understood if its close contact with action in favour of the poor is ignored. It presents a challenge to those who wield power with a theological method which states that the only way to derive theological truth is by starting where people are, because it is paying attention to the lives of the poor and particularly oppressed people that one will find God. 'If you want to do theology, you have to start where people are, particularly the people that the Bible is primarily concerned with, who are the dispossessed, the widow, the orphan, the stranger, the prostitute, the pimp, and the tax-collector.' This is an action involvement, 'Find out what they are saying, thinking and feeling and that is the stuff out of which the glimpses of God will emerge.'[16]

---

14 Williams R., 'Saving Time: thoughts on practice, patience and vision', *New Black-friars*, Vol. 73, No. 861, June, 1992, pp. 319-326.
15 Rowland C & Corner M., *Liberating Exegesis: The Challenge of Liberation Theology to Biblical Studies*, London, SPCK, 1990.
16 *Ibid.* p. 42.

There is presented a two-fold dynamic: that in the experience of oppression, hunger, poverty and death, God is speaking to all people today, and that God's presence amongst the millions unknown and unloved by humanity, but blessed in the eyes of God is confirmed by the witnesses of the Christian tradition. Rowland argues that the only way to fill the vacuous European edifice with insight and power is to be attentive to the experience of the poor and the injustices of their environment. The privileged status of the poor in the divine perspective is an evangelizing force operative within those who approach them. The Hope Community members have given eloquent testimony to this dynamic. It appears that the poor in the church are the structural source that assures the church of really being the agent of truth and justice. Since very few of the poor in Britain today find a home within the church, this would appear to necessitate the conversion of the historical church to which Rowland refers. Rowland emphasises the life-experience of the individual as both the starting point and the validating factor for reflection. He stresses that most liberation theologians are engaged in costly small-scale protests and programmes at the grassroots, which offer a glimpse of God's eschatological kingdom amidst the injustices of the old order. Rowland suggests that one of the contributions of a British liberation theology could be to interest ecumenical bodies in social questions around which different denominations might achieve an orthopraxis and divert their concerns from their search for an orthodoxy reflected in common consent to a series of doctrinal propositions. He asserts that the poor in Britain, as elsewhere in the world, are increasingly being seen as the objects of private charity rather than state provision. Thus society passes the task of listening to and articulating the concerns of the poor to private individuals who may or may not be thus inclined, but who will have comparatively little influence on the functioning of political policy, which determines much of the oppressive structures under which the poor continue to suffer. Indeed, a particularly insidious feature of such private charity is that emphasis is given to a reconciliation which breeds subservience, apathy and despair amongst the poor.

The harshness of the Christian gospel is easily made subservient to an ideology of reconciliation, which manipulates the principles of Christian love into a means of resisting any real challenge to the established order. Yet the uncompromising character of the call to discipleship sits uneasily alongside the comfortable *Sitz im Leben* from which the contemporary church in Britain so often presents the gospel. It seems inevitable in our contemporary context that reconciliation first involves conflict. Yet, 'the negative is always the condition of a greater positive, the cross a condition of the resurrection.'[17]

The consciousness of a need to seek within British shores for something that might engage the preferential option for the poor has taken various forms. One conference, endeavouring to search for a British Liberation Theology, invited two members of the estate along with the Hope Community leader to a meeting in Crewe. The participation of the residents from the estate was reported as being a vital part of the conference, and on their return they endeavoured to convey something of what had happened to those attending one of the Faith Alive meetings. For one of the participants it had been a very significant experience. 'It was brilliant. I thought they'd all be educated, and with degrees and that, but some were working with the homeless, some in Toxteth.' He went on to say, 'There were priests and nuns and sisters and ordinary people. They all seemed to have a vision but no one knew what it was. We were all looking for it. I kind of grasped it.' The commitment of all present at the meeting to an undefined notion – liberation theology – did not seem to impede this man's own concern to be involved. He had obviously perceived a common vision though the practical details might be obscure.

A more cynical friend involved in this conversation made suggestions based on his experience of the church. 'It'll be polite....have a cup of tea first. It's like a teacher explaining things to a child.'[18] Later in the evening when asked to expand this opinion he stressed that religion had been imposed in the past, that today it was rather a polite affair but that it had not yet reached the stage of a loving open possibility. He considered the churches to be still too enmeshed in disputes about details that seemed irrelevant to him, such as forms of liturgy and ritual. This view was further substantiated by the other participant at the conference who described the occasion of an informal eucharist. 'The best bit was when we all took a bit of bread broke it and gave it to your neighbour and said 'The body of Christ' – no fancy titbits etc. No one saying we don't do it that way in our church.'[19]

---

17   *Ibid.* p. 198.
18   Resident P.
19   Resident T.

This inclusive eucharist obviously made a profound impression on this resident. It was interesting to note that this part of the conference was not re-described in the feedback to the wider group, nor did it arise in discussions amongst the Community. To include such a possibility in the paraliturgical occasions of Community celebrations, could be to invoke concern about authentic liturgical practice. By contrast this resident was endeavouring to appeal to an interior sense of authenticity and integrity which he felt guarantees truth. 'People know the truth inside themselves, but some stand up and say you can't do things this way or that way.'[20] Both the residents were surprised at the way their views were listened to and respected. It was rare for them to encounter members of the churches who accepted criticism and even more rare to encounter an atmosphere of mutual trust.

Liberation appeared to one of the residents to have more to do with a certain unity and solidarity – opposed to any degree of individualist factionalism – which could then lead to freedom for individuals. The other participant was concerned to emphasise the radical Christian nature of such moves for solidarity. 'They kept on talking about liberation theology....basically it's hoping that sooner or later all people, races, creeds, feminists etc., will be free and equal.' He reflected that 'What came out was that all cliques are fighting their own corners but if all stuck together, everybody would be liberated. If you're fighting your own corner, you need help from others to be liberated.'[21] The other resident said, 'That's the way I see it as well. They seemed radical to me not conservative.'[22] The more outspoken participant was concerned to promote a form of exchange which could be clearly appropriated by all those present, and insisted that this should be the manner of converse, even when it proved disruptive to the flow of discussion. In this way he was insisting on a right to participate in the discourse. 'Most of the people there were very well-educated, all used long words, most of the conversation was over the top of my head.' In reaction, this resident said 'I got into the habit of stopping them and saying explain that. After that all spoke at a level we all could take in.' For him this was partly to list authenticity, 'When people use some big words I've got the drift of what they're saying. When I

---

20 *Ibid.*
21 Resident T.
22 Resident P.

stopped them in full flow, it's to see if they're hiding behind them long words they might not know themselves or use it out of context.'[23] It was apparent to the leader of the Community that the presence and contribution of the residents had a profound influence both on the course of the discussions and on other individual participants.

The conciliar and post conciliar contribution

Within the situation of Heath Town, what is evident in the lives and words and actions of the people is the presence of God at work among them. This sense of God actively at work in the world was affirmed by the deliberations of the Conciliar fathers at Vatican II. Indeed the hope and inspiration aroused by the Vatican Council appeared to promise a deeper identification with the mystery of God at work in this way. The documents *Lumen Gentium* and *Gaudium et Spes* indicated the way the Conciliar fathers regarded the role of the church and its involvement with the mystery of God at work in human lives and particularly in the lives of the poor.

The Dogmatic Constitution on the Church *Lumen Gentium*[24] begins with a section devoted to the 'mystery' of the church. As Paul VI described it 'a reality imbued with the hidden presence of God.'[25] This preliminary emphasis focuses attention away from the hierarchy and the institutional church, and challengingly gives priority to the mystery of God present in a much wider sense in the church. This is reinforced throughout the document by the dominant image of church as the 'people of God'. 'Primarily a people in whom God is present and through whom God acts on behalf of all humanity. The Church is not primarily a hierarchical institution, nor can it speak and act as if it were.'[26] Yet in practice one is forced to agree from experience with Adrian Hastings that the term

---

23 Resident T.
24 *Lumen Gentium*, Vatican II, November, 1964.
25 Pope Paul VI, 29 September, 1963.
26 McBrian R.P., 'Lumen Gentium', in Hastings A., [ed.], *Modern Catholicism: Vatican II and After,* London, SPCK, 1991, pp. 84-95.

people of God has not been welcomed, and indeed its practice appears to have been eroded in recent Vatican communications. 'Nothing has been more ominous in the doctrinal shift of the 1980s and 90s than the actual hostility to this term which can now be found in Roman teaching.'[27] *Lumen Gentium* teaches that the lay apostolate is a direct participation in the mission of the church and not simply a participation in the mission of the hierarchy. It also presents the church itself as a sacrament 'a sign and instrument, that is, of communion with God and of unity among all.'[28] The church is seen as both a sacrament of our union with God and with one another, but more than this, the same sacramental nature is also a witness to the world, and thus, 'for each and everyone the visible sacrament of this saving unity.'[29] Indeed, the call to contribute to the sanctification of created reality, our ordinary pragmatic living, is a fundamental mission that all are required to embrace, and 'proclaim, and this by [our] own example, humility and self-denial.'[30] Even more emphatically the church is called to encompass with her love as her first priority. 'All those who are afflicted by human misery and she recognises in those who are poor and who suffer, the image of her poor and suffering founder. She does all in her power to relieve their need and in them she strives to serve Christ.[31]

Church renewal and reform are an ongoing mission given fresh impetus in *Lumen Gentium*. The church is both holy and sinful and, in the pursuit of holiness, individuals and the body are called to follow 'the path of penance and renewal'. It is stressed that there is a 'common dignity' amongst members deriving from the egalitarian nature of their oneness in Christ. With unwonted clarity the Council fathers also emphasise the importance of the gifts of all to be used for the building up of the church. All are called to holiness, and thus the fundamental mission of members of the church is to sanctify reality. A renewed appreciation of the local church has reinforced the positive estimation of pastoral diversity and led to a new dynamism effecting pastoral practice. This has also resulted in a

---

27   *Ibid.* p. 58.
28   'Lumen Gentium', para 1, in Flannery A. [ed.], *Vatican II: The Conciliar and Post Conciliar and Post Conciliar Document*, Worcester, Fowler Wright, 1975, pp. 350-440.
29   *Ibid.* para. 9.
30   *Ibid.* para. 8.
31   *Ibid.*

parallel move to impose a recentralised policy. The consequences for our study is that with the impetus given to a more centralised role, the local diocesan hierarchy keep determinative control of the growth of local initiatives. In this way, though the Hope Community are encouraged at a local level, beyond this first stage of support, affirmation becomes at best avuncular and at worst what appears to be toleration. In neither case is the effect at local level held to be important enough to have any consequent effects with regard to ongoing reflection and policy making. The latter resides firmly in the hands of the clerical hierarchy.

Within the document *Gaudium et Spes*[32] is expressed a Christian anthropology which involves pastoral sensitivity, a loving awareness of humanity in its actual condition and a loving sense of responsibility to it. An attempt is made to integrate the personal quality of each human as created in the image of God with the equally constitutive social dimension of the human in relationship and structures. However, following the modern cultural sway within the West, the individual perspective still appears dominant subordinating the social. As McDonagh indicates 'A more complete Christian anthropology would have recognised that the person may only be person as person-in-relationships in structures, as person-in-community, and as in an immediate dialectic with a community-of-persons.'[33]

There appears here echoes of Hauerwas' plea for a church which will really be a church, a community of persons established by radical Christian belief, and bearing witness by their very presence as community. The model of the church as servant is prevalent within this document. A servant who shares intimately in the world, such that the joys and hopes, griefs and anguish, indeed all aspects of humanity, particularly the life of the poor, are vital ingredients of its concern. 'The joy and hope, the grief and anguish of the men of our time, especially of those who are poor or afflicted in any way, are the joy and hope, the grief and anguish of the followers of Christ as well.'[34]

---

32   'Gaudium et Spes', *Vatican II*.
33   McDonagh E. 'Gaudium et Spes' in Hastings A. [ed.], *Modern Catholicism, op. cit.,* p. 102.
34   'Gaudium et Spes', para. 1, in Flannery A. [ed.], *Vatican II: The Conciliar and Post Conciliar Documents, op. cit.* pp. 903-1014.

There is a strong emphasis on the importance of culture, and an openness to attempts to define or describe it. Cultural variation is affirmed and the need to link religion with different cultural settings. This acceptance of a form of pluralism was focused on the many different parts of the world where, prior to Vatican II, the imposition of Western culture, perhaps best exemplified by the Latin liturgy, was comprehensive. Here, there was a genuine attempt to open dialogue with particular cultures, and the non-European nations were the focus for this concern. This process of inculturation was considered necessary to assist interpretation of the signs of the times and discernment of God's activity in the world.

Inculturation was seen as most particularly pertinent to practice among the non-European nations. Yet an insidious collusion with the secular culture prevalent within Britain as a dominant ethos has become evident, as already indicated. The consequences have been an increased polarisation, not merely within British society, but specifically within or rather without the church. Those outside are, as it were, kept there by the very form of life which prevails within. Yet a more authentic inculturation within British society would mean involvement with the culture of the urban poor, to the extent that this might have some determining effect upon the life and work of the church within Britain.[35]

These two fundamental documents of Vatican II have been the source of ongoing contention, since their initial promulgation. Yet John Paul II's later encyclicals draw heavily upon them for authoritative reference. The incomplete anthropology of 'Gaudium et Spes' is specifically addressed by John Paul II in his first encyclical *Redemptor Hominis*.[36] At the heart of this document is a theological anthropology which defines Christ as the full measure of the human. In Christ is revealed the full potentiality of human beings. The church is declared to be a 'sign and safeguard of the transcendence of the human person'.[37] Simultaneously, the human being in the concrete circumstances of existence is the 'primary

---

35 'Unless understanding modifies the ways in which we evangelize and our responses to the people, it is difficult to see us doing anything other than imposing and enforcing our 'package' on others.' Gittens A.J., *Gifts and Strangers*, Mahwah, New Jersey, Paulist Press, 1989, p. 50.
36 John Paul II, *Redemptor Hominis*, London, Catholic Truth Society, 1979.
37 *Ibid.* para. 13.

and fundamental way for the Church.'[38] Thus the church understands the human in the light of its fulfilment as revealed in the mystery of Christ, proclaimed and protected by the Church.

In *Sollicitudo Rei Socialis*[39] the transcendence of the human being is re-emphasised, and the preferential option for the poor, which applies not only to the internal life of the church but also to its social responsibilities. 'This is an option or special form of primacy in the exercise of Christian charity to which the whole tradition of the Church bears witness. It affects the life of each Christian in as much as he or she seeks to imitate the life of Christ.'[40] The encyclical urges action to be undertaken according to local circumstances. It asserts that all concern for the poor must be translated into some form of meaningful action. 'The motivating concern for the poor – who are in the very meaningful term, 'the Lord's poor' – must be translated at all levels into concrete actions. Each local situation will show what reforms are most urgent and how they can be achieved.'[41]

In *Centesimus Annus*[42] John Paul II concludes the encyclical with a presentation of Christian anthropology which grounds the church's social vision and mission on the basis of a transcendent human dignity. 'The Church proclaims God and his mystery of salvation in Christ to every human being, and for that very reason reveals man to himself.' Against this background, 'In this light, and only in this light, does it concern itself with everything else, the human rights of the individual, and in particular of the working class.'[43] In stressing the mystery of God constantly at work within human lives, John Paul II has been cited as one of the foremost thinkers of conservative post-modern theology. Within his various encyclicals and other writings there are constant references also to the crisis of modern culture and the birth of a new cultural form. Indeed, as Rocco Buttiglione, a close friend of the Pope, stated '...the Pope is not 'pre-modern', as many of his critics portray him, but 'post-modern'. He doesn't attack Marxism or secularism because he thinks they're the wave

---

38   *Ibid.* para. 14.
39   John Paul II, *Sollicitudo Rei Socialis*, London, Catholic Truth Society, 1988.
40   *Ibid.* para. 42.
41   *Ibid.* para. 43.
42   John Paul II, *Centesimus Annus*, London, Catholic Truth Society, 1991.
43   *Ibid.* para. 54.

of the future...He sees their time as already having passed.'[44] Aware of the vast cultural deficiencies of East and West, John Paul II has been profoundly critical of both modern socialism and modern capitalism as socially mechanistic, geopolitically imperialist, and ecologically destructive. In his analysis of society the realm of politics follows that of culture. Accordingly, since modern culture exhibits such signs of turmoil and crisis, the primary task for him is not to struggle politically within the modern framework, but rather to seek a transformation at the cultural root. In consequence he continually reasserts the transcendent human dignity.

Holland indicates in some detail[45] how the Pope's critical analysis of modern culture is the key to his profound and urgent focus on the role of society as a tool of redemptive work. He outlines what he considers from the Pope's writings to be his potential strategy for the church, centred on the themes of culture, the laity, family and work, which aims to be a response to the contemporary cultural crisis. It is interesting to note the emphasis on the laity, building once more on the foundations laid by the Vatican documents *Lumen Gentium* and *Gaudium et Spes*. Culture is seen as the vital ground, the laity those who must embody this new vision and the family and the work-place the areas where is must be enacted. The context of this new vision is set in a framework which is both pre-modern in its attempt to restore the importance of the Christian transcendent meta-narrative, and post-modern in its stress on co-creativity with the divine.

Holland's own vision[46] takes into account the dramatic transformation in the Catholic Church, change he feels implicitly containing a post-liberal, post-Marxist, and even a post-modern, social and religious paradigm. He considers this contains the seeds of a new ecumenical Christian theology. Catholic transformation remains open to liberalism and to Marxism, but it begins to transform both from within. It does this by pro-

---

44   Buttiglione R., cited by Dionne E., in 'As Pope Confronts Dissenters, Whose Catholicism Will Prevail?' *New York Times*, December 23, 1986, cited in Holland J., 'The Cultural Vision of Pope John Paul II: Toward a Conservative/Liberal Postmodern Dialogue', in Griffin D., Beardsless W., Holland J. [eds.]. *Varieties of Postmodern Theology*, New York, New York University Press, 1989, pp. 95-127.
45   Outlined in Holland J., *The Postmodern Paradigm and Contemporary Catholicism, Ibid.* pp. 9-27.
46   Holland J., *op. cit.*

foundly shifting the fundamental vision. Community is at the foundation of this new vision, formation of community, tapping the roots, stirring the creative imagination.[47] For the post-modern paradigm, secularism is rejected and the sacred is rediscovered, disclosed in the creative communion across the natural and social ecology of time and space. Leadership remains important, but governance becomes the service of communal creativity. A new important root metaphor – the work of art. 'The root metaphor of the classical premodern period was organic [the body], housing a fortified, transcendent soul. The root metaphor of the modern period became mechanistic [the machine], initially in liberalism only a physical machine, later in Marxism a cybernetic machine. The root metaphor of the postmodern period becomes artistic [the work of art], expressed in the creative ecological communion of nature and history, across time and space, and flowing from the religious Mystery.'[48]

John Paul II's vision of the laity as the embodiment of a counter-cultural force is a call to the faithful within the church to effect such change through their exemplary manner of family life and work. In a not dissimilar manner, Hauerwas appeals to those within the church to focus their efforts on actually being church and in forming a real community where effective Christian witness will be enacted. In each case the attention is focused on the faithful within the Christian community fulfilling their Christian commitment in a more exemplary fashion. In contradistinction an alternative focus for the counter-cultural dynamic which both John Paul II and Hauerwas in their different ways espouse might be those outside the numbers of the faithful. Whatever consideration is given to the formation of the laity and clergy as specific tasks and particular foci of discourse, a more important focus for attention with regard to the activity of God in the world must also be the lives of the marginalised themselves. 'Many parishes have little room for the poor. Many local parishes help the poor, feed the poor, clothe the poor – but do not want the poor to become the parishioners or, even more threatening, the parishioners to become the poor.'[49] The dire local situation here portrayed

---

47   'For Holland the governing ideal of post-modern Catholicism will not be authoritarian but communitarian. The focal energies of Christian counterculture are not on the individual or the state, but on the community.' *Ibid.*
48   *Ibid.*
49   Faucher T., 'Outsiders need not apply', *The Tablet*, December 12, 1992, p. 1566.

gives some indication of the obstacles impeding any deeper involvement of local parishes with the poor or marginalised who live within parochial boundaries. Given the absence of such folk amongst most congregations, and with little encouragement from church leaders to associate with them, it is not surprising that alienation often based on fear is the consequent result. Of John Paul II's more recent vision, particularly re-emphasising the transcendent dignity of all human beings, there is little evidence of a comprehended view among the clergy. Thus the sense of ecclesiological and preceding theological cognitive dissonance is revealed.

It would appear that there is a need to look more closely here at the particular conflicting situation within the Roman Catholic Church. The Church's self-understanding is theoretically grounded in Vatican II and later papal documents, which redescribe the nature grace relationship or the old dualism of God and the world. Human history and experience is stated as being an indispensable locus revelationis for the church. This has radical implications for the church which, as the previous chapter indicated, in its hierarchical, institutional, sacramental form still tends to operate on the Vatican I 'ecclesia docens, ecclesia discens' model, with its implicit dualism predicated upon the division of nature and grace. Yet it is important to recall, as John Paul II asserted before his translation to the papacy, that the Council 'at no point repeats the traditional distinction between the Ecclesia docens, Ecclesia discens: this is evidently because it wished to avoid an insufficient consciousness of the universal sharing in the manus propheticum of Christ.'[50] It does appear that by virtue of their own discovery of the transcendent, the group in Heath Town are celebrating grace but have come to it in and through the sacrament of their own lives – their own 'categorical imperative'.

Foremost exponents of this emphasis on the transcendent within the context of ordinary life were de Lubac and Rahner whose insights permeated the deliberations of the Conciliar fathers at Vatican II. For de Lubac, human beings are a mystery in the very essence of their natures, because of their inherent relationship with God. 'Not because the infinite fullness of the mystery which touches him is actually in himself, for it is strictly inexhaustible, but because he is fundamentally a pour-soi purely in refer-

---

50   Wojtyla K., *Sources of Renewal: The Implementation of the Second Vatican Council*, London, Collins, 1980, p. 253.

ence to that fulness.'[51] De Lubac maintained that human beings could only be understood against the reference of the incomprehensible God and were always moving towards the obscurity of God. Thus a certain gratuitousness of the supernatural order is true both individually and collectively. It is gratuitous as far as each one of us is concerned. Its gratuitousness always remains both complete within itself and forever new. It remains gratuitous at every stage of preparation for the gift and at every stage of the giving of it.[52] God's freedom is characterised by this gratuitousness. Human beings exist as those who are the possible and potential recipients of immediate communication with God.

Widening the discourse with Rahner

Rahner's work is complementary in that his intention appeared to be to disclose the ultimately mystical character of all human subjectivity. His primary hermeneutical principle was a transcendental theological anthropology. Here he was concerned to show that being moved toward or 're-ferred'[53] to the absolute mystery of the self-communicating God is the condition of the possibility of human desires, actions and existence. According to McDade, Rahner's theological anthropology attempts 'to provide an ontologico-metaphysical account of the correlation of the mystery of the triune God and the mystery of humanity.'[54] What actually constitutes the creatureliness of human beings is the self-communication of God. Rahner describes the revelation of God in Jesus as the 'grammar' that brings to articulate expression the mystery of the God-world relationship. In an interview in 1974 he stated that the fundamental and basic

---

51 De Lubac H., *The Mystery of the Supernatural*, trans. Sheed R., London, Geoffrey Chapman, 1967, p. 275.
52 A fuller explanation of this point may be found *ibid.* pp. 309ff.
53 'referred' in the sense of a basic existential.
54 McDade J., 'Theology in the Post-Conciliar Period', in Hastings A. [ed.], *Modern Catholicism, op. cit.* pp. 422-443.

conception within Christian theology was 'the divinisation of the world through the Spirit of God'.[55]

The mystery of faith for Rahner consists in Mystery itself, indeed, the proximity of holy Mystery is the leitmotif of Rahner's entire theology. Human beings by their very nature have a dynamic drive towards mystery – inevitably have to do with mystery. Everyone has some experience of God's offer of himself at least implicitly and as such can also be the source of perceived experience of God. Thus there is the condition for reciprocal evangelisation. 'Man is therefore, because his real being, as spirit, is transcendence, the being of the holy mystery. Man is he who is always confronted with the holy mystery.'[56]

According to this anthropology all are inescapably religious. Our experience of God is given with and through human experiences in the world. This conception far from being ahistorical, as a number of his critics have argued, is actually rooted in concrete history where this transcendence is experienced as operative. Indeed, there is a basic reciprocal relationship between transcendence and history. 'History only becomes history in contrast to nature through what one calls transcendence. Transcendence is not the business of human beings alongside history, but is lived and realised in concrete history and in freedom.'[57] This lived reality in temporal entitative historicity involved the given dynamic self-communication of God. 'Right from the outset the human being is not only radically unequivocally open to God as the absolute mystery, surrendering to it, but also because of the dynamism of God's self-communication, what we call grace, the Holy Spirit, is also at work from the outset.'[58] Such an emphasis when applied to the concrete circumstances of the life of the people of Heath Town is able to authenticate the experience of grace at work in the lives of individuals and the corporate celebration of that in the paraliturgical gatherings. For it is to affirm the ongoing mysterious reality of God at work in the ordinary lives of the people. This is to appropriate a new theological approach in pragmatic

---

55   Imhof P. and Biallowons H. [eds.], *Karl Rahner in Dialogue, Conversations and Interviews 1965-1982*, trans. Egan H., New York, Crossroad, 1986, p. 126.

56   Rahner K., 'The concept of Mystery in Catholic Theology', *Theological Investigations 4: More Recent Writings*, trans. Smyth K., London, DLT, 1966, pp. 36-73.

57   Imhof P. and Biallowons H. [eds.], *Faith in a Wintry Season*, op. cit. p. 22.

58   *Ibid.* p. 25.

affairs, which underlay the proclamations of the Vatican council but which has yet to be concretely affirmed amongst local hierarchics within the church. The latter appear still to be operating under a previous theological imperative – as Rahner made clear – one which was founded upon a different appreciation of grace at work within the world.[59] Indeed, *Gaudium et Spes* itself stated that 'all persons of good will in whose hearts grace works in an unseen way....[are] associated with the paschal mystery in a way known to God.'[60] Accordingly, the operative fact of grace at work within the lives of the people of Heath Town cannot remain in the realms of abstract theory, but must fall within the reflective consideration of praxis. The mystery is that human beings are able to grasp that the incomprehensible really exists and is active in the everyday situations of their lives. It is at this level that it achieves a dynamic evangelistic thrust in the lives of the Hope Community members. It is at this level that it presents a challenge for reflective evaluation at all levels within the churches. It is precisely at this level that the institutional church in its actual pastoral practice, with its legalism and ritualism and what seems its concern about itself instead of God, can be an obstacle to such an experience of God. It is important that the church be both conscious of this possibility and take measures to avoid it. 'If the Church preaches the properly central features of Christianity in a thoroughly orthodox way, but at the same time in a completely modern way, then it avoids the danger that the Church is living for itself, instead of being a sign of salvation for all.'[61]

For Rahner the church still remains as the legitimate though not the sole embodiment of the pneumatic. Rahner himself subject to censure at

---

59   'At least at one time, grace, assisting grace, and the outward circumstances shaped by God's grace in human life were conceived extrinsically, as discrete realities that occurred now and then, and which could be lacking completely in the sinner or the unbeliever. My basic theological conviction is in opposition to this. What we call grace is obviously a reality which is God-given, unmerited, free, dialogical – in other words – supernatural. But for me grace is at the same time a reality which is so very much a part of the innermost core of human existence in decision and freedom, always and above all given in the form of an offer that is either accepted or rejected, that the human being cannot step out of this transcendental particularity of his being at all.' *Ibid.* p. 21.

60   'Gaudium et Spes' para. 22, in Flannery A. [ed.], *Vatican II: The Conciliar and Post Conciliar Documents, op. cit.* pp. 903-1014.

61   Imhof P. and Biallowons H., [eds.], *Faith in a Wintry Season, op. cit.* p. 174.

different stages of his career endeavoured to give some solace in such a situation of confrontative suffering. He stressed the importance of an ongoing relationship, despite its problematic quality.[62]

The ongoing commitment of the Hope Community members to remain within the church at a personal individual level, and work towards building bridges with the institution, has consequentially entailed the suffering which comes from being both misunderstood and ignored by the institutional church. In this context Williams helpfully brings to the fore the very fallible nature of the British church in its institutional form. He also stresses the theological reality that grace does not give innocence, it gives absolution to sinners. The church's peace is a grace-filled healed history, not a total harmony whose constructed and wounded character does not show. Today as at other times in its history, the church stands in need of that freedom of God drawing it towards metanoia. 'The Church actually articulated its gospel of peace by speaking the language of repentance: failure can be 'negotiated' into what is creative. But this means that the peace of the Church as an historical community is always in construction.' Williams continues, 'It does not promise a new and finished innocence in the order of time, but focuses the freedom of God constantly to draw that order back to difference that is nourishing, nor ruinous.'[63] Williams goes on to express his concern to keep in view the danger of setting the common life of the church too dramatically apart from the temporal ways in which the good is realised in a genuinely contingent world. He emphasises that this is not undertaken by minimising the mistakes of the church but rather by incorporating into its theological reflection its past failures. The consequence may be to highlight ongoing areas of dispute and conflict, but only in this way may there be moves toward real reconciliation. To utilise covert euphemisms in order to avoid contentious issues is to increase the possibility of festering sores within the

---

62 'For the person for whom the Church constitutes an inner moment of faith, it is not surprising that in relation to it we can have all kinds of experiences that are unfortunate, annoying and nerve-wracking, and that provoke us to protest. Such offences caused by the Church are and remain provisional and in the last analysis secondary...The point for me is that Christians remain in the Church in spite of all the anger that they might feel about it.' *Ibid.* pp. 142-143.

63 Williams R., 'Saving Time: Thought on Practice, Patience and Vision', *New Blackfriars*, Vol. 73, No. 861, June, 1992, pp. 319-326.

body. 'The imagining of 'total peace' must somehow be accessible to those whose history is not yet healed by the Church.'[64]

In this connection we might see not only the history of those who are marginalised, but for the purposes of this research also the history of those who work with the marginalised. The ambiguity surrounding the response of particularly Roman Catholic Church personnel to the work of the Hope Community raises a peculiar problematic given pronouncements by the hierarchy of England and Wales. With the exception of the issue of ordination, the previous decade has witnessed a more positive attitude towards and appreciation of the ministry of women in public pronouncements. In 1980 the response of the bishops to the National Pastoral Congress[65] indicated that they were both concerned to value the abilities of the female members of the church, and to offer support in the development of the ministries of the women.

Such an emphasis on the experience of women being brought to bear in a collaborative fashion upon pastoral planning and decision-making finds no echo in the previously recorded lack of enthusiasm by the local hierarchy for utilising the experience of the women of the Hope Community. Indeed, it was apparent that there was a singular lack of dialogue. 'Dialogue is a reciprocal relationship in which each party experiences the other side so that their communication becomes a true address and response in which each informs and learns...the other is a partner, someone to be taken seriously.' There is a risk involved 'both are aware of the

---

64   *Ibid.*

65   'We thank God for the many distinctive gifts and talents that women offer to the Church...Your particular gift for relationships makes you invaluable in any attempt to create communities. We believe that the time is overdue for more positive attitudes about your participation in the life of the Church and we recognise with regret that you have often been permitted to play mainly a limited, and often inferior part in the Church. We welcome the evidence that change has already begun...Traditional and unquestioned attitudes towards women and your role may have to be changed. We ourselves and our clergy may well have to be persuaded gently of our insensitivity and our assumptions of male dominance...You must not be excluded from the process of pastoral planning and decision-making. We assure you of our collaboration and support as you achieve your genuine role in the Church and society at large.' The Roman Catholic Bishops of England and Wales, *The Easter People*, London, St Paul Publications, 1980, para. 178.

possibility that the meanings of one may cause those of the other to be revised.'[66]

The picture thus presented is of the Hope Community as a group of women who have chosen to enter into the marginal status of the people on the estate by living alongside them, being also in the position of marginality within their own Christian affiliations. For the sisters within the Community the situation has a double poignancy the ambivalent nature of their support within their own province, is mirrored in the volatile nature of the support accorded by their official denominational representatives. The evident concern that has been expressed by the group with regard to their own sense of power and powerlessness with regard to the people with whom they live has an ironic counter-balance in their evident powerlessness in the face of the bureaucracy of their own church. As they continue to feel the need to authenticate the experience of the people on the estate, by listening to their stories and incorporating their experience into the activities of the Community, at the same time their voice appears to be denied in the counsels of their church, and their experience almost negated. 'The final indignity for anyone is to be forbidden one's own voice or to be robbed of one's own experience.'[67] Accordingly, for the Community there is the possibility of a deeper sense of solidarity with the people with whom they live, whose own experience is so often denied and whose voices are rarely heard within the counsels of those who hold authority in state or church.

How can there be an adequate communication of experience at a local level into the reflective evaluation and policy making of local dioceses? The question of present church structure and the dependence upon a uniform parish model is one which was raised by local clergy in interviews. There is no indication at a hierarchical level that any consideration is being given to the present and potential functioning of parishes and possibilities of alternative structures. Yet this very question was one which concerned Rahner as he sought to promote the Christian message, and for him the formation of alternatives not in opposition to but com-

---

66   Howe R., *The Miracle of Dialogue*, New York, Seabury, 1963, pp. 49-50, cited in Dulles A., *The Craft of Theology: From Symbol to System*, Dublin, Gill & MacMillan, 1992, p. 189.

67   Tracy D., *Plurality and Ambiguity: Hermeneutics, Religion, Hope*, London, SCM, 1988, p. 106.

plementary with existing parishes appeared to be one possible way forward. 'I think in our present concrete situation we ought to stress the formation of lively basic Christian communities not in opposition to normal parishes, but as lively, missionary communities from below that reach out beyond the purely ritual.'[68]

However, this issue also led him to question the predominant emphasis on parochial structure. His poetic suggestion was for Christian communities strategically placed to be 'oases' to refresh surrounding areas. 'To create flowering oases even if thereby, from a pastoral and ecclesiological point of view, there would be many areas of desert in between.'[69] Rather than attempting to provide overall coverage, Rahner's ideas centred on the attractive nature of living Christian communities, which would provide a cohesive and recognisable Christian presence in certain areas. Given the nature of his already expressed emphasis on the graced self-communication of God, the absence of such communities would not preclude the presence of God. 'I may not trust that God will make the Church present everywhere, even if there is no longer anywhere an unchallenged Christianity of a regional character. I hope with a Christian realism that God also really lives where I myself am not present.'[70] He continued by saying 'I would maintain that we should calmly try to create living, radically cohesive communities that resemble the life of the early Church, and I would hope that from their feeling of being something special there would arise a pronounced sense of mission.'[71] Rahner's very practical concern was the pragmatic reality that a church of limited resources could not tackle all possibilities. Nor could it be present everywhere. His concern was that where the church was present it should be a vital vibrant force, not a presence handicapped by an agenda it could not possibly fulfil. The situation of the over-worked clergy outlined in previous chapters give added weight to his arguments. 'The Church of today really has to have the courage to follow a certain strategy, instead of starting every imaginable approach on all possible fronts, approaches that immediately fail because they were undertaken with lim-

---

68   Imhof P & Biallowons H., [eds.], *Faith in a Wintry Season, op. cit.* p. 176.
69   *Ibid.* p. 192.
70   *Ibid.* p. 193.
71   *Ibid.* p. 193-4.

ited resources.'[72] He continues 'I'm arguing that the Church should judiciously employ its available, but looked at soberly, very limited potential for religious communities in the right places. That's where the weakness is.'[73]

To undertake such an evaluation and new initiatives in the area of the reform of the parochial structure would be a major change within the British church. It could be the potential for widespread communication and dialogue between the clergy, laity and religious in an unprecedented form. It would certainly involve a degree of risk and commitment to the potential within the church both within and without its boundaries. It would also involve the church re-evaluating what may be seen as its exclusive ecclesiology and the theology of grace which informs it.

If the contemporary church really does proclaim God at the deepest roots of a human being, forming and shaping things to reflect back his glory, this implies that divine grace is both personal and concrete and evinces the importance of solidarity on the part of the church with the most vulnerable in society. There are already various examples of such initiatives – of which the Hope Community is but one – which could act as both exemplary modes of presence and evaluated experiments for further reflection within the church. At the heart of any experimental[74] aspect of option for the poor lies a deliberate choice to enter in some degree into the world of those who are deprived – to share in a significant way in their experience of being mistreated, by-passed, or left helpless. It springs from compassion and involves a choice to deepen this compassion by sharing to some extent in the suffering of the poor. But the experience is not totally negative: by entering the world of deprived people one begins also to experience their hopes and their joys.

---

72 *Ibid.* p. 194.
73 *Ibid.*
74 'For the most part experiment is understood as dependent on a [more or less] express concession of the ecclesiastical legislator. And the latter offers only a certain choice of already [more or less] clearly known alternatives for experimentation, in order to decide which of them is better suited to a goal already fixed, so that the result cannot surprise the legislator. We frequently close ourselves up in the face of such experiments, if they become really serious, with an appeal to the unchangeable principles and convictions of Christianity.' Rahner K., 'Experiment in the Field of Christianity and Church', in *Opportunities for Faith: Elements of a Modern Spirituality*, trans.. Quinn E., London, 1974, pp. 214-222.

However, it may be that the church within its institutional form is trapped within a particular form of articulation of religious issues to such an extent that it is unable to appreciate the full religious significance of new questions. It does appear that the official church is failing people by not articulating their deepest religious instincts with them or even for them. This drawing forth of the gifted inner reality of a human being and affirming such God-given interiority might be likened to a form of empowerment, of vital importance, is the spiritual dimension and the ability to articulate explicitly deep Christian instincts. This kind of power inspires people to action but does not give any guarantee of immediate success. Yet there is a hunger for a coherent articulation of what the Spirit of God is saying in individual hearts. Although commitment to social change may be enthusiastically acclaimed, at the heart of the expression of the presence of God among the people of the Heath Town estate is a primary desire for the sense of God at work within the pain and sorrow and joy and hope of their ordinary lives.

Fruitful marginality

It does appear evident that if theology is not deliberately used to give power to people in this way, then it will almost certainly be used to take away power from them. A crucial question is whether those who hold authority in the church are prepared to trust the experience of the 'ordinary' Christian. A theology that is imposed makes slaves of people. A theology that is drawn out of people's own Christian experience by sensitive facilitation helps to set them free to be fully Christian, fully human, fully alive. This sensitive facilitation I suggest would include a profound critical listening to the people and their experience of God, and would be open to being transformed by such converse. For such a practice is to assert the recognition that change renewal or reform is super-eminently the work of the Holy Spirit. She is present in all living members of the church, in those 'above' as in those 'below'. She is above the one, below the other, and breathes where she wills. This is the ground of mystery upon which Rahner takes his transcendental anthropological stance.

Bishop Nichols made a similar assertion when he spoke of the spirit-led journey of the church into new modes of being.[75] There does appear to be a wide gap between the proclaimed social teaching within the Roman Catholic Church and the actual structures and policies of the church. However, this gap between theory and practice has widened, as Dorr indicates[76], precisely because the churches really listened to prophetic voices and through them allowed the Spirit to challenge the church. It is thus, in this way, a sign of hope. The contemporary need is to undertake the painful task of correcting our inadequacies and failures. It is proposed that this be undertaken by a concrete commitment to learn from the experience of those already involved amongst the marginalised and a willingness to let their experience reflectively effect evaluation and policy decisions.

As Hastings[77] so well illustrates those who live and work on the margins do not fit within a precise category, they are not quite clearly in or out of mainstream society. They can be viewed as unpredictable, bearers of power but also of possible pollution to the society as a whole. People such as these may be thought 'to be upsetting, or endangering the society, they need to be guarded against, but they may also be a source of blessing, of new strength and wisdom. Marginality may be a danger to the Church but it may also be a way in of divinity.[78] Marginal ministry Hastings sees as a main locus for the evangelical counsels. Here his views coincide with those of the leader of the Hope Community, situated at the social periphery there is the possibility to challenge and revitalise

---

75   'The patterns of our discovery of truth are Spirit-led. To know the truth, to be possessed by it, we must be open to it, and follow the Spirit. Following that Spirit will lead us by paths of death and resurrection: death to treasured half truths and self-understanding, resurrection to new life given in unexpected places, at the margins of our societies, in the shocking and unexpected, in pain and distress, and even in the routinely familiar. Our notions of power and security will be overturned for this Spirit-led search demands continual conversion, a radical re-orientation throughout our human family. Yet the truth, given in love, but often received only in pain, will set us free' Nichols V., Closing Reflections, Gospel and Culture Conference, 11-17 July, 1992, Swanwick.

76   Dorr D., The Social Justice Agenda: Justice, Ecology, Power and the Church, Dublin, Gill & MacMillan, 1991, p. 39ff.

77   Hastings A., The Faces of God: Essays on Church and Society, London, Geoffrey Chapman, 1975.

78   Ibid. p. 19.

society because there is the offering of a possible alternative. Freely chosen celibacy, poverty and obedience for the kingdom is significant by the sheer quality of meaning and joy they can radiate and for the potential protest power inherent within them. The patterns of fruitful marginality are many and varied[79] despite all the pain and opprobrium and perhaps the personal disaster that the state of marginality can bring with it. True marginality is inevitably painful and frustrating. Yet it is also a state which is necessary for the health of the church. The insight of those on the margins, particularly those who have chosen marginal status, has the value not only of the partial dissident, the anomaly, the person who has moved out from the regular working of the system without sundering all formal links. It also has the potential to bring to the attention of the church the richness of the life of God at work in very different ways from those within the institutional church, uncomfortable and messy as this may be to the hierarch.

Dialogue presupposes real conversation unless it is to become a form of abstruse discussion. Such conversation in its turn presupposes the ability to listen, in a profound and critical way. It is important that such listening be critical in order that a priority or option for the poor, whereby transformation for all participants within such converse is possible, is not hardened into an ideology which of its nature can distort and exploit the very basis of such exchange. It is not suggested that such attentive listening be in opposition to other ongoing active involvement in the life of the marginalised particularly in social and political terms. However, this dimension is one which is a vital ingredient and indeed presupposition for such active engagement. For it is asserted that such profound listening reflectively evaluated can promote a deeper appreciation and indeed responsible appropriation of the motivation for such activity. This dimension is not unknown within the life of the institutional church, indeed it receives in some quarters overt intellectual adherence. Yet within the pastoral practice and policy making of the church there is little sign of it receiving adequate consideration. If there is to be a real engagement of

---

79   The state of marginality as here expressed has resonance with that of liminality as particularly outlined in the work of the social anthropologist Victor Turner. The liminal individual faces the same kind of ambiguity in terms of the position vis á vis the society with which they co-exist at the boundary. Such persons also provide a potential challenge to the existing mores within such a society.

the church with those who live on the urban margins of society a revitalised understanding and practice of this dimension is imperative and a very real consequence could be the revivifying of those very social, political and economic initiatives already being undertaken by the church on the margins.

If human beings in their very essence are a transcendence towards mystery this must be an operational principle within all our engagement with individuals. For Rahner the profound choice with which everyone is confronted is whether they will try to ground their own lives and cling to their own securities, or whether they will surrender their lives into the silent and often terrifying dark Mystery whom we call God. This choice is also one which faces the church in its dealings with those on the margins, where God may often appear to be at work in a disconcertingly novel form. Here the question arises will the institution continue to cling to known secure ways of relating to those on the margins, ways which serve to alienate rather than include? Or will the church risk the relational mode of listening through those already established contacts on the margins? In so listening will those in authority within the church allow the possibility of transformation and policy modification by virtue of that experience?

For Rahner as O'Donnell[80] maintains, there is an ongoing paradox. On the one hand Christian existence is surrender to the Mystery beyond all things but on the other hand it is also finding God in all things. The Christian is neither merely ascetical and contemplative nor merely secular and active. Rather she must be contemplative in action. Only the lived integration of this tension adequately expresses the paradox of Christian existence. It is here in the dimension of spirituality that we may encounter the facilitative tool for such a mode of profound listening to which the church is called to give attention.

---

80   O'Donnell J., 'The Mystery of Faith in the Theology of Karl Rahner', *Heythrope Journal*, XXV, 1984, pp. 301-318.

Chapter 6

To Dialogue with the Outsider

Christianity….had its roots in humanity and is consequently human. Ah yes, it had its roots in humanity. But where does humanity have its roots? It is human, precisely because there is in humanity something of the divine. And if there is something divine in humanity, under what conditions and in what manner is it to be found there? There you have the question that must never be lost to sight.[1]

The previous chapter, in establishing as fundamental the transcendental anthropology of Rahner, contended that we approach all individuals as already standing within the orbit of the mystery of God's self-communication. It was further asserted that in order to apprehend this reality a profound critical listening is an imperative for the church both to advocate and to incorporate. Such a listening will ground the discourse. This chapter will endeavour to give further justification for such a model of a listening church, and postulate a means of facilitating this in terms of encouraging awareness of the contemplative dimension. It is important to emphasise the lack of polarisation within what is asserted. The recommendation of a mode of listening is suggested as an underdeveloped dimension not an alternative to anything or everything else: a critical listening and hearing which leads into discerned action.

A further question that is addressed is the nature of the relationship of this proposed mode with the teaching authority in the church. A crucial consideration is how to assure the reverence for hearing what is coming from marginalised people and being open to transformation by that, alongside reverencing the reality of what the tradition enables us to carry forward via the magisterium. Here again what is emphasised is the lack of polarisation: both features are considered essential for an authentic expression of contemporary Christian involvement on the urban margins. There is no attempt to divorce listening from action undertaken or to assert an individualistic listening option which supersedes tradition or

---

1   Laberthonniere L., cited in Daly G., *Transcendence and Immanence*, Oxford, Clarendon, 1980, p. 231.

145

the teaching authority in the church. Yet it may be that a priority option for prior listening may be necessary in order to guarantee the integrity of our active teaching and participatory modes of being. 'So often the Church can act like another professional agency, deciding what can be done for the poor without even consulting them, and possibly finding God at work there.'[2]

If the mystery of God at work on the margins is to be apprehended by the church, then in order to listen and hear members must engage in conversation with those who are deprived of a voice in any other arena of society. Individuals can so often become the objects of language and a converse from which they suffer exclusion. Indeed it becomes a prominent responsibility for the church to be engaged in such conversation, as Austin Smith asserts, the greatest act of marginalisation is, 'the control and manipulation of the conversation which is both at the heart of and indeed creative of the world in which we find ourselves.'[3] Smith sees the avoidance of such responsibility by the Church as a radical failure, for the word of God requires both the engagement of human experience and of its very nature gives added depth to such experience. 'I do believe there to be a radical failure to bring alive a conversation, based upon God's word and the word of human experience in harmonious reciprocal service.' He continues 'There is a sense in which the word of God must be articulated by the word of God spoken in human words.' He concludes, 'And there is also a profound sense in which the word of God must deepen human experience, stretch it to its transcendent horizons, when it is expressed in human words.'[4] Human experience as here indicated is that which occurs both within and without the institutional church, and includes the outsider – even the stormy petrel heralding the approach of troubled times. A conversation involving such potentially disturbing elements requires a flexibility which cannot be predetermined. In the concrete such interaction may be messy, provisional, inexact, frustrating and full of unintended errors. a conversation which offers hope of fulfilment in action and arises from action, tests the depths of our sincerity and commitment. In authentic conversation we are challenged at a very pro-

---

2   A Religious sister in a comparable peripheral housing estate in Scotland.
3   Smith A., *Journeying with God: Paradigms of Power and Powerlessness*, London, Sheed and Ward, 1990, p. 145.
4   *Ibid.*

found level about our language. We are challenged to examine our language, to be precise, to avoid evasive formulations, to say what we mean – what we really mean – to speak as authentically as is given us to be able to do. With regard to the engagement of the church upon the margins it is not advocated that the institution should engage in major direct involvement advocating new and populous programmes, but rather might encourage the converse already actively present. Here there might be a certain 'entrusting' of those already at work in this area and an openness on the part of the institution to being transformed by the fruit of this exchange.

It is because language is the middle ground for understanding and agreement between people that conversation is of such importance as the potential for real discourse. For Gadamer, language always of its nature is conversation. The ontological characteristic of hermeneutical conversation he cites as the concept of understanding as a transcendental and universal reflection.[5] The conversation of humankind with its tradition is for Gadamer the inexhaustible source of new instances of self-understanding. Such understanding is envisaged as guaranteed by necessary processes of critical revision, critical and by implication also fallible, thus ongoing reflection becomes a vital requirement for the process.

Drawing Tracy into the discourse

This process, Tracy considers, is one in which we are in pursuit not of certainty but of understanding, and in our following of this course we have the knowledge that our interpretations also will prove inadequate and will need to be supplanted. Indeed, what may seem a weakness here is rather the strength of a reflective sense that is able to continue the process of interpretation towards an ever fuller understanding. 'The groping,

---

5   Here we might note in passing the criticism of the ontological self-conception of hermeneutics which Gadamer explicates as formulated by Habermas. However, as Ricoeur has stressed, Habermas' critique does not invalidate Gadamer's claim. His desire for a depth hermeneutics still is, as Ricoeur maintains, a form of hermeneutics.

tentative even sometimes stumbling character of the interpretations of both the tradition and the signs of the times....are not therefore a weakness but a strength.'[6]

Tracy asserts that discerning the signs of the times can lead to interpreting the tradition anew, both to retrieve often forgotten, even repressed, disclosive and transformative aspects of the tradition, and also to interpret the tradition not only with a hermeneutics of retrieval but also of critique and suspicion. He stresses that in any concrete case of theological interpretation there is need to allow for the kind of interaction that is genuine conversation – a real interaction between the tradition and the situation.[7] Here in a novel form he sees the correlation of the results of all these interpretations as mutually critical in both theory and praxis. It is significant that he, 'does not suggest either the dilution of Christian experiences into general human experiences or the 'Christianisation' of all human experiences.'[8] Rather he acknowledges that both of these distinct though related sets of experiences are ambiguous and both call for critical interpretation. In *The Analogical Imagination*[9] Tracy emphasises that the heart of any hermeneutical position is the recognition that all interpretation is a mediation of past and present, a translation carried on within the effective history of a tradition to retrieve its sometimes strange, sometimes familiar meanings. He sees a predicament here not just theological but a common human predicament: how to deal with the risk of interpretation both of the Christian tradition and the world in which that tradition finds ongoing development.

He explores the difficulties surrounding authentic conversation as distinct from idle chatter, mere debate, gossip or non-negotiable confrontation. For him, real conversation occurs only when the interlocutors in the conversation move past self-consciousness and self-aggrandisement into joint reflection upon the subject matter of the conversation.

6   Tracy D., 'Project X: Retrospect and Prospect', *Concilium*, 170, 1983, p. 30-36.

7   For Tracy, as Jeanrond maintains, the context for his theory of human conversation is a postmodern one. See Jeanrond W., 'Review of Tracy D., Plurality and Ambiguity: Hermeneutics, Religion and Hope', *Religious Studies Review*, Vol. 15, No. 3, July, 1989, pp. 218-221.

8   Jeanrond W., *Theological Hermeneutics: Development and Significance*, London, Macmillan, 1991, p. 174.

9   Tracy D., *The Analogical Imagination: Christian Theology and the Culture of Pluralism*, London, SCM, 1981, pp. 99-229.

Real conversation occurs only when the participants allow the question, the subject matter, to be of prime importance. In such circumstances, anxiety about the individual's self-image becomes unimportant and understanding can ensue. This occurs not as the result of any personal achievement but in the ordinary give-and-take movement of the conversation itself. Thus understanding happens in a 'deeply subjective yet intersubjective, shareable, public, indeed historical movement of authentic conversation.'[10] Within such a dynamic interaction, there may also be the added element of what Tracy terms a 'classic'. 'Every classic is a text, event, image, person or symbol which unites particularity of origin and expression with a disclosure of meaning and truth available in principle to all human beings.'[11]

According to Tracy, any classic employs some explicit model of Christian self-transcendence, implying some form of intense journey. This involves a risk that the subject matter of the classic articulates a question which is worth asking and a response worth considering. Classics he cites as those texts that bear an excess and permanence of meaning, yet which always resist a definitive interpretation. He stresses that it is important to be open to converse with the classics of our tradition. This conversation might then enable the manifestation of new modes of being in the world, and of potentially new projects for our common life in this world. For him there is the conviction that if the religious classics are classics at all, they can be trusted to evoke a wide range of responses, including the shock of recognition of God religiously named faith. He states that explicitly religious classic expressions will involve a claim to truth as the event of a disclosure-concealment of the whole of reality by the power of the whole – as in some sense, a radical and finally gracious mystery. This involved the realised experience of a recognition as that response of trust called faith to the reality of the whole disclosed in the religious classic. This reality is experienced as liberating the individual to trust that there is an ultimate wholeness – that how we ought to live, and how things in reality are, are finally one.

Though the classic referred to by Tracy is predominantly a text, analogously I would argue it may be used in reference to an experience, and in this case the experience of those on the margins of society. Here,

---

10   *Ibid.* p. 101.
11   *Ibid.* p. 133.

just as in a text, there are demands necessitating constant interpretation and the actual experience bears a certain kind of timelessness – namely the timelessness of a classic expression radically rooted in its own historical time and calling to any individual historicity. However, it is vital that there should be ongoing reflection and indeed constant reinterpretation by later finite, historical, temporal beings who will risk asking questions and listening, critically and tactfully, in order to elicit responses to actualise and guarantee authenticity. In the same manner with regard to the experience of those on the margins, there is a primary need for ongoing reflection and critical reappropriation of that experience in the light of the church's contemporary understanding.

To interact with a classic text Tracy asserts is to be subject to a generative and evocative power and to converse with difference and otherness. It is asserted analogously that in contemporary society otherness and difference are primary characteristics of those who live on the margins of society. The experience here manifested is such as is apprehended by those who have chosen to live and work there as both disclosive of the reality of the mystery of God at work there, and involving a transformative truth, if approached in openness and reverence. Here is encountered Tracy's emphasis upon truth as event of disclosure, the manifestation of truth.[12] Within the British churches there may be a need to learn how to be open to the challenge of what Tracy describes as 'less intense classics'[13] – the ordinary practices, beliefs and everyday rituals. Genuine conversation, according to Tracy, can only occur when the participants are prepared to face the reality of otherness. It is here that he recommends an 'analogical imagination'[14] as the most appropriate strategy for a genuine participation in such conversation, and reasserts the need to use the language of 'disclosure-concealment'. 'The people reveal God to me most when they come out with things that are so simple and yet so profound, and when they seem to put that understanding into little acts of generosity, when there is no incentive to do that.'[15] Tracy empha-

---

12   Tracy D., *Plurality and Ambiguity: Hermeneutics, Religion, Hope*, London, SCM, 1988, p. 28.
13   *Ibid.* p. 97.
14   'The phrase can remind conversation partners that difference and otherness once interpreted as other and as different are thereby acknowledged as in some way possible and in the end analogous.' *Ibid.* p. 93.
15   Fieldworker D.

150

sises that there is a natural hermeneutical competence, which is available to all those who are willing to risk their own present understanding being subject to change. Within such a sphere there is no room for élitism since any human being can interpret the religious classic.[16] 'That natural competence belongs to all those who assume that, to understand any classic and its claim to attention, we must be prepared to risk our present understanding' He concludes 'It is the competence of anyone willing to confront critically and be confronted by any classic.'[17]

Although within the hermeneutical tradition, as Tracy re-emphasises, priority is given to understanding in the process of interpretation, yet there is an essential dialectic of understanding-explanation-understanding. In this manner the process is always incomplete, because leading on to the next stage which is either the attempt to understand or to interpret based upon such understanding. A prior dimension, as previously asserted, is that of listening in order to hear in order to understand. However, at each stage what is required is that openness that refuses to foreclose on any stage of the process, but which is continually open to transformation through the discourse. Such a mode of being, it is argued, does not lead to a paralysis of indecision, but rather to discerned action, which of its nature is open to ongoing reflection and thus to ongoing discernment.

Here Rahner[18] has helpfully focused attention on the existence of God's absolute mystery as the ultimate horizon to all thinking and living. Thus, the human being is understood as always already within that horizon of ultimate mystery. At this point Rahner has redescribed such a person as a potential hearer of a possible revelation from this horizon,

---

16   c.f. 'Any human being can interpret the religious classic because any human being can ask the fundamental questions that are part of the very attempt to become human at all, those questions that the religious classics address. These are 'questions' provoked by radical contingency and mortality, the question of whether I too experience moments that bear some family resemblance to those 'consolations without cause' of which the mystics wrote.' Tracy D., *Plurality and Ambiguity, op. cit.* p. 86.

17   *Ibid.* p. 103.

18   Reference in Tracy D., *Plurality and Ambiguity, op. cit.* p. 109.

namely the self-manifestation of the mystery of God by the power of ultimate mystery itself.[19]

Accordingly, since we are always already in the presence of absolute mystery, we are thus all in fact hearers of a possible revelation or self-manifestation from the freedom of absolute mystery. Indeed, we are all therefore open to understanding that mystery in attending to the reality proclaimed through each other. Here we find ourselves in a world beyond the domain of technically controlled comprehensibility, but encountering the uncontrollable incomprehensibility of an experience of radical mystery.[20] Yet our openness to this mystery we cannot control evokes a freedom which is sensed as gracious gift, and which further empowers life. Here we move into the dimension of growing trust, wonder and an increased reverence for the reality of that mystery at work in the lives of all human beings. 'That same sense of radical giftedness both fascinates and frightens as it shocks and transforms the self to believe what one dare not otherwise believe'. Namely 'that reality is finally gracious, that the deepest longings of our minds and hearts for wholeness in ourselves, with others, with history and nature, is the case.'[21]

Tracy emphasises the all encompassing features of this mystery and the consequences for ourselves as individuals – primarily the shattering of false illusions – and the world which we inhabit. 'When it is believable, religious faith manifests a sense of the radical mystery of all reality: the mystery we are to ourselves, the mystery of history, nature, and the cosmos, they mystery above all, of Ultimate Reality.' Indeed when plausi-

---

19   'In the actual experience of that self-manifestation of God in Jesus Christ, the Christian believer now, according to Rahner, recognises that the concrete revelation is a pure gift or grace from the incomprehensible God of Love. Then the believer 'recognises' that all reality is graced by that gift: that all reality partakes in a 'transcendental' revelation disclosed in the categorial revelation of God's own self-manifestation in Jesus Christ, that revelation as 'transcendental' is always already present in this concretely graced world, that revelation as 'categorical' is present in the gratuity of God's self-manifestation in the events of 'salvation history' decisively present, for Rahner, in the event of the manifestation of who God is and who we are in Jesus Christ.' Tracy D., *The Analogical Imagination, op. cit.,* p. 162 c.f. Rahner K., *Foundations of Christian Faith: An Introduction to the Idea of Christianity,* London, DLT, 1978, pp. 153-62 and 206-228.

20   For one of the Hope Community members life on the estate was 'like a secret that was going to unfold'. Fieldworker C. *op. cit.*

21   Tracy D., *The Analogical Imagination, op. cit.,* p. 177.

ble, 'religious hope frees us from our temperamental inclinations to either pessimism or optimism.' And when active 'religious love frees us from the illusion that to be a human being means to become an ego attempting mastery and control of all others.'[22]

Such a revelation of the mystery of our reality and the interaction with Ultimate Reality may lead through greater obscurity to manifest a deeper sense of ultimate mystery. Within such a context, silence may be the most appropriate kind of speech for evoking this necessary sense of the radical mystery. Silence may indeed be the final and most adequate mode of discourse for religion. Or at best, dialectical speech like silence may prove the only relatively adequate form of expression. For that sense of mystery personally appropriated will take the respondent beyond all previously realised experiences and beyond the powers of expression possible to any finite human being caught up in a disclosure of the infinite by the infinite.

Indeed, it would appear that at this juncture there exists an obligation to hear what is being said, even if such hearing obliges an encounter with what is different and possibly lacking in civility. When engaged with those on the margins the middle class mores of polite courtesies may be singularly lacking. The reason Tracy gives for the importance of such engagement is that 'the oppressed are the ones most likely to hear clearly... Among our contemporaries their readings are those the rest of us most need to hear.'[23] Such a need to hear is also rooted in the need to acknowledge our ambiguous relationship towards power and knowledge in our own converse. This implies also the willingness to enter into critical conflict with our own experience.

The complimentarity of tradition and experience

The interrelated nature and challenge of the tradition and contemporary experience, which only in this mutual exposure and confrontation can

---

22   Tracy D., *Plurality and Ambiguity, op. cit.*, p. 107.
23   *Ibid.* p. 104.

contribute to a discourse, which addresses contemporary men and women, is emphasised by Jeanrond.

> Only if the interpretation of the Christian tradition reveals the power of this tradition to be a continuously meaningful challenge to our understanding of being in this world, and only if this interpretation is a critical act of appropriation i.e., an activity guided by a hermeneutics of retrieval and suspicion, will the disclosure of Christian revelation have any possibility of succeeding to address contemporary men and women.[24]

Yet this appears to be a call to a renewed freedom at the heart of Christian proclamation. A freedom rooted in a revitalised experience of faith. Here Jeanrond sees the apparent withering away of formal support structures as something to be welcomed, a necessary breaching of the walls which have precluded real responsibility being collaboratively exercised. 'That the formal dogmatic support structures of this faith are more and more losing their authority is not a disaster.' Instead the situation 'provides all Christians with the unique possibility of accepting their critical and constructive responsibilities for participating in God's creative project.' He cites the primary concern as being 'the actualisation of a challenging message in our generation according to our best abilities – the Church as a community of responsive and responsible fellow builders.'[25]

In order to assist the reality of co-responsibility, it is necessary to appreciate the prevailing modes of analysis with the church. It does appear that there are distinctive types of clarificatory processes or analysis which are peculiar to religious institutions. However, as Douglas perceptively highlights, these can be misconstrued, and what may look like weakness and inability may be in fact an active attempt to protect a particular status quo. 'Persistent short-sightedness, selectivity and tolerated contradictions are usually not so much signs of perceptual weakness as signs of strong intention to protect certain values and their accompanying institutional forms.'[26] If the church's tradition is to be a dynamic rather than a static partner in the dialogue with human experience, it requires a renewed sense of its own transformative heritage. As O'Donoghue ar-

---

24 Jeanrond W., *Theological Hermeneutics, op. cit.,* p. 175.
25 *Ibid.,* p. 173-4.
26 Douglas M., *Risk Acceptability According to the Social Sciences,* London, Routledge & Kegan Paul, 1986, p. 3.

gues,[27] by its very nature tradition is dynamic, selective and creative. Indeed he asserts that the more dynamic a community is, the more faithful to the tradition it is. 'Tradition is the past as enduring. Christianity of its very nature is always growing and renewing itself by the creative assimilation of the past.' Indeed he asserts, 'the process of growth and renewal is at any stage only true to itself if it emerges within the living process of tradition.'[28]

There is a simple and obvious principle that all genuine renewal must present a vital link with the tradition. However, in the past, tradition appeared to be associated with much that was both negative and proscriptive. The language and tone of 'anathema sit' appeared integral to the tradition of the Roman Catholic Church prior to Vatican II. Indeed, it was this feature of church life which contributed to Weil's reluctance to commit herself to Christianity and in particular the Roman Catholic tradition. She had little patience with pronounced anathemas on all who did not conform to selective spiritual mechanisms. She stressed that the insurmountable object for her was not the existence of such terms but the way they have been employed. She preferred to identify herself with the outsider. 'I remain beside all those things which cannot enter the Church.'[29] She loved the church as a guardian of truth, but as an institution she abhorred it.[30]

With a new impetus given by the Council Fathers at Vatican II, the rigidity of such an approach has been ameliorated. Post-Vatican II has seen a period in which critical growth has occurred involving perceptible transformation of the Church. Indeed, for many it has appeared to involve a period of crisis in which the organism seems to be breaking up or destroying itself. Rather than seeing such a time as destructive, O'Donoghue maintains that this is the time for the true potential of the

---

27   O'Donoghue N., *Heaven in Ordinarie*, Edinburgh, T & T Clark, 1979.
28   *Ibid.*, p. 123.
29   Weil S., *Waiting for God, op. cit.*, p. 28.
30   'I recognise that, as the steward of the sacraments and guardian of sacred texts, the church has the task of formulating judgments on a few essential points, but only as a guide-line for the faithful. I do not recognise her right to set up as being the truth the commentaries with which she surrounds the mysteries of faith, and much less still the right to use intimidation when in imposing these commentaries, she exercises her power to deprive people of the sacraments.' Raper D. [ed.], *Gateway to God*, London, Collins, 1978, p. 72.

church to be realised. 'It is in these times of critical growth that the organism is most truly identical with itself it is opening up its own proper dimensions.' He continues 'Those who would see its identity in static terms are in fact falsifying its nature and if they were allowed to have their way the organism would die.'[31]

For O'Donoghue, the church rather than dominating by prohibitive rigidity was called to influence by charity, by service, by self-sacrifice. His conviction is that the deepest bond which binds together the people of God is the bond of charity, and this bond, being of its nature universal, is alone capable of binding the world together. Yet this is not to diminish the place of the institution and to exalt the experience of the individual. What appears necessary is a renewed ecclesial authenticity, only possible within the creative tension of human experience interacting with authority and tradition.

For O'Donoghue there is an additional element in the correlation of tradition and experience: this is the dimension of mysticism. Here he asserts there is always an inherent tension with formal theology. The mystical tends to find the limits and structures of systematic theology confining and usually moves more easily in the open space of fundamental ontology. It may be, as O'Donoghue so poignantly asserts, a question of looking afresh and with steady gaze towards the distant horizon which unfolds into infinity, while at the same time allowing the inward eye to grope falteringly down into the interior depths. 'A lowering of the eyes into those depths downwards that become as we look heights upward and a refusal to allow one's vision to be obscured by the clouds and mists that lie over the human landscape.'[32]

Attentive waiting and listening

A vital ingredient in the stance of both the institution and those engaged on the margins in this converse is the ability to wait. A reverent waiting upon the people and the reality of God at work within their lives. 'It takes

---

31   O'Donoghue N., *Heaven in Ordinarie, op. cit.,* p. 130.
32   O'Donoghue N., *Heaven in Ordinarie, op. cit.,* p. 191.

a long time for relationships to build up. Slowly, slowly, slowly, trust is built up.'[33] Such waiting, as Weil powerfully asserted, is a presence within the experience that is open, in silence, to the divine initiative. She regarded waiting – a spiritual variant of what she termed 'attention' – as the very foundation of the life of the soul. 'Waiting is a higher form of attention, it is then an ability to 'read' what is supernatural in things,'[34]

This superior form of reading she asserted to be essentially a mystical experience. She believed that prolonged waiting in an outward and inward void would necessarily be followed by mystical experience. For her, waiting involved a tension, it was not a state of passivity but of readiness, an ascesis leading ultimately into the supernatural reality that underlies the emptiness of natural desire. She was certain that if waiting were sincere and thorough it could not be frustrated, and taken to its highest degree it was the same as prayer, presupposing faith and love. There was also for her a link with humility, which she saw as both the root of love and also as attentive patience. Waiting silently and patiently was for her the attitude of greatest humility, and in this stance the individual is conformed to the divine image. 'God waits patiently until at last I am willing to consent to love him. Time is God's waiting as a beggar for our love.[35] By waiting humbly we are made similar to God.' For Weil 'humility is a certain relation of the soul to time. It is an acceptance of waiting. Humility partakes in God's patience. The perfected soul waits for the good in silence and humility like God's own.'[36]

This waiting encounters the limits of human horizons and awaits there the divine initiative. For Weil there was no possibility of apprehending the transcendent mystery at work within the world without awaiting the leading of the spirit of God into that mystery. 'There is no entry into the transcendent until the human being waits at this threshold, which he can make no move to cross, without turning away and without knowing what he wants, in fixed, unwavering attention.'[37] Yet it is important to stress her insistence that 'earthly things are the criteria of

---

33   Fieldworker C.
34   Cabaud J., *Simone Weil: A Fellowship in Love*, London, Harvill Press, 1944, p. 286.
35   This sense of the divine vulnerability into which the individual is drawn is a theme taken up again in the following chapter.
36   Weil S., *First and Last Notebooks*, trans. Rees R., London, OUP, 1970, p. 141.
37   *Ibid.*, p. 335.

spiritual things', and here, as Winch[38] asserts, it is very clear that she is not attempting to construct a metaphysics of the spiritual but rather a certain way of regarding the earthly. Thus analogously, the waiting stance of the church through those engaged on the margins is to perceive the divine initiative at work there. In being open to receive the fruit of this experience of interaction, there is the possibility of incorporating this within the life of the church.

To remain within this stance of motionless waiting does not mean, as Weil was concerned to reiterate an abstaining from action. It was rather an attentive spiritual immobility that did not preclude from material action but gave added impetus to such action. For her the hardest effort was to maintain such a steady gaze directed towards God, bringing it back when it has wandered and fixing it sometimes with all the intensity of which any individual might be capable. This required, for her, a constant conversion. 'We must constantly renew within ourselves the vow of adherence to that part of us which calls for God, even when it is still only infinitely small.'[39] For Weil, such a stance was a form of obedience to God and was one to be adopted whatever the vicissitudes of life. 'In our acts of obedience to God we are passive: there is only waiting, attention, silence, immobility, constant through suffering and joy.'[40] For Weil, attention animated by desire was the whole foundation of religious practice. Indeed O'Donoghue stresses that the importance of Simone Weil focuses on her message of waiting and her whole spirituality centres around the Abba prayer as the way into the fullness of waiting. Here she speaks of attention rather than listening – loving attention.

There is a call for an ever deeper and ever more finely tuned listening. A new depth of listening, an inward listening from the foundation of the human heart. Here a childlike open-eyed wonder and the ability to wait are fundamental dispositions and are essential in an individual's openness to God and to other human beings. 'Man open to God is man open to man. And this means listening as it means seeing.'[41] This listening is not a merely passive or receptive stance, but it is rooted in the activity of being, and in this mode it shares in the divine initiative. 'In

38   Winch P., *Simone Weil 'The Just Balance'*, Cambridge, CUP, 1989, p. 199ff.
39   Raper D., [ed.], *Gateway to God, op. cit.,* p. 83.
40   Weil S., *Waiting on God, op. cit.,* p. 126.
41   O'Donoghue N., *Heaven in Ordinarie, op. cit.,* p. 111.

the appropriation of my listening self, I am not passive or merely receptive. I am active not according to the lesser and derivative activity of doing but in the primary activity of being.' He continues, 'Listening is a primary aspect of being, so that we can describe infinite being as infinite listening. God is perfect listening, the perfect listener. Our listening is a participation in his listening.'[42]

If this is a call to a new depth of listening, it is a call to ever deeper, ever finer listening – involved human listening – listening from the heart. At this level is encountered the contemplative dimension where all reflection has its proper place. It is to be in touch with the infinity of inner space within which individuals are drawn on, not into passivity, but into a more attuned and deeper listening. This too is the level of divine reciprocity, where we both hear and are heard as we listen and are listened to. 'We are in our listening as being towards him, as being towards Being, he is in his listening Being towards us. For all true listening is loving.'[43] This inner sanctum is the place where freedom may be found and so emphasises the importance of listening to the resonances within which the voices of conscience mingle with the subtle whisperings of self-deceit. 'And so my freedom expresses itself, reveals itself as an ever deeper listening, an ever deepening being as listener, a discovery of my being in its aspect of listening being.' He continues, 'In listening to my own being in its self-disclosing fullness, I become more fully listening being, more fully open to my own centre, to that Being in which I am centred and grounded.'[44]

The vital necessity of listening to one's own inner reality is interrelated with the ability to give effective utterance. It is only those who are able to listen at the different levels of self, others and God who are able to speak of any of these realities. 'It would seem that only those who know how to listen know how to speak. For in order truly to speak, from out of my own truth, I must be able to listen to myself.' He emphasises, 'If I do not listen to others I won't listen to myself and vice versa. As the inner depths reveal themselves we are forced into the ways of the mystics or we turn away.'[45]

---

42 *Ibid.* p.114.
43 *Ibid.* p.117.
44 *Ibid.* p.118.
45 *Ibid.* p.120.

Powerlessness and Prayer

It is at this juncture that we become aware of that radical weakness which is the foundation of strength and we find ourselves upon the ground of the passion, where the anguish of Gethsemane leads inevitably to the agony of the cross. To some extent this is the experience of all those who risk the reality of that interior journey. Yet it is a progress always to the ultimate reality of resurrection. As O'Donoghue states: 'In the inner 'garden of the agony' we can only wait and listen where listening is prayer and prayer is listening. In this darkness, in great anguish, freedom and love are being, as it were, reborn in us.' The consequence of this is that 'I am utterly alone in this final darkness, completely free, for there is nothing to plan or do to distract me from my freedom. And in the deepest darkness, God has vanished.' Within this 'As I listen to the beating of my heart, in that immeasurable poignancy of the end of my little being, the only voice that reaches me is that of love, love that is fully gratuitous, entirely free, that goes forth naked into the eternal void, into the primal chaos.' This he identifies as 'a narrow gate beyond which [but not yet seen] lies the Kingdom of Heaven. In entering this Kingdom we share in creating it, we share in creating ourselves.' And the final paradox 'In losing life we find it. We have listened to his voice in the very depths of our inner selfs, where he is entirely himself, not as power but as utter giving, as love.'[46]

Von Balthasar has powerfully explicated the importance of this radical weakness of God in the person of Christ and the lesson apparent throughout his ministry.[47] He states that the boundless love of God, as Jesus discloses this and portrays it, is poor. It is not only meek and humble but powerless. The father in the parable 'must' let the younger son go. It is only to the sinful woman whose life is shattered that 'much' can be forgiven. Prayer appears to be in the air, and as it were the protective covering, in which the 'poor son' can live in its 'defencelessness'. He also asserts, that as with the apostle Paul so with ourselves, the apostle's weakness is not a human weakness, but the weakness of Christ: the paradox of the relationship between human failure and God's power is ulti-

---

46   *Ibid.*, p. 119.
47   Von Balthasar H., *The Glory of the Lord: A Theological Aesthetics VII*, trans. Davies O., Louth A., McNeil B., Edinburgh, T & T Clark, 1989, p. 351ff.

mately not an anthropological paradox, but a christological paradox.[48] In a not dissimilar manner, O'Donoghue asserts that the true listener sifts things as Mary did, and perceives something of the breath of the spirit of God. Such a contemplative attitude may be more akin to wrestling with God than with any intellectual envisioning of the world.

This tussling in darkness with powerlessness and helplessness is a feature of life on the margins with which those who choose to work there are inevitably confronted.[49] Many who have no choice but to live on the margins become trapped in a cycle of fear and alienation. Within the dependencies which are common to all people, it has become clear that they may become doubly dependent because so many choices are removed from them, and the power of choice is such a basic human freedom. The power to choose divides us, and communion in a truly shared spirituality will necessitate a struggle mutually to share power over destiny. Certainly, it appears tied to contemporary work on the theology of weakness, brokenness, vulnerability and failure – the cross. The gospel story witnesses to the power of God situated squarely within the reality of powerlessness. The paradox of cross and resurrection, death and life defies manipulation, and challenges evasion. There we encounter the meaning of Christian hope and simultaneously the stark reality of human suffering. As one fieldworker working with prostitutes states, 'I'm aware, as I listen to others speaking, of their life's pain, of the sense of helplessness. This is what I notice most, when I'm helpless, I am vulnerable, somehow then the pain can be absorbed, integrated, productive, if I give it time, gentleness and patience.'[50]

The gospel calls us to a new translation of the reality and experience of power. This may include a trusting vulnerability, which of its nature

---

48   *Ibid.,* p. 492.
49   'Fundamental to any spirituality is powerlessness and helplessness. It was only when I came to live here and when I'd been here sometime, that for the first time in my life I realised what Christianity was about, and I didn't like it. I find it very hard to face powerlessness and helplessness. All my life I've some kind of control, some kind of support, some kind of security, and I still have it. I'm a sister and there's an order behind me....I live and work with people who are helpless at lease in the system, not in person. What really is spirituality for me is how these people go on, going on.' Fieldworker in a comparable situation of living on a peripheral housing estate.
50   Fieldworker secondary source.

transforms everyday situations, releasing the possibility of change and growth. It may be a presence which exists and suffers with the people. The character of love in presence is fundamentally an offer of self to the other person, in ways that often resist the cold conceptualisation of language. Indeed, God's incarnate love knows no boundaries and the body of Christ is alive in the most unexpected places where humble service meets human need. And perhaps this is poetically described by one man who has lived all his life on the margins who stated,

> There's a power in weakness as though God's made some gentle folk weak but as though he's given them a little magic dust for emergencies. It's a beautiful thing. They've got a hidden supply. Even though they appear to be weak and don't trouble anyone, should an emergency come, they've got the strength. That's what God wants us all to be, I think, weak in that sense. The strength is really in the weakness.[51]

This awareness of powerlessness and helplessness on the part of those who have chosen to work on the margins has prompted a deepened awareness of the need for prayer. Accordingly, the very structure of the Community's week has been determined by such specified times for prayer. Core members see this basic prayer structure as very much a support or a framework for their weekly activities. As one sister indicated, the prayer is an integral part of the teamwork which she finds so supportive. 'What I value most is the prayer life, this is very good and the peak of the team work. I find the prayer meetings together very sustaining and life-giving.[52] One of the older lay women who lived for two years with the Community, expressed her own understanding of what such structured community prayer means to her in the following terms. 'The regular prayer on a daily basis is very important to me, although at times it's a drag every morning. I know that I need that space. Personally, prayer is a struggle.' She went on to say, 'When I first came I was totally silenced by what I saw. I didn't know what to think or feel. I was numb. So the coming before God in that silence is just a relief.' For her 'it was an experience of handing all the gunge over to him. We all do carry a lot of people's questions, hurt, anger, pain.'[53]

---

51   Resident P.
52   Fieldworker D.
53   Fieldworker C.

162

A deepening contemplative stance is crucial, for those who work amongst the marginalised. This is particularly acute if there is to be a real attunement to what is emerging from the poor. In order to be able to listen at such depth, it appears important to be prepared to risk the ongoing darkness of one's own inner depths. Here, in the acknowledged reality of one's own incoherence before the mystery of God at work, there is the foundation for a deeper involvement with God and with other human beings. From that position of essential vulnerability and powerlessness in our own contemplative depths, the clarity of resonance with others is peculiarly powerful.[54] The powerlessness of that level extends to our inability to articulate any understanding of our position. Such incoherence and powerlessness is the common lot of many who live on the margins.

In the life of faith there comes a time when prayer life shifts from a more active sensible form to one where the emphasis is more on receptivity. When this shift occurs within those working on the margins, it is a shift which may give deeper insight and receptivity both to God and to the people with whom they work. The great temptation may be to run from this into more frenetic activity, for what the individual is being called into is something beyond the realm of sensible comprehension, something which is not controlled and where the sense of God may be less and less apparent in prayer.

Mansfield gives added emphasis to the development of prayer in this way.[55] While acknowledging the uniquely personal way God works with any individual, he outlines the movement of prayer from a more active meditative/discursive phase to a more receptive and contemplative way. He elaborates by stating that at the more ordinary level of experience, contemplation seems like nothing at all in comparison to the earlier, satisfying time. But with regard to the working of God, it is, if one remains perseveringly and with longing, allowing God to come more immediately – God who is mystery, who could never be encompassed by our knowing

---

54 Perhaps the analogy of fasting may be useful here – undertaken prayerfully, this practice may not only give greater freedom in prayer, but may also lead to a greater attunement and clarity when involved in spiritual direction or indeed undertaking theological reflection. It is something to do with being less cluttered, and consequently more open to receive.

55 Mansfield D., 'The Exercises and contemplative prayer', in Sheldrake P. [ed.], *The Way of Ignatius: Contemporary Approaches to the Spiritual Exercises*, London, SPCK, 1991, pp. 191-202.

or reached by our effort to live, but who will now deeply communicate God's own understanding and love in the more intimate divine self-giving. In the active, more outward orientation of one's life, it is where all that is done will be more directly under the influence of grace, being ordered more purely and consistently to God.

The time of prayer is a matter of just being there in weakness, but coming to it with belief and hope in the faithfulness of God, the divine purposes and mysterious approach in love. This is but the beginning of an endless road, the whole landscape of the mystery of God, hardly glimpsed before, and over which we are to travel with even purer faith, being led onward to a greater communion in the divine life. There will be deeper suffering, due to increasingly painful self-awareness, to the wound of the longing for God, and to the extreme aridity arising from the sense of God's seeming remoteness as even our depths are purified. Yet God, unceasingly faithful, enables us as God alone can do, to abide more and more in divine life. Everything is given to God, but in a way which is dark and difficult, because so utterly beyond what can be comprehended, until our knowing and loving is taken up more fully into that of God. All of the concrete circumstances of life are involved in this transformation, so dark to us, but being accomplished divinely, as we are brought to let go of our own direction in life and can therefore be led securely.

It is before this God and in the face of the reality of the cross that the darkness of much that appears a chaotic void on the margins begins to have some inchoate and imperceptibly conscious form. The primary scandal appears to speak across the centuries to all situations of gross in-humanity. 'His incomprehensible cross is set up above our life and this scandal reveals the true, liberating and beatifying significance of our life.'[56] The passion of humanity is taken up into God's passion, and where there is passion, there is love and suffering, and where there is love and suffering, there a Trinitarian pattern is evident. In such contempla-tion, it becomes evident that there is a deep desire within God to be united with humanity. A growing conviction of this reality is what en-ables a deeper entry into the pain of the world and the sorrow of God. Here it is the divine pathos which engenders compassion, and the vision of a radical weakness which is the ground of strength.

---

56   Rahner K., 'The Spirituality of the church of the future', in *Theological Investiga-tions 20*, trans. By E. Quinn, London, DLT, 1981, pp. 143-153.

According to Julian of Norwich, the Lord is 'the ground of your beseeching'. If our beseeching has its place and its influence at the very source itself, than all influences do in fact flow peacefully together. By prayer individuals are involving themselves in the providence that guides the live of all. Here it is important to rediscover a religious hermeneutics of suspicion within religion itself. Such a discovery was one which O'Donoghue asserts Teresa of Avila was cognisant of when she attempted to reformulate the stages for the mystical journey and warned about ecstasies and visions. In a similar manner John of the Cross insisted that a dark night of the soul awaits any attempt to follow the mystical way. Such paths are only advocated for the mature and oft humbled spirit. At this juncture it is the dawning recognition of the wild glory of God's love for which the heart was made which determines the path, and along this way it becomes increasingly apparent that the world is charged with the grandeur of God, as Hopkins so eloquently asserted.

A possible way forward

According to Rahner, the Christian of the future will be a mystic or will not exist at all. This implies a genuine experience of God, emerging from the very heart of our existence.[57]

Within this context of faith, Rahner stresses the importance both of the individual and communal experience of God. The former is necessitated in order to confirm the courage necessary for those decisions which are contrary to public opinion. Such a solitary courage however can exist only if it lives out of a wholly personal experience of God and his Spirit. However, the communitarian dimension is also necessary and the possibility of a communal spiritual discernment. This communal element includes an integral commitment to the church. Such an attachment avoids

---

57 'The ultimate conviction and decision of faith comes in the last resort from the experience of God, of his Spirit, of his freedom, bursting out of the very heart of human existence and able to be really experienced there.' Rahner K., 'The spirituality of the church of the future', in *Theological Investigations 20, op. cit.*

the possibility of élitist arrogance based upon arbitrary opinions or the uncertainties of unbelief.

In order to guarantee this open form of spirituality in the church of the future, it is suggested that a unified formation experience for ministry is necessary in order for the church to find a deeper way to enter into the yearning of the human spirit in the world. The way in which we structure the educational or formation system of any institution will determine the way in which that institution will pursue its mission in life. Thus there is the need for a whole programme of formation development for total ministry in the midst of the poor.[58] Indeed, Rahner proposes that the criteria for choosing those who should be called into ministry and given responsibility in the future will be very different – possibly shocking – to more conventional minds.[59] Rahner builds upon this novel insight by insisting that the preacher of the future will need the sensitivity to proceed with gentle caution feeling the way step by step. This stands in stark contrast to what he portrays as an attitude which is too easily prompted into hasty and ill-advised words, without the grace to recognise the difficulty there is in attesting to real faith and not merely its historical and social objectives and relics.

In order to promote the necessary sensitivity and attunement to the reality of God at work in the world and in the mystery of human lives, both Rahner and Tracy advocate a return to the study of the spiritual classics. Here, in the very foundation of the masters of the spiritual life, there is the call to reverence the working of God and the directing force of the Holy Spirit in human lives. Thus engagement with the spiritual classic texts is a vital dynamic, prompting further engagement both with an individual's own experience and growth in openness but also in propelling that deeper involvement with those who are marginalised. The minimal priority given to consideration of the spiritual classics within formation

---

58   Austin Smith maintains that the voice on the pavement decides for you what and where the Kingdom is and what it should be about.

59   'If in the immediate future we want to choose a capable parish priest or bishop from a number of men, we ought to ask if he has ever succeeded in getting a hearing from the 'neopagans' and made at least one or two of these into Christians. The best missionary in a non-Catholic diaspora situation would be the best candidate for an office in the Church, even though he has hitherto acted perhaps very unconventionally and – for some merely tradition Christians – 'scandalously'.' Rahner K., *The Shape of the Church to Come*, trans. Quinn E., London, SPCK, 1974, p. 33.

programmes is bewailed by Rahner. 'Where in the priests' seminaries are the ancient classics of the spiritual life read with the conviction that even today they still have something to tell us? Where is there an understanding of the logic of existential decision in which, over and above all purely 'objective' reasoning, a person asks about the will of God as it holds precisely for him and is every time unique?'[60] This is the means which Rahner advocates in order to ensure that the church remains as it must remain: the church of mystery and of 'the evangelical joy of redeemed freedom'. Only when human beings know that they are worth infinitely more than is immediately evident – namely, as loved inheritors of the infinite God of unlimited freedom and bliss – can they really grow and flourish. Otherwise they slowly stifle in their own finiteness and all lofty talk about human dignity and duty comes to sound increasingly hollow. Accordingly, the church is concerned always and at all times with God and with the reality of his presence amongst real human beings.

Within this context, Rahner asserts the importance of trust within the church – trust as given to concrete human beings: such trust being in terms of those with whom we co-operate in the service of the church's mission. In the particular instance of the context of this book, trust in those who in the name of the church choose to live and work on the margins. Trust however also has to be placed in the office-holders of the church. Here trust has something to do with granting another a prior claim on our own life and action, a placing of ourselves at another's disposal without an ultimate reinsurance. Yet this must be a reciprocal process, particularly when looking towards any possibility of reconciliation between the church and the urban margins. A principle of trust is that we venture out to 'the other', forsake ourselves and our own security, and advance towards the other. On behalf of the church, those who work on the margins have made such a commitment, and here trusting involves an advance without security. It is essentially the risk of being disappointed, exploited, and of having their own uprightness turned into a weapon against themselves. If the church is truly to 'entrust' in its name those who work upon the margins, then a truly human effort involving the institutional hierarchy and the fieldworkers concerned will also require the ongoing provision of grace. 'Trust is possible to the Church but this is a

---

60 *Ibid.*, p. 85. An additional concern for Rahner is the lack of spiritual direction available in these formation centres for priests. *Ibid.*

miracle of God's grace, the folly of the cross, the imitation of the cruci- fied, the faith that unarmed, foolish-seeming love will be victorious.'[61] Tracy indicates that a new solidarity of human beings is necessary as a foundation for the transformation of the world and as the context in which historical experiences are interpreted and eschatological possibilities con- ceived. Tracy's model of a conversation, both with contemporary human beings and with the classic expressions of past centuries, represents a constructive attempt to provide a basis for human solidarity in thought and action in our somewhat chaotic culture. I have suggested an exten- sion of this model, and thus a widening of the discourse, both to conver- sation with those on the urban margins and by a re-engagement with the classic spiritual tradition.

If truth in its primordial sense is manifestation, then it is imperative to listen more profoundly in order to perceive all aspects of that mystery in our universe. Tracy insists that any responsible 'analogical imagina- tion' must respect the otherness of the fellow interpreter, of God, and oc- casionally even of the interpreting self. Only that respect can release the energy for genuine conversation and also for such possible manifestations of the truth of all reality. For Tracy 'truth as manifestation' is a lifting of the veil covering our perceptions of reality, which may happen in genuine conversation. Yet the demands of such authentic conversation are costly both in terms of participation and the effort of solidarity so involved. Although the Roman Catholic Church is the context out of which Tracy develops his thought, it is a context which still appears to refuse to recog- nise the communicative equality of all.

Rahner also indicates concern that the perspective of the Christian and the church is one that recognises such equality of communication grounded as it is in the mystery of God's prevenient grace operative above and beyond the boundaries of the church. Throughout his work the threads of this understanding are operative, and in his later years the

---

61   Rahner K., *Opportunities for Faith: Elements of a Modern Spirituality*, trans. Quinn E., London, SPCK, 1974, pp. 199-203.

theme is renewed with added vigour.[62] For him the manifestation of this truth in the lives of men and women reconfirmed the mysterious reality of God's presence within the world, a presence which is both inexhaustible and uncontrollable. Yet which may be perceived through a willingness to enter into conversation, to listen, to await the gift of recognition. Here the cultivation of the contemplative dimension, the willingness to be drawn beyond the frontiers of our intuitive insight, is the precondition for such recognition and the root of all energy for engagement in action. Here in the contemplative dimension reflection is consubstantial with action. 'Look at the eyes of the man or woman who has pondered the word of God in his heart night and day, see the depth, the peace, the contemplative quietness and gentleness, deeper radiance.'[63] It is from the wellspring of the contemplative dimension that compassion is born, and this provides the existential dynamism for action. For God mysteriously calls all human beings to himself, the very ground of existence yet intimate and personal, but he does so in order to send them back with renewed energy into the action necessary for the building of the kingdom.[64]

Such willingness to enter into an individual's own interior depths was the path Weil advocated. Her preoccupation with the Lord's prayer evinces her sense that this prayer enables our deeper listening, for we can listen fully only in the atmosphere of full forgiveness – purifying darkness. This dimension of forgiveness is vital to the life of the church both in the acceptance and the giving thereof. It is here that the church crucially witnesses to the God whose very nature it is to forgive. Thus the absence of this sphere or its restrictive employment evinces a pharisaical community as opposed to the church of the kingdom. As O'Donoghue emphasises the readiness to forgive and to be forgiven are signs of real

---

62 'The Christian message of God, who offers himself as himself....as our eternal life, is offered and brought to us as a message beyond earthly hopes and fears, beyond optimism and pessimism, but only on the absolutely indispensable condition that we succeed by God's grace in leaving God's transcendence [if we may put it this way] unexhausted.' – Rahner K., 'The inexhaustible transcendence of God and our concern for the future', in *Theological Investigations 20, op. cit.,* pp. 173-186.

63 O'Donoghue N., *Heaven in Ordinarie, op. cit.,* p. 113.

64 'The man of prayer enters ever more deeply into the human condition and he knows that the 'living water' which he receives is not for himself alone but for the whole world.' *Ibid.,* p. 95.

maturity.[65] 'A paradox is that it is only in so far as we learn to be for-given that we can thus radically forgive, and conversely it is only when we learn radical forgiving that we can open ourselves to the light of radi-cal forgiveness.' Such forgiveness, he continues, 'bears not on this or that offence or ugliness of behaviour but rather on our innermost secret self, as needing acceptance in its very being.'[66]

Forgiveness is founded upon truth and sincerity and has a personal and communitarian dimension. In its celebration it can usher in creativ-ity, since it is a reflection in human terms of a central divine attribute. The way into forgiveness is the way of prayer, and here reconciliation is only real in an atmosphere of truth. Yet it is reconciliation that lies at the heart of forgiveness and for this to be effected it requires that willingness to own vulnerability and to be open to either rejection or acceptance. It is also to gain an increasing clarity of sight with regard to the reality of God at work in those around us, and to own both the dark energy in opposition to, and the deep desire for, God within us. It is to become aware of our own deepest selves and the potential for true freedom and for enslave-ment within us. Here we encounter the forgiveness of Christ. 'The for-giveness of Christ is the bringing forth of that deeper self where our true freedom dwells.' O'Donoghue argues that 'To accept this forgiveness is to cast away all masks and pretences, and to walk free and entirely vul-nerable both to the light of Christ and the menacing darkness of the world.' And forgiveness and faith as inter-linked 'to accept forgiveness is to accept my deepest truth and my deepest freedom. My deepest free-dom is the freedom to be loved, to be, as it were, at the mercy of those who love me.'[67]

God's reconciliation becomes available to us, as we place ourselves within the tension of these apparent opposites. However, there is a ten-dency within the church to want to resolve all dilemmas neatly, to remove tensions, to draw back from situations which are ambiguous. Such a path of privatised and controlled existence constrains and restrains the interior life, and removes the individual from involvement with others while cre-ating exclusivity amongst any group or institution. By contrast, it does

---

65 O'Donoghue N., *The Holy Mountain: Approaches to the Mystery of Prayer*, Dub-lin, Dominican Publications, 1983, p. 80ff.
66 *Ibid.*, p. 89.
67 *Ibid.*, p. 88-89

appear that a basic movement of the spirit of God is one from contradiction to paradox, from looking at life in terms of irreconcilable opposites to seeking a deeper reconciliation through all, and this, as Moule asserts, is an infinite process.[68]

Reconciliation is not a once and for all event, but a way of psychological and spiritual formation that takes a lifetime. As with an individual, so with the church. It will always be the church in need of reconciliation, a church of sinners called to offer reconciliation to others. This task is entrusted to her as Rahner makes clear only by the grace of God, which enables the church always in need of reconciliation to be also a church which is indefectibly holy.[69] A feature of such reconciliation is also the ability of the Church to move beyond its boundaries to welcome those without. In our contemporary world it does appear that the delicate balance between mystery and meaning, reverence and action, has been perilously upset. It is difficult to hold firm to the view that reverence of God implies that same reverence being extended to the whole of humanity. Heschel[70] emphasises the Jewish view that wherever one sees a trace of man there also is the presence of God. Yet our vision proscribes that possibility being extended beyond the range of those we consider 'acceptable'. We do not expect to encounter unwashed saints for example! Such limited vision makes it profoundly difficult to be more than merely 'charitable' to marginalised individuals we encounter. The consequence of such behaviour is that those on the margins are only really known, by those prepared to spend time and energy living with and listening to them – most of us prefer more comfortable berths elsewhere. Yet when it comes to that communication with God which we call prayer, and which

---

68 'There can never be an end absolutely to this reconciliation, for it is the living God at work.' Moule C., *The Sacrifice of Christ*, London, Hodder & Stoughton, 1957, p. 32 cited in Leech K., *True God: An Exploration in Spiritual Theology*, London, Sheldon Press, 1985, p. 106.

69 'If the Church is holy not only institutionally but also 'subjectively' and her holiness is a reality already present here and now, and not a mere juridical claim or an eschatological hope for future credit, then God gives this holiness to the Church in so far as he grants to her and her members the possibility and the reality of constantly fleeing from their sinful state to the mercy of God which alone makes holy.' Rahner K., 'The sinful church in the decrees of Vatican II', in *Theological Investigations 6*, trans. Karl H. and Kruger B., London, DLT, 1969, pp. 270-292.

70 Heschel A., *The Insecurity of Freedom*, New York, Shocken Books, 1972.

Heschel refers to as a 'condensation of the soul',[71] it would seem that it is the weakest within our society, those who may be less in control of their personal lives – the elderly, those with less education, women and those with less income – who are more likely to enter into deep prayer.[72] It would seem that our capacity to recognise the reality of the transcendent wholly Other who is God is in proportion to our ability to recognise the image of God in the person who is not like ourselves – indeed who is the human wholly Other.

In our complex cultural matrix, redolent with polysyllabic platitudes and vacuous hyperbole, it seems that only childlike simplicity can shake our complacent arrogance. The child as the essential symbol of one who is powerless, dependent, needy, little and poor. Few acts of Jesus are more radical, or countercultural, than his blessing of children. An individual of this simplicity is open both to forgive and receive forgiveness, elements essential for any real spiritual growth. This openness may also stand as a sign of prophetic witness, and, as Heschel reminds us, prophecy is the voice that God has lent to all silent agony 'a voice to the plundered poor, and to the profaned riches of the world.'[73] As for the person who sounds such a note of prophecy, 'A prophet is a person who holds God and men in one thought at one time, at all times. Our tragedy begins with the segregation of God, with the bifurcation of the sacred and secular.' Heschel continues, 'We worry more about the purity of dogma than about the integrity of love.' Finally he states, 'We think of God in the past tense and refuse to realise that God is always present and never, never past, that God may be more intimately present in slums than in mansions, with those who are smarting under the abuse of the callous.'[74]

The faithful prophet is a lonely calling, focused around a theology of the cross, and looking to a Kingdom which involves the ability to see God within those people and experiences which he would regard as ordinary and of no account. It is a dynamic, prophetic spirituality which will sustain life on the margins. The foundation for any operational practice must necessarily include such a spirituality which provides the ontological

---

71   *Ibid.* p. 254.
72   Poloma M. and Gallup G., *Varieties of Prayer – A Survey Report*, Philadelphia, Trinity Press International, 1991. Here such findings are statistically revealed.
73   Heschel A., *The Insecurity of Freedom*, op. cit., p. 11ff.
74   *Ibid.*, pp. 92-93.

grounding for ongoing discernment. 'The forms and tasks of life are many but holiness is one – that sanctity which is cultivated by all who act under God's Spirit and, obeying the Father's voice and adoring God the Father in spirit and in truth, follow Christ, poor, humble and cross-bearing.'[75]

This path is one which leads to reconciliation within an individual, amongst individuals, in a communal celebration and pushing the boundaries of the church to an inclusive encounter – involving a renewed interaction with the Christian tradition and a revitalised engagement with the contemporary world – a truly fruitful discourse.

---

75   'Lumen Gentium', para. 41, in Flannery A. [ed.], *Vatican II: The Conciliar and Post Conciliar Documents*, Worcester, Fowler Wright, 1975, pp. 350-440.

Chapter 7

Re-engaging the Spiritual Tradition

Reply of Eternal Wisdom: 'If thou wouldst see Me in My uncreated Divinity, thou shouldst learn to know Me in My suffering humanity.'[1]

It has become evident that in the lives, words, and actions of the people of Heath Town the presence of God is at work. It does appear that by virtue of their own discovery of the transcendent, the people are celebrating grace but have come to it in and through the sacrament of their own lives – their own 'categorical imperative.' Chapter 3 illustrated the sense of faith evident amongst the people on the estate and the effects of this upon the members of the Hope Community. It also indicated the way in which through the Community celebrations a regular attempt was made to celebrate the transcendent human dignity of the individual and the reality of grace in the daily life of the people.

This operative fact of grace at work within the lives of the people of Heath Town cannot remain in the realm of abstract theory, but must fall within the reflective consideration of praxis. The mystery is that human beings are able to grasp that the incomprehensible really exists and is active in the everyday situations of their lives. It is at this level that it achieves a dynamic evangelistic thrust in the lives of Hope Community members. It is also at this level that it present a challenge for reflective evaluation at all levels within the churches. It is precisely at this level that the institutional church in its actual pastoral practice, may be an obstacle to such an experience of God. Here it is important to acknowledge the fallible nature of the Church in its institutional form, called always to conversion and holiness and needing to incorporate into its theological reflection the reality of past failure.

The original question underlying this book – whether it is possible to have a shared spirituality between those who work on the urban margins

---

1   Suso J., *Little Book of Eternal Wisdom and Little Book of Truth*, trans. Clark J., London, Faber & Faber, 1953, p. 49.

and marginalised people themselves – has a positive response, though not unequivocally so. The empirical work revealed that where time is expended in widening the discourse and listening to the experience of those who live on the margins, the potential for reciprocal transformation exists. As an individual's life experience unfolds and is heard and sustained in ordinary daily contacts, the growth in self-worth, self-confidence and the ability to articulate experience of God becomes more evident. At the same time those who listen and hear are aware of themselves being evangelised as they recognise God at work amongst the people in ways very different from the forms they may have traditionally encountered. Nevertheless, ambiguity marks this inter-relationship. The Hope Community ongoingly encounters the tension of maintaining the egalitarian nature of the interaction, such that they do not fall into the dual disasters of either imposing their own views in any given situation or, conscious of this possibility, abnegating any personal contribution which in turn may contribute to a state of paralysis into which both Community members and residents are inextricably drawn. The planning of the Community Celebrations are a clear example of this. The very consistency of this internal debate helps to validate the authenticity of the core group response. However, this internal forum is also effected by the pressures from external forces, notably the hierarchies of the Congregation and denomination to which the members of the Community who are religious sisters belong. Here, there is a persistent expectation of some tangible signs of success emerging in predictable forms, namely the increase in church membership through the efforts of the Community. Although at local level such expectations have ceased to be a primary focus, and support has been given for what is regarded as novel forms of involvement with the local residents, at a diocesan level little is known of the actual working of the Community and less understood.

There does appear to be a gender specific issue here. The all female composition of the Hope Community, both religious sisters and lay women is a significant factor in the primordial feature of the life and work of the Community, namely the willingness and ability to exercise the listening faculty. Indeed, this fundamental approach is the foundation for all the many activities in which the Community are involved. The dynamic for the latter resides in the energies expended upon the former. It is the very prominence given to this listening which enables the Community to engage in activities with real credibility from the viewpoint of local residents. This approach stands in stark contrast to the existing mode of involvement of representatives of the institutional church in the area, who are constrained by the traditional forms they have inherited – even the physical forms of the buildings they must endeavour to preserve.

It may be that this mode of listening is a characteristic more usually associated with women. It may be a vital form of availability to the people from which the official Church might learn. The Community does not claim to be or do more than this, an easy and normal engagement with people in the affairs of their daily lives. Yet it does appear a vital ingredient, if there is to be a real possibility of a shared spirituality on the urban margins. An important feature of this kind of ministry appears to be the notable lack of structure involved. Indeed, it might be seen as a ministry that precedes structure, yet not in a way that poses a threat to existing structures within the church, primarily because the Community are missioned by the institutional church under the auspices of the Provincial of the Congregation to which the sisters of the Community belong.

Further exploration of other individuals and groups working on the margins might give corroborative evidence of the gender specific nature of such involvement. If an operative feminine dynamic proves to be the case, then it is certainly a factor which requires both acknowledgement by the official Church and could be valuably incorporated in the recognition and encouragement of such a ministry by women, and in the attempt to learn from women's experience in order to incorporate such an approach into male ministry. The consequences of this could have far-ranging repercussions not just for those who work on the margins, but all engaged in any form of ministry within the Church.

It is important to emphasise the lack of polarisation within what is proposed. It is suggested that the listening mode is an underdeveloped dimension, not an alternative to anything or everything else. It is a critical listening, leading into discerned action. An important question here involves the relationship of this proposed mode with the teaching authority of the church. A crucial issue is how to interrelate the reverence for hearing what is coming from the people and being open to transformation by that, with reverencing the reality of what tradition and authority enables us to carry forward. Again there is a potential false polarisation here: it is not either/or, but crucially, in the language of the Vatican documents, together/with. Yet it may be necessary to make a priority option for prior listening in order to guarantee the integrity of active teaching and participatory modes of being. Conceivably the official church can exercise its divine authority without nervously clutching control. The need to keep control of a process is not something that is required by an authentic authority. Both the gospel and a sane pastoral strategy would appear to exclude the need to keep control.

Such a listening mode involves ongoing engagement in dialogue through conversation. Dialogue implies a mutual exchange of views between diverse parties who do not fully agree, but who respect and are prepared to learn from one another. Indeed the presupposition is the openness to the possibility of modification of views through the undertaking of such converse. Dialogue presupposes real conversation unless it is to become abstruse discussion and such conversation presupposes the ability to listen, in a profound and critical way. It is important that such listening be critical in order that a priority or option for the poor whereby transformation for all participants within such converse is possible, is not hardened into an ideology which of its nature can distort and exploit the very basis of such exchange. It is not suggested that such attentive listening be in opposition to other ongoing active involvement in the life of the marginalised, particularly in social and political terms. However, this dimension is one which is a vital ingredient and indeed presupposition for such active engagement. For such profound listening reflectively evaluated can promote a deeper appreciation and indeed responsible appropriation of the motivation for such activity. This dimension is not unknown within the life of the institutional church, indeed it receives in some quarters overt intellectual adherence. Yet within the pastoral practice and policy making of the church, there is little sign of it receiving adequate consideration. If there is to be a real engagement of the church with those who live on the urban margins of society, a revitalised understanding and practice of this dimension is imperative and a very real consequence could be the revivifying of those very social, political and economic initiatives already being undertaken by the church on the margins. It is important to emphasise that, although commitment to social change may be enthusiastically acclaimed, at the heart of the expression of the reality of the presence of God among the people of the Heath Town estate is a primary desire for and sense of God at work within the pain and sorrow, joy and hope of their ordinary lives.

The actual form of this listening is engagement in conversation and dialogue widening the discourse. The facilitating tool of this is a deeper engagement with the contemplative dimension. These factors point in-exorably towards a spiritual hermeneutic of the urban margins. In con-versation there is the potential for real discourse and here the incorpora-tion of the 'classic' element united the particularity of origin and expres-sion with a disclosure of meaning and truth available in principle to all. Indeed, Tracy argues most convincingly for a natural hermeneutical com-petence which is universally available. According to him, any classic employs some explicit model of Christian self-transcendence implying some form of intense journey. This involves a risk that the subject matter of the classic articulates a question which is worth asking and a response worth considering. In developing Tracy's use of the 'classic' to cover the experience of the marginalised, I have argued that, just as in a text, there are demands necessitating constant interpretation and the actual experi-ence bears a certain kind of timelessness – namely the timelessness of a classic expression radically rooted in its own historical time and calling to an individual historicity. There is a primary need for ongoing reflection and critical reappropriation of that experience in the light of the Church's contemporary understanding.

To interact with a classic text, Tracy asserts, is to be subject to a generative and evocative power and to converse with difference and oth-erness. I have argued analogously that in contemporary society otherness and difference are primary characteristics of those who live on the mar-gins of society. The experience here manifested is such as is appre-hended by those who have chosen to live and work there as both disclo-sive of the mystery of God at work there, and involving a transformative truth if approached in openness and reverence.

If human beings in their very essence are a transcendence towards mystery, this must be an operational principle within engagement with individuals. For Rahner the profound choice with which everyone is con-fronted is whether they will try to ground their own lives and cling to their own securities, or whether they will surrender their lives into the silent and often terrifying dark Mystery whom we call God. This choice is also one which faces the church in its dealings with those on the mar-gins where God may often appear to be at work in a disconcertingly novel form. Here the question arises will the institution continue to cling to know secure ways of relating to those on the margins, ways which serve to alienate rather than include? Or will the church risk the relational mode of listening through those already established contacts on the margins? In so listening, will those in authority within the church allow the possibility of transformation and policy modification by virtue of that experience?

An insidious collusion is evident within the secular culture prevalent as a dominant ethos. The consequences of this are increased polarisation not merely within British society but specifically within or rather 'without' the church. Those outside are, as it were, kept there by the very forms of life which prevail within. However, a more authentic inculturation within British society would mean the reality of involvement with the culture of the urban poor to the extent that this might have some determining effect upon the life and work of the church within Britain. This would widen the social discourse into hitherto unchartered territory.

Looking at the contemporary Christian calls to renew the face of the church, it is evident for example that the Pope is not struggling politically within the modern framework of cultural debate. Rather he is seeking a transformation at the cultural root. In consequence he continues to reiterate a fundamental feature of the Vatican II documents, evident within his later encyclicals – namely the mystery of God at work within the world and the transcendent human dignity of every person.

John Paul II's vision of the laity as the embodiment of a counter-cultural force is a call to the faithful within the church to effect such change through their exemplary manner of family life and work. In a not dissimilar manner, Hauerwas appeals to those within the church to focus their efforts on actually being church and in forming a real community where effective Christian witness will be enacted. In each case the attention is focused on the faithful within the Christian community fulfilling their Christian commitment in a more exemplary fashion. Meanwhile as the forces of modernism and postmodernism swirl within contemporary Britain, individual desires seem paramount for those with the financial means or acumen to achieve them. Those outside this enclave, estranged by the very existence of those within, continue the slide towards non-person status. It is within this group, those outside the numbers of the faithful, that it is here suggested a focus might be found for the counter-cultural dynamic which both John Paul II and Hauerwas in their different ways espouse. I would contend that whatever consideration is given to the formation of the laity and clergy as specific tasks, a more particular focus for attention with regard to the activity of God in the world must also be the lives of the marginalised themselves.

How can there be an adequate communication of experience at a local level into the reflective evaluation and policy making of local dioceses? One problem centres on the church's dependence on existing parochial structures. A church of limited resources as Rahner maintained – and as local clergy confirmed – cannot tackle all possibilities. Rahner's concern was that where the church is present, it should be a vital vibrant force, not a presence handicapped by an agenda it cannot possibly fulfil. This points the way to a suggestion of evaluation of contemporary parochial needs and the encouragement of new initiatives alongside the possible reform of parochial structures. Here there is the potential for widespread communication and dialogue between clergy, laity and religious in an unprecedented form. However, this involves a degree of risk and commitment to the potential both within and without the boundaries of the church. Also this might lead to the re-evaluation of what may be seen as its exclusive ecclesiology and the theology of grace which informs it.

There is a contemporary need to undertake the painful task of correcting our inadequacies and failures. It is proposed that this be undertaken by a concrete commitment to learn from the experience of those already involved amongst the marginalised and a willingness to let their experience reflectively effect evaluation and policy decisions. A question arises whether those who hold authority within the church are prepared to trust the experience of those who live on the margins and those who work with them. A theology that is drawn out of people's own experience by sensitive facilitation helps to set them free to be fully Christian, fully human, fully alive. This sensitive facilitation would include a profound critical listening to the people and their experience of God and would be open to being transformed by that converse. For such a practice is to assert the recognition that change, renewal or reform is super-eminently the work of the Holy Spirit.

There is necessarily a dialectical tension between individual and general experience. Here Weil's emphasis upon the attentive waiting stance may be of crucial importance. Those who work on the margins are called to wait attentively in their listening to those with whom they work before embarking upon discerned action. Analogously, the waiting stance of the church through those engaged on the margins is to perceive the divine initiative at work there, while the stance of the institution is also to receive back from those so engaged the fruit of their experience.

This requires an expansion of the dimension of listening involving a new depth, and an ever-finer attunement. It impels towards a level of darkness powerlessness and helplessness. Here the facilitating tool for such a listening critically involves a deepening contemplative stance.[2] This is a particularly acute need if there is to be a real attunement to what is emerging from the marginalised. In order to be able to listen at such depth, it appears important to be prepared to risk the ongoing darkness of one's own inner depths. Here in the acknowledged reality of one's own incoherence before the mystery of God at work there is the foundation for a deeper involvement with God and other human beings. From that position of essential vulnerability and powerlessness in our own contemplative depths, the clarity of resonance with others – particularly the marginalised – is peculiarly powerful. Indeed before God, and in the face of the reality of the cross, the darkness of much that appears a chaotic void on the margins begins to have some inchoate and imperceptibly conscious form.

Re-engaging the Tradition

Within this chapter we draw into the discourse the 'classics' of the spiritual tradition. We explore the integrated nature of contemplation and action as advocated by previous generations. A particular focus of attention is the contribution of Ignatian Spirituality with the classic text of the Spiritual Exercises. Discernment is a keynote, as the potential is explored for a renewed spirituality and a renewed asceticism arising from the tradition in interaction with the contemporary world. Here reconciliation, both individual and communal, proves to be a dynamic for deeper con-

---

2   Conversation with Dr Noel O'Donoghue has indicated, there are three levels of contemplation as outlined within the spiritual classics: active, passive and mystical. Within this chapter no attempt is made to outline all three in detail. What is indicated is that the inner journey may involve all three and, across this contemplative spectrum, there is the possibility of a more powerful encounter with an individual's own powerlessness and vulnerability before God and a subsequently more acute 'hearing' and consequent listening to the experience of the marginalised.

templation and propitious action. Authentic interpretation of either the classic text or the experience of the marginalised depends on the moral authenticity of the interpreter. However, I have argued that beyond moral integrity, authentic interpretation requires a purification of the spirit.[3] The context of consideration of the spiritual tradition is the experience of encounter upon the margins.

The mysterious presence of God at work amongst the marginalised, evangelising those who live and work on the margins, has been the focus of consideration in these chapters. For fieldworkers interviewed, reflection upon their experience has produced a convergence of opinion that they have learned so much of God through the people. This epiphany of God within the poor and marginalised is perceived and responded to by those who come from very different backgrounds, from the security of religious life, or from the potentially equally secure shelter of middle class family life.

Having focused upon the interactive experience of life and work with the marginalised, it is appropriate now to attend to what the classics of the spiritual tradition emphasise as key factors in the integration of contemplation and action. According to Underhill,[4] the germ of that same transcendent life of the great mystics is present, latent within all human beings. Thus each in his or her own measure may, according to the capacity for openness to the grace of God, be drawn into a mystical trajectory. 'this spark of the soul, once we permit its emergence will conform in little and according to its measure, to those laws of organic growth, those inexorable conditions of transcendence which govern the mystic way.'[5] For Underhill, the possibilities for such a drawing into the contemplative way demand great love and desire for God coupled with self-discipline, courage and generosity. Yet she asserted that the writings of the cognoscenti of the spiritual life evoke a chord of recognition, for they speak of a reality embedded deep within us.

---

3   Veale J., 'Dominant Orthodoxies', *Milltown Studies*, No. 30, Autumn, 1992, pp. 62-63.
4   Underhill E., *Mysticism*, London, Methuen and Co Ltd., 1940.
5   *Ibid.* p. 445.

Historical Transcendence

In a commensurable manner is Rahner's emphasis on the commonality of the mystery of God at work in human beings. Both Underhill and Rahner reassert the deep chord within human beings which resounds to a divine note.[6] There is at this depth an ontological unity[7] between God and the deepest self. Here the work of Anderson[8] may be of particular significance in his assertion that it is not the immanence of God which has the deepest bond with humanity but rather the transcendence of God, seen in terms of historical lived transcendence. Thus he inverts the traditional metaphysical framework for one in which transcendence not immanence is the key factor for divine human relations and the axiomatic point of departure. He does not envisage the 'otherness' of God creating a great gulf between God and humanity but rather as sustaining the work of creation through the incarnate Word and the Spirit in real historical terms. Thus the transcendence of God does not involve a remote abstraction from the world but rather a direct engaged presence with humanity in the world. 'Divine transcendence is not a quality of being which is defined by abstracting from a non-divine creation or nature. Transcendence is difference in solidarity, and as such, it is the extrinsic rather than the intrinsic reality of being.'[9] This solidarity is both personal in terms of the individual's involvement with God and also communal in terms of the interelatedness of all humanity with one another and with God. '...the 'difference' or the transcendence of God, can only be expressed in solidarity with humanity. Lived transcendence is an incarnational life which involves complete solidarity with an absolute difference.'[10]

Kenosis becomes revealed as the depth of divine transcendence experienced as an intra-divine relation into which human beings are incor-

---

6   One of the members of the Hope Community a young laywoman made the point that 'I felt much nearer to God when I was with...people who were in the dirt in a sense.' Fieldworker C.

7   Here ontological unity is not equated with ontological identity.

8   In particular Anderson R., *Historical Transcendence and the Reality of God*, London, Geoffrey Chapman, 1975, and Anderson R., [ed.], *Theological Foundations for Ministry*, Edinburgh, T & T Clark, 1979.

9   Anderson R., *Historical Transcendence and the Reality of God, op. cit.*, p. 260.

10   *Ibid.* and p. 261.

porated with their full humanity. Anderson speaks of the 'kenotic community' as the solidarity which the church has with all human beings. It is the incarnational solidarity which permits no distinctions to be made between the Christian and the world by limiting the incarnation to the church. Indeed he stresses that the church which denies its involvement with the world has ceased to be true to its Lord. It becomes an 'untruthful' Church and no longer has the 'incarnational credibility' that is the mark of Christ himself.'[11] The Christian is seen as incomplete without the world loving within it as Christ loved. The kenotic community is cited as being not just the church assuming a position of humility, rather it is Christ in solidarity with the world in a living tension.[12] This calls into question whether it is possible to make distinctions at the boundaries of a church which is called into such a solidarity. 'The Church [the body of Christ], a refugee with the refugees, with no outer wall to separate saint from sinner, with no inner sanctuary to be guarded against profanation, is nonetheless the place which is also the presence of the living God.' In this manner Anderson ties the possibility of hope for the world directly to the reality of the eschaton as the gift of God's own life to humanity. Thus lived transcendence also radicalises the conditions under which humanity lives for it has its source in the life of God.

Underhill emphasises that true mysticism[13] is active and practical not passive and theoretical. For her it is an organic life-process not a speculative project. A keynote of mysticism seems to be that eager outgoing activity driven by the generosity of love to an ongoing engagement with

---

11 *Ibid.*, p. 274.
12 'The distinction between Christ and man is absolute while at the same time there is a solidarity with man which is permanent. This is the implication of the kenosis when considered as the historical transcendence of God through the Incarnate Logos. The kenotic community, considered incarnationally, is the foundation of all human community and the Church can never deny its common participation in this community without denying Christ himself.' *Ibid.*, p. 259.
13 Underhill cites three elements which characterise the mystic way: '1. Mysticism is a transformative approach to life rather than a theoretical 'playing' with ideas. 2. Mysticism involves spiritual activity representing the individual's absorption and deepening relationship with God. 3. The mystic's dominant life-emotion becomes love leading to progressively strengthened dedication of will toward the things of God: the expression of his will in daily life: service to him through work, relationships and everyday choices: and sacrifices of the physical/mental body.' Sinetor M., *Ordinary People as Monks and Mystics*, New York, Paulist Press, 1986, p. 77.

the world. '..the great mystics tell us, not how they speculate, but how they acted. The paradoxical 'quiet' of the contemplative is but the outward stillness essential to inward work.'[14] Classical criteria stress the inter-relatedness of contemplation, mysticism and action. Indeed action is seen as the overflow of mysticism and 'non-action' as the most powerful action of all. This paradox lies at the heart of mysticism and indeed at the heart of all contemplation. There is a peculiar fecundity about this contemplative dimension which flows forth into discerned action. Within Augustine's work, the study and pursuit of wisdom lies in action and in contemplation, so that one part may be called 'active', the other 'contemplative'.[15] Gregory the Great lays it down that the one who ordinarily carries on the good works of the active life, but also strives to recollect himself and raise himself to contemplation, is not failing in leading a contemplative life. Meanwhile it is St Bernard who carries on the imagery of spiritual marriage to spiritual fecundity.

It is Ruysbroeck who stresses that contemplation is highly intellectual and yet mystical. Though he does not use the imagery of 'fecundity' for him also, as for Bernard, the final state, the result of the highest contemplation, is that the contemplative is inspired with zeal to labour actively for God's glory. 'In contemplation God comes to us without ceasing and demands of us both action and fruition, in such a way that the one never impedes but always strengthens the other.'[16]

In conversation with Eckhart

Although, as Woods[17] indicates the levels of comprehension are severely strained by Eckhart, nevertheless through that very pressure upon the in-

---

14   Underhill E., *Mysticism, op. cit.,* p. 83.
15   It is important to acknowledge that within the Fathers action does not necessarily signify 'ministry'. Often in the Fathers the 'vita activa' refers to the *ascetical* aspect of the Christian life, viz what we can do, what we do. As distinct from receptivity before what God is doing.
16   Ruysbroeck, 'Adornment ii 65', cited in Butler C., *Western Mysticism*, London, Constable & Co Ltd., 1922, p. 173.
17   Woods R., *Eckhart's Way*, Wilmington Delaware, Michael Glazier, 1986, p. 10.

telligibility of language, he sought to walk a precarious course along 'The nether borders of the unnameable Mystery we call God.'[18] Eckhart explicates the paradoxical mystery of God, who is both utterly beyond human comprehension and yet who is the ground of all human reality which, as created in the image and likeness of God, enjoys a privileged region of communion with God that Eckhart often referred to as the ground or abyss of the soul. Indeed, Woods cites him as stating 'I have a power in my soul which is ever receptive to God.'[19] Yet within such mystical intuition and direct apprehension of the mystery of God, Eckhart stresses the very ordinary nature of God's appearing in the world. For him God does not generally ravish the soul with ecstatic delights, but rather communicates his loving presence through the pragmatic events of ordinary experience. It is striking that in Eckhart's writings there is a consistent emphasis upon the Christian's work in this world, and this is so even after an experience of union with God. 'Eckhart insists that 'perfected' disciples, the true mystics, pass back unnoticed into the human milieu where, one in will and work with God, they energise and hallow the experience and activities of their fellow citizens and saints.'[20] Eckhart asserted that true holiness was more a quality of being, and this very being is the source from which flows all the good we achieve in action. For him, contemplation was brought to perfection through loving activity in the world, amidst ordinary human concerns. Indeed, he urged his disciples to cultivate a mystical spirituality that expressed itself actively in the world. This insistence on the priority of contemplation in action, and the reality of the presence of God throughout humanity, motivated the conclusion of one sermon when he stated, 'I say humanity is as perfect in the poorest and most wretched as in pope or emperor, for I hold humanity more dear in itself than the man I carry about with me.'[21]

For Eckhart the individual was capable of a simple receptivity to God and by the grace of God was gradually transformed into the shape of the one contemplated and drawn into his mission within the world. This was no mere private interiorisation of a Christian vocation but recognition of the integrated nature of activity, motive and desire. Thus a contempo-

---

18   *Ibid.*
19   *Ibid.* p. 58
20   Woods R., *Eckhart's Way, op. cit.,* p. 84.
21   *Ibid.* p. 216.

rary Dominican gives articulation to the voice of the Meister for the twentieth century. 'He calls us freshly to transformation, to a rebirth into God-centred contemplation of the world's weal and woes, to a greater, freer commitment to social justice, inclusive love and effective action.'[22]

Many medieval writers wrote about the relationship between action and contemplation in life. Yet these were not necessarily seen as competitive features of life, but rather there was discussion around the proper relationship between the active and contemplative dimensions. For Francis of Assisi the primary motivation was always the example of Christ. Although Christ went apart to pray, the majority of time was spent in a very public ministry. Accordingly, Francis is reported as saying, 'Because we should do everything according to the pattern shown to us in him as on the heights of the mountain, it seems more pleasing to God that I interrupt my quiet and go out to labour.'[23] Bonaventure, wrote of the way action and contemplation were integrated in Francis. 'Therefore when in his compassion he had worked for the salvation of others, he could then leave behind the restlessness of the crowds and seek out hidden places of quiet and solitude.'[24] The highest mystical experience has, as one of its effects, the sending back of the one who achieves it to the active life with an enhanced zeal to work for the good of others. Catherine of Siena was not concerned with the soul's ascent to God in itself, but rather with the means by which personal sanctity could help the church in the world. Her concept of holiness was the self-knowledge and awareness of one's own nothingness before God, which could lead to a love which was united to Christ's own saving love, and to his mission bringing to others the good news of that redemptive love.

The reason for this overflow of the contemplative dimension into the realm of action lies in the very nature of that deepened relationship with God which – rooted and grounded in love – cannot be confined but involves a participation in the loving work of God. It is a question of entering into a participation in that love of which God himself remains the only possible subject. It is most often experienced not in the ecstatic visions of the few but in the habitual performance of the humblest daily duties. Here there occurs a vivid consciousness of the presence of God

---

22   *Ibid.* p. 219.
23   Bonaventure Legenda Maior XII, 1, cited *Ibid.*, p. 81.
24   Bonaventure Legenda Maior XIII, 1, cited *Ibid.*, p. 82.

within all the circumstances of life. In a similar manner members of the Hope Community find themselves involved in the daily lives of the residents of the estate.

Julian of Norwich enters the discourse

An outstanding example of such an integrated Christian, for whom daily life and religious experience and reflection on that experience were all aspects of one whole, is Julian of Norwich. Her emphasis on experience was as day by day contact with the love of God which enables individuals to make steady unspectacular progress both in the knowledge of self and in responding to the love of God which liberates individuals to respond in turn to others. During her time as an anchoress at Norwich, she appeared to divide her time between prayer and worship and a quiet ministry to the local poor who sought her presence. One author[25] surmises that Julian wrote especially for women and particularly those who suffer from exploitation or from situations of hopelessness or helplessness.[26] For Julian the path to life is one of humility and compassion which she sees as rooted in the 'kindness' of God, which is built into human nature created by God. For her the message of love which she received was intended always for the poor and uneducated, who would have been most troubled during her times by the questions of judgement, death and suffering and how to live amidst a world beset by turmoil and uncertainty. Julian's message of hope was that by our very creation we share in the divine nature through the love of God. This love is the foundation and meaning of all things. 'Love was his meaning. Who showed it to you? Love. What did he show you? Love. Why did he show it? For love.' She continued 'Hold yourself in it, and you shall understand and know more of the

---

25   Pelphrey B., *Christ our Mother: Julian of Norwich*, Wilmington delaware, Michael Glazier, 1989.

26   In this she seems peculiarly appropriate for those whose ministry involves them with the lives of single mothers, girls on the streets, and any area in which women are exploited.

same, but you will never understand or know anything else in it, forever.'[27]

Julian's central message appeared to be that the most one could say of God was that he loves. It was this love which Christ offered to sinners and outcasts within the society of his time and which has been the compelling attraction across generations. The paradigm of the crucified Christ is the focus of her spirituality and of her advocation of the inward quest. This is not undertaken as some self-indulgent exercise, for the improvement of her own soul, rather she reflected upon her experience and shared it with others.

Accordingly, human lives are meant to be a process of growing into maturity in that love, and being drawn increasingly into the likeness of God in whose image all are made. For Julian human nature is inextricably 'knit' to God, hidden there as God is also hidden within our nature. Even sin, according to Julian, does not destroy the union of our essential substance with God, for she sees the image of God as the inalienable essence of what it is to be human. Sin may cloud or distort such relatedness but it cannot be utterly destroyed.

Julian's awareness of sin was focused in a sense of fragmentation between what she referred to as the substance of the individual, which was inextricably bound to God, and the sensuality, which was often distorted by the motions of sinfulness. Yet still she asserted we long for God in our inmost being, even when our lives are so fragmented and misfocused such that we do not recognise the longing for what it is. For Julian, the church's reason for existence is to enable human beings, broken and distorted, to be made whole in the love of God. In order for this to be effected, she saw it as necessary that there should be a concrete means of the renunciation of sin enabling real repentance. Here she stressed the value of confession and penance as a means to facilitate this. She saw the sacramental means of the church as the way of renewing that longing for God to which she would always respond. Indeed three keynotes of her writings are found here. The desire for true contrition, compassion and a deepened longing for God. 'By contrition we are made clean, by compassion we are made ready, and by true longing for God we are made worthy. These are three means, as I understand, through which all souls

---

27   Julian of Norwich, Long Text chapter 86, cited Pelphrey B., *Christ our Mother, op. cit.,* p. 258.

come to heaven.' And amazingly the wounds of sin become the means of honour. 'Though he be healed, his wounds are not seen by God as wounds but as honours...For he regards sin as sorrow and pains for his lovers, to whom for love he assigns no blame.'[28]

Julian was convinced that God was dynamically involved with all things. Indeed, that it was part of the unchanging humility of God and a feature of his divine compassion that he suffered with humanity and that the desire of God was for all humanity to be brought to a state of holiness.[29] Accordingly, even in her emphasis upon the importance of penitence for the individual, it is not for the individual alone. Rather she sees the true penitent as one who is not only sorrowful for his own sins, but for the sins of all and thus shares in something of the divine sense of contrition. Here individual passion and suffering become part of that divine compassion which longs for the whole world to be redeemed. Here too, there is awakened something of the joy and inner peace seen as gift of the spirit of God. 'For Julian inner peace stems from the encounter with God at work in all things. It is therefore an engagement with everything in this world, loving it as God loves it, for the sake of God who is at work there.'

All experiences of suffering Julian saw as potential opportunities to learn more of the grace of God. They are a call to a greater dependence upon God and a corresponding deeper faith in the loving compassion of God for all. 'He did not say: You will not be troubled, you will not be belaboured, you will not be disquieted; but he said: You will not be overcome.'[30]

The incomprehensible dignity of ordinary life is reiterated time and again in the work of those known as spiritual masters in the Christian tradition. It is amidst this reality that true faith is enacted. Faith does not add to life an alien dimension of supernatural reality to supersede mundane reality. Faith and grace are not alien. Neither does it abolish the

---

28   *Ibid.*, p. 200.
29   This egalitarian sense of all humanity brought before God is echoed in a contemporary form by the street that one of the Hope Community members lays on the equality of men and women. 'I strongly feel that women and men are equal in the eyes of God...so why should the women here be existing almost as slaves, grateful for any attention from the greatest blackguard on the estate?' Fieldworker D.
30   Julian of Norwich, Long Text 68, cited in Jantzen G., *Julian of Norwich, op. cit.,* p. 213.

often dull ordinariness, where there can be more sadness and disappointment than success and happiness. Yet what it does do is to draw our attention to the roots of this life which might be overlooked. Faith is a response that God elicits by his presence and grace. As Rahner states, 'Faith proclaims the radical character of freedom, of responsibility, of love, hope, guilt, forgiveness, and the ultimate ground of their radicalness it calls God. It is God who has always established himself within this life as its ultimate depth.' In our concrete activities our relationship with our neighbour, of our miserable daily duties, of our capacity for forgiveness, of our acceptance of life's dark disappointments of our resignation in the face of death.'[31]

In conversation with Teresa of Avila

This focus on the ordinary was one well understood by Teresa of Avila. For her the attempt to stammer out the unutterable with regard to her relationship with God was rooted amidst all the problems and ambiguities of daily life. Teresa's advice to others was to focus on the reality of what true love of neighbour might mean for them in daily life rather than endeavouring to examine the quality of their relationship with God. 'We cannot be sure if we are loving God, although we may have good reasons for believing that we are, but we can know quite well if we are loving our neighbour. And be certain that, the further advanced you find you are in this, the greater the love you will have for God.'[32]

This love is focused in the heart, and it is this level which is the ground of all mystical experience for Teresa as O'Donogue makes clear.[33] He stresses that preparation for this is in the form of a pedagogy of the

---

31   Rahner K., *Opportunities for Faith: Elements of a Modern Spirituality*, trans. Quinn E., London, SPCK, 1974, p. 8.

32   Teresa of Avila, The Interior Castle, fifth mansion, chapter 3. Cited in Peers E. A., *The Complete Works of St Teresa*, Vol. II., London, Sheed & Ward, 1946, p. 261.

33   O'Donoghue N., *Mystics For Our Time*, Edinburgh, T & T Clark, 1989, p. 48ff.

heart, as Teresa's writings exemplify.[34] This use of water as a motif for the growth of prayer, and indeed the given nature of contemplative and mystical experience, dominates Teresa's writings. It is God himself who, as the source of water refreshes the interior life of the individual. Such a source of life may be earnestly sought and yet cannot be commandeered or controlled. So Teresa emphasises the gratuitous nature of prayer and consolation therein. As O'Donoghue explicates, 'The water stands for the glow and power and illuminative splendour of the Divine presence, which can be touched and glimpsed painfully in the ordinary ways of prayer beginning with the early fervours and sweetnesses which have a light and transient quality.'[35]

Even the heights of mystical union namely the spiritual marriage, Teresa emphasised, had as its effect to cause in the soul an intense longing to serve God by striving to gain souls for him. This irrevocable bond between the highest contemplation and the involvement in active service[36] of others is a recurrent feature through the writings of all those acclaimed in the spiritual tradition.

With regard to the more dramatic phenomena associated with mysticism and indeed present in the life of Teresa herself, she makes it very clear, as Williams[37] emphasises, that the criteria for authenticity either of a life or of phenomenon associated with that life lies not in the nature of any particular experience, but rather in the way it is related to any pattern of concrete behaviour and the development of dispositions and decisions within that life. 'Mysticism is demystified and mystical experience as such is accorded no particular authority. Its authority – as Teresa implicitly argues in the Life – has to be displayed in the shape of the vocation of

---

34   'The Interior Castle traces the steps of this pedagogy, its phases, its pitfalls, its basic principles, its point of crisis when ordinary prayer yields place to mystical or, as Teresa calls it, supernatural prayer.' *Ibid.,* p. 49.

35   'This presence of God is greatly sought and deeply longed for in the ordinary ways of prayer, but it comes only painfully and grudgingly as one waters or irrigates the parches earth, until the time comes, when the heavens open, the rain falls and the whole garden of the soul is filled with the life-giving water of the Divine presence.' *Ibid.,* p. 76.

36   There is a revered tradition also that pure union with God it itself the best service of other members of the Body of Christ. This is fundamental for cloistered contemplatives.

37   Williams R., *Teresa of Avila*, London, Geoffrey Chapman, 1991, p. 147ff.

which it is part.'[38] The incarnational mode of God's working with humanity is to the fore in Teresa's work, according to Williams, and he asserts that her view of her calling focuses on that kenotic move which led to the abandonment of divine status in order to become 'defenceless, dishonoured and unpriviledged'. The heart of her commitment to reform the Carmelites, Williams maintains, lay in the desire to imitate Christ. Within this very active phase of her life, there is a call out of the purely contemplative domain to become at times a nomad in her attempts to reform the Carmelite order. Yet here again there is the emphasis upon the union that matters most being union with the divine will and not in itself an experience of divine absorption. In this manner Teresa is likened to Eckhart.[39] 'For both, intimacy with God is conceived as assimilation to a God whose life is itself a move to mission. God is not God except as the one who sends the Son.'[40]

Teresa's focus in her espousal of the need to learn the ways of prayer, and to be able to discern amidst its consolations and desolations, is to be more adequately prepared for loving service within the world. If God should draw an individual into the way of mysticism it involves no position detached from the world. Rather it calls for an attitude of detachment which refuses to accept anything less than God and by God Himself is led back into the concerns of the world. Thus an individual continues the creative action of God within the world through any increase of faith, hope and love.[41] For Teresa there was nothing contradictory about being actively absorbed in the world and at the same time

---

38   *Ibid.,* p. 148.
39   There is also a comparable emphasis in Ignatius – see later in the chapter.
40   Williams R., *Teresa of Avila, op. cit.,* p. 160.
41   'We may and must detach ourselves from all that keeps us from God: but the God with whom we are finally united is the God whose being is directed in love toward the world which we must then re-enter equipped to engage with other human beings with something of God's whole-heartedness because we have been stripped of certain modes of self-protectiveness, of an understanding of our worth or lovableness as resting on prestige, achievement or uniformity. The way of perfection leads back to taking our active place in the human community.' *Ibid.*

wholly exposed to the reality of God.[42] For her there was no attempt to use activity as a form of defence against God or conversely to use the contemplative focus as a defence against the inherent risks and tribulation of activity.

Here also, like Julian before her and Ignatius after, Teresa emphasises the indispensable nature of the church in the developing spiritual life. The sacramental action of the church witnesses to the love of God made manifest in Christ. Yet this did not mean that Teresa felt the church was above criticism, rather the church was criticable in the manner in which it was exercising its authority and remaining faithful to its Lord. 'If the contemplative radical like Teresa questions the Church's practice, even in some respects the Church's method of practising authority, she does so in the name of what the Church itself 'authoritatively' does and says.'[43]

John of the Cross enters the discourse

Teresa's contemporary and collaborator in the reform of the Carmelite monasteries, John of the Cross, also stressed this fundamental link between action and contemplation. There is no real spirituality which is not deeply concerned with the poor, suffering, and marginalised. Yet time and again John appears to be drawing his readers back to the mode of waiting upon God prior to any doing. He stressed that the Christian experience of growth in relationship with God is growth in obscurity involving pain and struggle. It is a movement into darkness and dispossession, but it is in this manner a following of Christ and in being thus dispossessed the individual is shared out for all, in imitation of Christ. Yet the

---

42 cf. 'Behind the competent practicality of the person living in union is a continuing experience [so Teresa sees it] of living on the edge of ecstasy, undergoing moments of piercing intimacy and seeing into the heart of theological mysteries. The point is that such intensity and such perception are no longer alien to the soul that has completed its journey, and so no long interrupt the flow of thought and action.' *Ibid.,* p. 162.

43 *Ibid.*

195

foundation for what appears a dour programme is love and though John appears uncompromising in his demand for individual renunciation, paradoxically this is aligned as Collins[44] makes clear with his manifestly overflowing joy in created goodness and beauty.

Always the initiative belongs to God, and the writings of John reemphasise the total gratuitousness of all God's gifts. Indeed the very disposition of receptivity is itself a feature of prevenient grace and establishes that attentiveness which it also sustains.[45] 'A certain loving gaze into the dark reaches of faith where God is known to dwell, an activity which, for all its simplicity and its 'confused and general' nature is something which the person can discern and faithfully maintain.' Sustenance now comes for the grace of God. 'It is a condition of strong sensitive spiritual attunement to the divine mystery.'[46] In this attunement – this simple dark gaze of contemplative faith – there is a deeper openness to God and to other human beings. For John there is no other way for a person to become whole than by committing self to God's loving transforming will. Here the false darkness of unmortified desire must give way before the pure and simple light of God. Within this new mode of attentiveness, a novel form of spiritual ascesis comes to the fore, involving a deeper acceptance of an inner austerity which God has initiated. There is the need to discern the authenticity of the contemplative darkness experienced at this time and indeed the finely discerning nature of John's experiential knowledge is apparent in his writings.

Throughout his works, as Collins makes clear, John always emphasises the working of grace as a living personal relationship between God and the human person. It is this intimacy which draws the individual to an 'habitual sense of the need for purification.'[47] John's most renowned image is that of night and the two dark nights of the senses and the spirit. Without undertaking a full exploration of the literature abounding on these, it is important for our purposes to give them some consideration. Although two nights are described, they are – as it were – interwoven. The purification of the senses begun in the earlier phases only comes to

44   Collins R., *John of the Cross*, Collegeville, Minnesota, The Liturgical Press, 1990, p. 60ff.
45   Fieldworker C.
46   Collins R., *John of the Cross, op. cit.,* p. 70.
47   *Ibid.,* p. 90.

its perfection in the radical refinement of the spirit. As Collins states, 'If we envisage the grace of God moving progressively inwards, then the divinisation of the outward sensitive life is not accomplished until the light has reached the innermost substance of the soul and from there irradiates the whole person.'[48] In this process there is a move into what is referred to as the passive night of the spirit. Here there is ultimately an ontological purification to which, John asserts, few are called. It appears to involve a true experiential knowledge of one's real lack of spiritual integrity. Finally full mystical union brings into one the work of God and the individual's free co-operation with that work. Here there is the fulfilment of human life and freedom in the freedom and life of God. Yet the way to this final freedom is through the reality of an individual's own weakness and deep poverty. Although an orientation towards transcendence is a fundamental feature of human life, as ongoingly asserted in this work, individuals are themselves unable to realise that transcendent life or even by their own efforts to dispose themselves for this. It is the graced gift of God which draws them to holiness and paradoxically the more they are drawn into a humble awareness of this reality the more they are infused with that divine spirit. Such awareness, far from breeding a spirit of worthlessness, depression and disintegration, flowers mysteriously into real spiritual growth in joy and peace through this apparent emptiness.[49]

Indeed it may be that the hope which is able to risk all is the sign of a profound security. This drawing towards self-transcendence is seen by John as a sign of authenticity for any particular experience of God. On the part of the individual it consists in this steady attentiveness to the dark and sensorily-deprived region where God is spiritually 'sensed'. For John this is the stance of contemplative faith and is the only means both to union with God and to true knowledge of oneself and the world which one inhabits. Yet always John ties this understanding to the normative guidance of the church, stressing that the genuine mystic will always have a concern to avoid self-delusion and thus will want to test any individual

---

48   *Ibid.*, p. 81.
49   'In the way of spiritual emptiness the soul asserts nothing of its own. It recognises the voice of the Beloved as the unique source of all meaning, and so, freely relinquishing control of its life to Him, enters into a region not of uncertainty but instead of great mystery.' *Ibid.*, p. 95.

experience against the belief of the church. Thus what may be seen as an intimate personal dark night of the soul has also a necessary ecclesial dimension and context.

It is the graced gift of faith which creates both an implacable thirst for God within the individual and also assists that vision of the mysterious unseen presence of God in all, such that all creation is 'charged with the grandeur of God', as Hopkins so powerfully portrayed. It is an ongoing paradox of this state that the more the individual is aware of his or her own emptiness and powerlessness – drawn into real spiritual poverty – the more consistently the power of God is operative within that life. It is a consistent theme in John's work that, '…by being true, through free consent to his necessary ontological passivity under God, a person enters into the full possession of his own powers. For, like everything else, these are held only as a gift from God.'[50]

There is here enacted the ontological reality of an individual being changed by the power of divine love. It is that love which works the transformation and which draws the individual into that purifying trajectory where desire, born out of love and sustained by love, brings to light the roots of sin which vitiate that mysterious union with the divine.[51] The suffering involved in such transformation is thus the result of loving desire not masochism. It is a mysterious sharing in the being of Christ, and in its reconciling reality it witnesses to the transformation of the disfigurement of sin into the marks of love. It is a deep involvement in the forgiveness of Christ.[52] The eventual 'logic' of this progression is the emer-

---

50   *Ibid.*, p. 140.
51   'The deep reaches of the 'deep caverns' – the ground of desire co-extensive with the soul's very being made in the image of God – are revealed by the light of grace. The more a soul is purified by the fire of love, the clearer will be its spiritual vision of all things, including itself. This is not a speculative philosophical insight. It is the experience of radical 'emptiness' by which love prepares the will, straining its capacity to ever greater limits in anticipation of an ever greater fruition. It takes the form of consuming desire.' *Ibid.*, p. 143.
52   c.f. O'Donoghue remarks 'The forgiveness of Christ is the bringing forth of that deeper self where our true freedom dwells. To accept this forgiveness is to cast away all masks and pretences, and to walk free and entirely vulnerable both to the light of Christ and the menacing darkness of the world. To accept forgiveness is to accept my deepest truth and my deepest freedom.' O'Donoghue N., *The Holy Mountain: Approaches to the Mystery of Prayer*, Dublin, Dominican Publications, 1983, p. 88-89.

gence of true action from such passivity, of flourishing life from death and of an abundant fullness from the emptiness of dispossession.

Widening the discourse with Therese of Lisieux

The divine love is most supremely expressed in the light which issues from the Cross, such was the inspiration of the later Carmelite Therese of Lisieux. Her vision of that radical weakness which is also the foundation of strength echoes the work of John of the Cross and Teresa of Avila. The condition of this divine love into which human beings are drawn is that humility and lowliness which rejoices in the infinite capacity of God to both delight in and work through such 'nothingness'. As O'Donoghue asserts, 'For Therese one thing alone remained when all was gone: love. Love, naked, poor, unsupported by the promise of future joy and glory.'[53]

The insistence and re-insistence upon the primacy of love was the foundation of Therese's own understanding of her vocation, her 'Little Way', and the context for all her instructions to others. A child-like trust combined with a deep sensitivity, vulnerability and openness to a God she imaged as simple, clear, intimate and loving, stood in stark contrast to the piety of the age in which she lived. For her the offering of an individual to God was as an act of loving trust not a desire for suffering. Such loving trust was crystalised for her in an inner attitude of 'remaining little', knowing that God sustained her at each moment. 'To remain little is to discover one's own nothingness, it is to always await the good God, it is not to afflict oneself with one's faults. To be disquieted about nothing.'[54] Therese's realisation that her vocation was one of love was rooted not in a volitional act of the will but in a personal relationship of trust in God. Here she used so often the familiar scriptural texts,[55] which spoke of the trust of the young child who sleeps without fear in a parent's arms. Prayer for Therese was a simple turning of the heart towards God. 'For

---

53   O'Donoghue N., *Heaven in Ordinarie*, Edinburgh, T & T Clark, 1979, p. 80.
54   Therese of Lisieux, cited in O'Conner P., *In Search of Therese*, Wilmington Delaware, Michael Glazier, 1987, p. 96.
55   c.f. Isaiah 66 12, Psalm 131.

me, prayer is an aspiration of the heart, it is a simple glance directed to heaven, it is a cry of gratitude and love in the midst of trial as well as joy.'[56] Yet this sense of union, this simple gaze of love, which appeared to stand in stark contrast to the more pronounced notions of growth in the spiritual life, as advocated by Teresa and John, was not arrived at without the familiar way of purification. For Therese this took the form of an emphasis upon detachment. John cautioned against dependence on anything that might weigh down the spirit, and particularly anxiety, guilt and fear. Therese adopted a habit of detachment which she adhered to strictly, which was incisive and all-inclusive but which was not seen as an end in itself. The end was the freedom of a greater openness to God. For her this detachment meant a continuous resistance to clinging to things, people, emotions, impulses, ideas, habits, preoccupations, indeed anything. She said of herself, 'Jesus has given me the grace of not being any more attached to the goods of the mind and heart than to those of earth.'[57] It was the way of love which drew her along the path of detachment, and this love was to find its flowering in relationships with others, such that it could be seen as a pathway to sanctity for ordinary people. Her emphasis was always to look for the positive good in others rather than the negative capabilities. 'Charity consists in bearing with the faults of others, in not being surprised at their weakness, in being edified by the smallest acts of virtue we see them practice.'[58]

Therese saw that it was in the darkness of littleness and weakness that the greatness and glory of God could shine more brightly. Thus she could state that she was not only reconciled to her weakness and imperfections but could also find her joy in them. Within the practice of detachment can be seen the paradox of all Christian asceticism where all the focus is upon making more room for the God whose goodness she always relied upon. 'Sanctity consists in a disposition of the heart, which leaves us little and humble in God's arms, aware of our weakness and trusting unto folly in His fatherly goodness.'[59] However, as O'Donoghue empha-

---

56 Therese of Lisieux, cited in O'Connor P., *In Search of Therese, op. cit.,* p. 114.
57 *Ibid.,* p. 44.
58 *Ibid.,* p. 165.
59 Therese of Lisieux, cited in Von Balthasar H., *Therese of Lisieux: The Story of a Mission,* trans. Nicholl D., London, Sheed & Ward, 1953, p. 175.

sises[60], such a progress involved the actuality of the Father consistently being of supreme importance. That is why the way of detachment was so important and indeed in this lies the true greatness of the 'Little Way' for true detachment and the consequently purified spirit is great through the enrichment of grace. This process, just as the way outlined by John, is a never-ending one drawing beyond all finite limits, as O'Donoghue makes clear.

O'Donoghue argues powerfully that at the end of her life Therese underwent such a 'death of the spirit' as that of Gethsemane and Calvary. Linked with her terrible physical sufferings, there came an inner darkness which quenched her little way of trust and plunged her into the terror of non-existence, and non-belief.[61] This experience though rare,[62] has peculiar relevance for those who work upon the margins, particularly in situations where goodness and generosity can co-exist with the most perfidious violence and vice. An interior contemplative living with, experiencing of, the desolation of the violent and the addict [of whatever kind] and the un-faith and the disenchanted with religion, is a necessary condition for effective Christlike presence to the marginalised.

---

60 O'Donoghe N., *Heaven in Ordinarie, op. cit.*, p. 72ff.
61 'Central to the Gethsemane experience is a sense of loss and forsakenness. It is only because one had, somehow, opened out to the [positive] Infinite that one discovers within that space whereby the awful chasm of the negative infinite opens up.' *Ibid.* p. 80 c.f. 'Therese did not simply accept the night of nothingness for her ownmost self, she lived this annihilation day after day, hour after hour, sometimes in the total aloneness of nights of pain, alone with the pain of total unmaking and undoing...all through this time she had to support the faith of the whole world as it surrounded her in her enclosed convent, microcosmically and therefore cosmically. It is almost terrifying to see, as one reads her last conversations so carefully preserved by her sisters, how they have unconsciously succeeded in pushing her into the position of being their guide and support. More and more she is the one source of light for them all, ever more profoundly so as she sinks ever more deeply into physical dissolution and total inner darkness.' O'Donoghue N., *Mystics For Our Times, op. cit.,* p. 123.
62 There are gradations of participation in such a contemplative grace or vocation.

The specific contribution of Ignatius Loyola to the discourse

Von Balthasar draws attention to the striking resemblance of Therese's views with those of Ignatius Loyola, especially in the emphasis given to the paradox underlying human actions and dispositions and connecting human and divine choice. Thus the stress which Ignatius laid upon the discernment of spirits aims at this disciplined testing of an individual's feelings, emotions, values, heart. The human heart is envisaged by Ignatius as a battleground where God and evil are drawing to conflicting discipleship. An individual can notice the repercussions of these dialogical relationships in his or her own experience, and is able to discern what is of God from what is not. However, in order to develop such discerning ability, it is essential to become aware of all that goes on within the heart trusting that God will lead. Ignatius believed that an inner spiritual dynamic resides in the heart, originating from the working of the Holy Spirit within.

Two vital characteristics within Ignatian spirituality are 'indifference' and 'finding God in all things'. As Rahner makes clear,[63] the first is the presupposition of the second. Indifference is that state of attentive equanimity which stands in readiness for every drawing from God, realising that since God is always greater than any way in which we experience him, there must be ongoing detachment from all particular ways of encountering him. As Rahner states, 'The characteristic of Ignatian piety is something formal, an ultimate attitude towards all thoughts, practices, and ways.' He continues 'an ultimate reserve and coolness towards all particular ways, because all possession of God must leave God as greater beyond all possession of him.'[64]

From this kind of detachment, this indifference, there arises the openness to being continually available to changing situations, seeking God in and through all. It involves the tension of always being open to the leading of the spirit of God and finding rest only in this attentive mobility. '...prepared in *indiferencia* to seek him and him alone, always him

---

63   Rahner K., 'The Ignatian mysticism of joy in the world', *Theological Investigations 3: The Theology of the Spiritual Life*, trans. Karl H. & Kruger B., London, DLT, 1967, p. 277-293.

64   *Ibid.*

alone but also him everywhere, also in the world: in *actione contemplativus*.[65] The more deeply one is united with God, there is a consequent deepening of that relationship with all God's creation. Thus the contemplative individual becomes creative, totally self-giving, radically concerned about others – in short spiritually fecund. Such indifference is the foundation of discernment – a way of life – the basis of mysticism in action. This inner alertness was an essential part of Ignatius' mysticism of discernment. To seek and find God's will requires an acute sensitivity, a mystical sensitivity, to the least sign of God's will. Obviously, in order to hold oneself poised in that openness of spirit, in readiness to follow the leading of the spirit, there is the need for liberation from inordinate affections and attachments. Accordingly, Ignatius, as with the other mystics under consideration, advocated the necessity of being open to the healing of all that was inwardly fragmented, in order to be more open to service in the reconciling mission of Christ within the world. 'Ignatian spirituality and mysticism find God in all things in order to love and serve God in all things. It is a mysticism of joy in the world because it serves God in and through this world.'[66]

What appears unavoidable is some form of purification and illumination, whether this is seen in terms of a dark night as in John of the Cross or in the more homely terms of Julian of Norwich. In this connection, the Spiritual Exercises[67] are as Rahner indicates a 'mystagogical help.'[68] They are a departure, not an end in themselves. They assist the flowering of a disposition that of *'discreta caritas'* which is ongoingly open to being purified. Thus they are able to lead individuals at whatever stage of their spiritual development into deeper dimensions of the spiri-

---

65 *Ibid.*

66 'This meticulous search to find God's will and to carry it out perfectly accounts for Ignatius' frequent examination of conscience and for his sensitivity to his least fault.' Egan H., *Ignatius Loyola the Mystic*, Wilmington Delaware, Michael Glazier, 1987, p. 122.

67 'By the term 'Spiritual Exercises' is meant every method of examination of conscience, of meditation, of contemplation, of vocal and mental prayer, and of other spiritual activities...every way of preparing and disposing the soul to rid itself of all inordinate attachments, and, after their removal, of seeking and finding the will of God in the disposition of our life for the salvation of our soul.' Puhl L., *The Spiritual Exercises of St Ignatius*, Chicago, Loyola University Press, 1950, Ex.1.

68 Rahner K., *Ignatius of Loyola*, trans. Ockenden R., London, Collins, 1979, p. 16.

tual life. Here, the more deeply individuals are united with God, the more deeply too they are united to others in loving service within the world. Thus there appears a mysticism of daily life requiring radical fidelity to pragmatic demands and through all radical surrender to the mysterious God who grounds all life. Here again is presented the truth that God's self-communication grounds all reality not as an extrinsic pervasive force but as intrinsic to human nature.[69] For Ignatius this realisation led him to the desire to follow God's will through all the circumstances of life.

Loving reverence for God, reverential surrender to God, and reverential humility for God and others were graced gifts that Ignatius himself sought and advocated for those who made the Spiritual Exercises. For such gifts moved the focal point of life from the individual to God. These gifts of reverence, humility and loving surrender also set the context for discernment, decision and confirmation. Reverential love for God and all creatures is a deeply mystical view of creation and its proper relationship to God. As Egan makes clear, 'A person with the contemplative view of loving reverence uses creatures as God meant them to be used. Reverential love of creatures is actually their fulfilment.'[70] Ignatian mysticism – particularly as witnessed in the Spiritual Exercises is focused upon a progressive simplification of prayer, a growing transparency towards deep contemplation.[71]

It is significant that what caused one of the young lay women to join the Hope Community for two years was an experience of making the Spiritual Exercises. The Exercises were also an aid for the leader of the Community and an ongoing influence for her in life. The more an individual becomes aware of the presence of God within their lives, and a sense of that loving drawing to God and others, the greater will become the awareness of the lack of indifference and sensitivity to sinfulness. This is an unending process but one of deep consolation. 'In the continuing experience of finding God in all things, the further discovery of unexpected sinfulness can become a joyful means of entering into a

---

69   'Contemporary theology stresses that God communicates himself as the mystery who haunts, illuminates and loves us at the roots of our being, even before we begin to seek him.' Egan H., *Ignatius Loyola the Mystic, op. cit.* p.108 c.f., references to Rahner K. in chapters 5 and 6.
70   Puhl L., *The Spiritual Exercises of St Ignatius, op. cit.* Ex. 233.
71   Egan H., *Ignatius Loyola the Mystic, op. cit.,* p. 144.

deeper knowledge of God.'[72] As Veale maintains, the grace of the first week of the Exercises leads to a realistic sense of self and an openness that can stand without dissimulation before the loving goodness of God. It involves both a radical appropriation of personal involvement in sinful social structures which may well – and beneficially – evoke a sense of complicity and powerlessness, and consideration of an individual's own personal sinfulness. What is desired in prayer is a deep interior knowledge of the particular sinfulness that lies at the core of all an individual's sins. 'The conjunction of 'the disorder of my actions' and 'a knowledge of the world' may find some affinity with a contemporary theology of sin that sees men and women as structuring their world by their choices and being made by the world they structure.'[73] Complicity in social structures, which are inherently sinful affect individuals in the form in which they have directly benefited from a system which has proved unjust for others. 'There is a constant dynamic linking an individual's recognition of the sinfulness of the world with an unease at what has been going on in his or her deepest self.'[74]

Thus conversion in these circumstances involves a fundamental shift from the illusory assumptions of autonomy involving those self-sufficient egocentric behaviour patterns to a reflective openness and commitment of love to God which involves an outworking in the lives of others. This is authentic growth in freedom.[75] As Egan makes clear, Ignatius offers within the first week an 'architectonic view of the mystery of iniquity.'[76] This mystery of sin is presented in the context of the crucified Christ.

---

72 Veale J., 'The First Week: Practical Questions' in Sheldrake P., [ed.], *The Way of Ignatius Loyola: Contemporary Approaches to the Spiritual Exercises*, London, SPCK, 1991, pp. 53-65.

73 *Ibid.*

74 McVerry P., 'The First Week and Social Sin', in Sheldrake P. [ed.], *The Way of Ignatius Loyola: Contemporary Approaches to the Spiritual Exercises*, London, SPCK, 1991, pp. 53-65.

75 'We can only be free if we surrender ourselves to God. We can only enjoy life if we surrender our illusion of control over it to God. We can only enjoy our friends if we surrender them to God. To the extent that we are gripped by the illusion that we can control our own destinies, to that extent fear for ourselves predominates over love for others and God and when fear predominates we are not free.' Barry W., *Now Choose Life – Conversion on the Way to Life*, New Jersey, Paulist Press, 1990, p. 111.

76 Egan H., *Ignatius Loyola the Mystic, op. cit.,* p. 99.

The movement of this week is towards profound wonder at the loving mercy of God and personal re-appropriation of redemption history. The discernment of spirits is ultimately not a discernment of the heart on the basis of generalised moral criteria, but an attunement to the will of God an endeavouring to seek that will within the circumstances of daily life. This inevitably leads to embracing the foolishness of the cross.[77] This is to acknowledge that the cross of Christ is an inevitable part of Christian existence. Indeed it is the Christian symbol of success shattering the illusions of other forms of success. The gospel call is to live in freedom from illusions, to question assumptions that cripple the imagination and imprison in fear, to challenge injustices. 'To be a fool for Christ's sake means to risk being honest in a world where dishonesty seems in favour, being courageous where caution is a way of life. Those who choose to follow Jesus will suffer some dying, but death is not what they choose.'[78]

The second week of the Exercise involves consideration of various mysteries of the life of Christ from the Incarnation onwards, and within this context certain key Exercises. The Kingdom of Christ exercise emphasises that to be with Christ is to serve and brings to the fore this mysticism of service which was prefigured in the Principle and Foundation which began the Exercises. The Two Standards meditation continues this dynamic drawing of the retreatant into focus upon Christ's call and the ramifications of enlisting under his standard, where even poverty insults and humiliation may be a vital way of experiencing the reality of God at work in the world. What the individual making the Exercises is seeking at this time is a basic discernment – to know the deceits of the enemy in order to resist them and the way of Christ in order to follow. The important Triple Colloquy is the solemnising of a desire to follow more closely along the way of Christ in the highest spiritual poverty, and if it is in accord with the will of God into the way of actual physical poverty and humiliation. The Three Classes of Person and the Three modes of Humility,

---

77   'Because Ignatius encounters this God in Jesus Christ, he commits himself to the cross and to the foolishness of Christ. For all this foolishness of the Cross is for him only an expression and a putting into practice of the readiness to follow that free God even when he calls us out of the world, out of its inner meaning and its light into his own light, in which it seems to us as though we were entering into the night.' Rahner K., 'The Ignatian Mysticism of joy in the world', in *Theological Investigations 3, op. cit.,* pp. 277-293.

78   Barry W., *Now Choose Life, op. cit.,* pp. 94-95.

involve a drawing to a more literal following of the poor and humble Christ. Here is stressed the importance of that radical humility which always has a social dimension. To be with Christ to serve means to embrace the poor, humble reviled Christ of the Kingdom, the Two Standards and The Three modes of Humility in the circumstances of life. In practising such a discipleship of the poor and humble Christ, it may involve the acceptance of life on the fringes of society. As Rahner indicated when he had Ignatius address contemporary Jesuits, 'You should be men who seek to forget themselves for God's sake, who are disciples of the poor and humble Jesus, who preach his gospel, who stand by the poor and homeless in the fight for more justice for them.'[79] The Ignatian mysticism of service is focused upon the poor and humble Christ. Indeed, the specific concrete decision or 'election' to be made during the Exercises involves some deepened following of the poor and humiliated Christ. It was during this time of the Second and Third weeks that the leader of the Hope Community in her retreat found herself constantly being drawn back to her experience on the estate, and in this way reflective clarity also began to emerge. 'The Exercises helped me make sense of my experience.'[80]

The exercises of the third and fourth weeks deepen and confirm the decision of this second week. In the third week the context is the Passion and death of Christ, whilst in the fourth the background is the Resurrection. Thus there is a drawing into both the sorrow and joy of Christ whilst maintaining that openness for confirmation of a decision made.

The dynamic throughout these weeks is a Christocentric one. The grace desired from the second week is 'an intimate knowledge of our Lord who has become man for me, that I may love him more and follow him more closely.'[81] The inner awakening of this deeper relationship with Christ has a correlation with an exterior outworking, namely service. Yet the dynamic is one, an interior Christocentric appreciation and exterior Christocentric operation. 'Ignatius uses the outer word of salvation

---

79   Rahner K., *Ignatius of Loyola, op. cit.,* p. 35.
80   Fieldworker A. *op. cit.*
81   Puhl L., *The Spiritual Exercises, op. cit.* Ex. 104.

history to deepen, and set in motion the inner word of God's universal self-communication.'[82]

Throughout the Exercises there is a gradual growing appreciation of the need for discernment as a life-long process. Genuine docility to the spirit of God is an art which is only learned through many years of trial and error. Only gradually does there emerge a delicate sensitivity to the inner motions of grace so as to be able to distinguish and be moved by the spirit of God. It is expected indeed, treated as ordinary in the Exercises that there should be considerable interior movements, and sometimes violent alternations of consolation and desolation. Both affectivity and reason are engaged in discernment. Ignatius' rules for discernment take this into account as Egan clarifies.[83] Ignatius sought to find the will of God primarily through docility to interior lights and motions of grace, but without neglecting the use of reason, enlightened by the truths of faith.[84]

The stress which Ignatius laid on exterior confirmation should not be minimised, particularly as on many occasions he saw this confirmation as coming from the church. Here is glimpsed something of the ecclesial dimension to his mysticism. He did not make the mistake of equating his own feelings with the will of God. For Ignatius even the most convincing interior mystical experiences had to be congruent with the doctrinal and sacramental reality of the church. His loyalty to church authority, doctrine and practices ensured that his mysticism like those individuals already considered was validated by the church. For Ignatius the church was the visible embodiment of the Lord to whose greater service he was committed. He experienced the will of God through the authority of the

---

82 'Only the inspired outer word of revelation correctly interprets the inner word, but only in the light of the inner word can the genuine salvific meaning and significance of the outer word be found' Egan H., *Ignatius Loyola the Mystic, op. cit.,* p. 109.

83 'The rules for the discernment of spirits...focus not only on affectivity but also on knowledge, understanding, the unmasking of 'false reasonings, seemingly serious reasons subtleties' [Ex. Nos. 315, 324] and the thoughts that spring from consolation and desolation [Ex. 317]. The exercitant must discern that the evil spirit counsels during desolation [Ex. 318] that God gives 'true knowledge and understanding' [Ex. 322] that the evil one may suggest 'good and holy thoughts' [Ex. 322] and that 'we must pay attention to the course of our thought' [Ex. 333-334].' Egan H., *Ignatius Loyola the Mystic, op. cit.,* p. 164.

84 In this context it is important to refute attempts at too marked a separation between the operation of the Holy Spirit interiorly and the intelligent operation of the subject. Ignatius maintained a healthy reverence for the operation of intelligence.

church. Yet his was a critical reverence for church authority. This is seen most clearly in Ignatius' own life and his involvement with church authorities.

Ignatius always remained a man of the church in its tangible institutionalised form. Unconditional loyalty to the institutional church and a critical detachment towards her spiritually was a genuine possibility for him and his companions. His reason for such devotion to the church, as Rahner explicates,[85] was his desire 'to help souls' a desire which reached its fulfilment when others were helped to grow in faith, hope, love – a deeper relationship to God. All else was subordinated to this end and was subject to change and left to the gradual revelation and prompting of grace. Rahner's suggestion of what Ignatius might say to contemporary Jesuits about their relationship with the church and indeed with the structural forms of power which accrue therein, focuses significantly upon the example of the poor and humble Jesus. Discipleship in these terms would prove irreconcilable with a way of life dependent upon secular or ecclesiastical power. 'Jesus alone can preserve you from the fascination of power which exists in a thousand forms in the Church and which will always remain there.' He continued 'he alone can rescue you from the only too plausible thought that basically you can only serve mankind by having power, he alone can make the Holy Cross of his powerlessness understandable and acceptable.'[86]

The all-consuming desire to be with Christ to serve is a hallmark of Ignatian mysticism. Discernment lay at the centre of this understanding, a guarantee of integrity and assisting what Egan calls the 'ascetical dimension of mysticism and the mystical dimension of asceticism.'[87] This was a discerning love, the determining principle governing mission and eventually the spiritual vitality of the Society of Jesus. This discerning love was the interior law of love inspired by the Holy Spirit.[88] Ignatius lived and harmonised the tension of mystical familiarity with God and pragmatic service. In this way Egan sees him as a 'creative prototype' for contemporary theological reflection.

---

85   Rahner K., *Ignatius of Loyola, op. cit.,* p. 26.

86   *Ibid.* p. 23.

87   Egan H., *Ignatius Loyola the Mystic, op. cit.,* p. 205.

88   c.f. Loyola St Ignatius, *The Constitutions of the Society of Jesus,* trans. Ganss G., St Louis, Institute of Jesuit Sources, 1970, para. 134.

Speaking of the contemporary members of the Society of Jesus and their ongoing discernment of mission, Veale makes the point that the primary instrument of authentic interpretation is the living body of its members when they are united with God, with one another and with the spirit of the Ignatian legacy. 'To the extent that the members are not united with the source, the spirit that is incarnated is inauthentic.' He continues 'the sources are not for speculative contemplation or for academic discourse but for contemplative decision and action. It is discerning love made concrete in apostolic action that embodies the original spirit, gives flesh to the word.'[89] This insight could also be applied more widely to the church, particularly for all involved in ministry on the margins, but also extended to those in any form of ministry. Here, it is seen as essential that there is ongoing union with the source in terms of experienced contemplative prayer, and involvement with the tradition of spiritual guidance within the Church. Such ongoing engagement assists the consistent purification of spirit necessary for authentic discernment with regard to action. 'The authentic source is a daily rediscovery and an unending search.' Here the traditional Ignatian dispositions are imperative.[90]

The very term 'mystical' has become a designation for an obscure knowledge of God beyond the reach of the intellect. It is conceived as appertaining to the deepest level of an individual which is open and submissive to the activity of God at work. Yet as a term it has, as Williams indicates,[91] become too loosely associated with various peculiar forms of experience or states of mind. Mysticism has also been juxtaposed over against other more rational and particularly institutional forms of religious life. This concentration on a particular phenomenological core and states of consciousness is not the focus for the spiritual writers that have been under consideration. Instead, clearly presented from the tradition, is the interrelated nature of contemplation and action and the spiritual fecundity of the deeper forms of contemplation and mysticism. Integral to this is the need for that ongoing purification of spirit which safeguards

---

89   Veale J., 'Dominant Orthodoxies', in *Milltown Studies*, No., 30, Autumn, 1992, pp. 43-65.
90   '…a thoroughly right and pure intention, which in turn presupposes in the searcher 'his greater abnegation and continual mortification in all things possible. The final hermeneutic is the Cross.' *Ibid.*
91   Williams R., *Teresa of Avila, op. cit.,* p. 143ff.

authentic discernment and thus subsequent action, and a fidelity to the Church which expresses itself in critical loving reverence. The importance of the grace gift of humility within such an outlook is starkly evident enabling a deeper drawing into the kenosis of Christ.

Humility as graced gift of God dissolves self-conceit, chastens arrogance, and pierces self-absorption. It opens an individual in greater simplicity to others. In this way, it in some small measure mirrors God's humility and faithfulness in being unconditionally accessible to human beings. Growth in this gifted understanding is an inexhaustible path, as Underhill so clearly indicated.[92] It is to accept the unlimited possibilities and also the responsibilities of such a way of life. It involves ongoing tension in an unrelaxed effort to be open both to the call to deeper union with God and to co-creative activity in the world. Indeed the effect on the individual is a transformation of being.[93]

All the mystics here considered demand this determined deliberate action, the insertion of the ongoingly purified and transformed individual within the commonplace minutiae of life. There is a call to participate in the redemptive work of God in reconciling what is in discord.

> They want to heal the disharmony between the actual and the real, and since in the white-hot radiance of that faith, hope and charity which burns in them, they discern such a reconciliation to be possible, they are able to work for it with a singleness of purpose and an invincible optimism denied to others.[94]

This vocation to participation in the redemptive work of Christ is particularly apparent upon the margins. Here, in a very specific way, it would appear that there is a call for individuals to become agents of God's love to a despised and rejected people. However, this risky enterprise inevitably involves a degree of unplanned and uncontrolled suffering. As already considered, this can take the form of physical discomfort

---

92 Underhill E., *Practical Mysticism for Normal People*, London, J.M. Dent and Sons Ltd., 1940.
93 'The spark of spiritual stuff, that high special power or character of human nature, by which you may first desire, then tend to, then achieve contact with Reality, is as it were fertilised by this profound communion with its origin, becomes strong and vigorous, invades and transmutes the whole personality and makes of it, not a 'dreamy mystic' but an active and impassioned servant of the Eternal Wisdom.' *Ibid.*, p. 151.
94 *Ibid.*, p. 156.

with the deterioration of health due to poor living conditions. It may occasionally involve the threat of physical violence. It certainly involves
the misunderstanding and lack of support evinced in the hierarchical levels of a religious congregation and the local hierarchy of a denominational tradition. Finally it may involve the stark confrontation of an individual's own basis of faith and understanding of a spirituality which is
rooted in powerlessness and vulnerability. Here the willingness to embark upon the personal inner journey and the openness to ongoing purification of desire are the guarantees of authenticity of life as contemplation
is gradually integrated with action. From this vantage point, discerned
action and a fidelity to the Church, which is expressed in critical loving
reverence, may arise and be transformative both of the individual and the
institution. The Spiritual tradition gives clear evidence of individuals
who have participated in such transformations.

Chapter 8

Towards a Spiritual Hermeneutic

The Sea of Faith
Was once, too,
at the full and round earth's shore
Lay like the folds of a bright girdle furl'd,
But now I only hear
Its melancholy, long, withdrawing rear,
Retreating to the breath of the night-wind, down the vast edges drear
And naked shingles of the world.

And we are here as on a darkling plain
Swept with confused alarms of struggle and flight,
Where ignorant armies clash by night.[1]

My beloved spoke, saying to me:
'Arise my love
my fair one, come away.
For see, the winter is past,
the rains are over and gone,
the vines appear on the earth,
the season of birdsong is come
and the coo of the turtledove
is heard in our land.'[2]

Winter or Spring are two contrasting seasons. One appearing to be the
denuding of life and an entry into the barrenness of slumber and death,
but in reality the precursor to the new life of Spring. Thus Winter may be
seen as pregnant with Spring and no matter how long the gestation period, the promise of life is contained within the semblance of death.
Matthew Arnold's bewailing of the lack of faith within the land, in contrast to previous generations, seems far removed from the joyous accla-

---

1   Arnold M., *Dover Beach*, 1: 21.
2   Song of Songs, chapter 2 v10-12, trans. Munro J., unpublished PhD thesis, Univer-
     sity of Edinburgh, 1992.

213

mation of the writer of the Song of Songs. The former a wail of seeming desolation, the latter the heralding of true consolation. In a nor dissimilar manner, the immediate impression of the Heath Town Estate is one in which Arnold's sense of a loss of faith might appear an accurate description. Even the physical impression of the place serves to convey this, as the residents so powerfully indicated.[3] Yet during the time of the existence of the Hope Community, the members have seen a gradual but remarkable transformation take place in the lives of some of the people of the estate. This includes a growth in self-esteem and in the ability to articulate the experience of God in their lives, and a realisation that 'they have a contribution to make to their own becoming and to the human community.'[4] Such a transformation has more resonance with the note of hope and joy prevalent in the words of the writer of the Song of Songs. This hope is fundamental to the existence of the Hope Community, and is the guiding light of their aims and policies.

However, this transformation is a reciprocal process. Engaged in conversation with residents and employing the critical listening faculty, Community members have been confronted with the presence of God amongst the people. Thus the hope so poignantly expressed in the very name of the Community is not only centred on the potential within marginalised people for growth and development, but also the hope that is engendered amongst the Community by their deepening appreciation of God as experienced through their encounter with the people of the estate.

It is this experience which inspires hope and has renewed a desire for prayer. Thus the incarnation of this hope amongst Community members has been both facilitated by, and given further impetus to, that personal and communal willingness to engage more deeply with the contemplative dimension. This openness to risk the interior journey and encounter the powerlessness and emptiness that humbly awaits God's plenitude has profoundly nourished the sense of prayer and forged a deeper solidarity with those who are marginalised. In turn the very being and presence of the Community members impelled by such a dynamic has drawn forth further evidence of God at work amongst the people, and enabled the residents to celebrate something of this reality in their lives.

---

3   See Chapter 1.
4   Fieldworker A.

A choice is increasingly presented to contemporary individuals and the church whether to be motivated by a depressed sense of the lack of faith within society and particularly amongst those on the margins and to confine effort and vision in an introverted focus upon a diminishing group of devotees, or whether to look closely, listen intently and be open to surprise and wonder as the mystery of God already at work upon the margins is apprehended. If the latter vision is but glimpsed, it leads into paths of more profound risk for individuals and the church. It leads deeper into the contemplative way, not as a withdrawal from the world into an enclosed environment, but rooted firmly in and with the marginalised and giving fresh impetus to proclamation of the gospel. It leads increasingly to a humble awareness of God at work beyond institutional boundaries enticing individuals to believe.

The previous chapter illustrated how the spiritual tradition substantiates the integrated nature of contemplation and action. Indeed there is abundant evidence that the deeper individuals are drawn into their own contemplative depths the more empowered are they for authentic and effective ministry, particularly amongst the marginalised. Openness to some form of ongoing purification of desire I have argued is a crucial factor upon this inner journey, assisting that consistent discernment of motivation which supports authentic action with and on behalf of the marginalised, without succumbing to manipulation or exploitation. In this chapter it is necessary to consider in more detail the process of that interior journey and the qualities engendered along the way vital for a contemporary spiritual hermeneutic. In such consideration, interaction with the work of Merton proves invaluable.

Unless there is a more profound human understanding derived from that exploration of the inner ground of human existence, loving activity will tend to be superficial and deceptive. Thus there is a direct correlation between the deepening of an individual's interior life and the expansion of the capacity to understand and serve others. There are no shortcuts in this process, for it appears part of the human condition that we are slow to relinquish either mental or material comfort. 'God's will is for us to become agents of love, and this is sufficiently difficult and risky for us to be sure that it will involve suffering, the kind of suffering we cannot control.'[5]   This openness is the starting point for the interior journey. It involves some generosity even magnanimity in the risk of embarking upon something unknown and uncontrolled. Here there is a drawing into a depth of solitude which confronts the fear of loneliness. Gradually there emerges a developing sense of powerlessness and helplessness, even apparent emptiness as the level of contemplative prayer deepens. Here a process of purification, of motivation, desires and ultimately spirit, leads into a growing freedom. At the heart of the journey the arrogance which sought to bring God to the marginalised is transformed through the shock of recognition of God already present into a humble receptivity of God's presence. At this juncture, the possibilities for reciprocal transformation are most evident, as those who work on the margins are evangelised by the people with whom they work and are in this process enabled freely to contribute to a shared spirituality.

The risk of beginning the journey

Those who seek authentic action on the margins are bound to risk exploring the inner waste of their own being and here to know the seasons of their own hearts, the fullness of consolation and the emptiness of desolation. Ontological reality lies here. There is a call to an integrating acceptance of the mystery at the heart of life and gratitude for the dimension of giftedness within. Here is encountered the paschal mystery of the contemplative dimension, where one lets go of needs and fears in order to receive gratefully the mystery of God's gift of self. Knowledge of God is paradoxically a knowledge of self as utterly dependent on God's saving knowledge. In its essence, it appears as more akin to an ongoing discovery of something mysteriously concealed. This interior exploration requires the listening heart. As already indicated, listening necessitates hearing, and both lead into understanding and reach into interior truth. For there to be understanding it must be found within a shared context

---

5   'It is no use choosing crosses that look congenial, because the point of the true bearing of the cross is the displacing of our self-oriented desire by openness to God.' Williams R., *Teresa of Avila*, London, Geoffrey Chapman, 1991, p. 95.

involving participation and the shared taking of time. Understanding of its very nature is both practical and credential, prompting appropriate responses, and the best of such responses is always a furthering of the understanding or a gesture in this direction. The ambience for this hearing, listening and responding involves patience and the spending of time. Understanding is always an open and provisional matter with an unfinished quality promoting further effort and denying the possibility of foreclosure or complacent arrogance. It is always reformable and corrigible and only by denying this interior freedom can it be said to have arrived at some complete or privileged point. The process is characterised by a certain raggedness and unfinished nature as the attempt is made to connect with what is not self. It involves a constant re-appropriation of self and extension of self in a way that is always unfinished and provisional.[6]

The risk of vulnerability is an important preliminary step upon the interior journey. Shared provisionality and shared vulnerability are near the heart of conscious selfhood. There must be a renouncing of the self as a solitary claimant. Always, what individuals say and do depends also on others. This is the nature of real discourse. Thus the speaking of one may be the silencing of another in a power-play or struggle for dominance. The aim sought is a single simple story giving life not competing monologues. The way of such a community is learned patiently over time by trial and error and the willingness to forgive. Over time there arises a discovery of the mysteriousness of selfhood out of trying to communicate and taking time to be less opaque. Here the very core of humanity is revealed in the difficulty.

We bring ourselves to speech and consciousness by struggling to see the other. Ourselves and the other are interrelated. We are constantly deciding what can and cannot be said in a world of listeners. The interlocutor is of vital importance here for we do not know what we want consistently without the mediation of others. We are constantly on the brink of adversarial conjunction. There is an unavoidable separateness in order to have a sense of distinction. It is important to stress the other who listens, perceives, respects with the solidity of human otherness. This is

---

6   I am indebted for this insight to Bishop Rowan Williams and notes made during the Gunning Lectures of 1993, delivered at the University of Edinburgh Divinity Faculty, New College.

what the church is called to mediate, an interest beyond rivalry and a deep reverence for the mystery of God at work within the other.

The personal response is essential here. There is always a risk involved and the journey is endless. Upon this way there is required a disposition which is willing to accept more perfectly what is already known and glimpsed though obscurely – re-realised interior truth. Thus the contemplative way into which God himself draws individuals is not an escape from potential conflict, anguish, doubt and even in some forms death. Rather it involves the willingness to live with ongoing questions, questions which paradoxically appear to bring life-giving energies.

Many people suffer because of the false supposition on which they have based their lives: that supposition is that there should be no fear or loneliness, no confusion or doubt. But these sufferings can only be dealt with creatively when they are understood as wounds integral to the human condition. Therefore ministry is a very confronting service. It does not allow people to live with illusions of immortality and wholeness. It keeps reminding others that they are mortal and broken, but also that with the recognition of this condition, liberation starts. 'The deep inexpressible certitude of the contemplative experience awakens a tragic anguish and opens many questions in the depth of the heart like wounds that cannot stop bleeding.'[7]

The risk of beginning the interior journey is mirrored in the risk of active involvement with those on the urban margins. In each case there are common characteristics. An open disposition is the invaluable foundation for acceptance of others, and interiorly leads to growing self-acceptance. The willingness to spend time listening to marginalised individuals is paralleled by the desire to spend time waiting upon God. The messiness and provisionality of life on the margins finds its counterpart on the interior journey where divine imperatives appear far removed from human tidiness. Finally, the raw revelation of vulnerability in daily life is also a necessary interior prerequisite for that mysterious discovery of selfhood rooted in divine intimacy. It is imperative that both forms of engagement are seen as necessary for the individual or the church if seeking involvement with the marginalised.

---

7   Merton T., *New Seeds of Contemplation*, London, Burns and Oates, 1962, p. 12.

Loneliness and solitude

'What do I find most difficult? The loneliness of it. I sometimes feel very alone.'[8] The experience of the leader of the Hope Community in her work on the estate at times results in a deep sense of loneliness. In a similar manner one characteristic of the inner journey is the experience of loneliness, each individual walks a solitary path. Yet loneliness if honestly acknowledged and confronted can come to be a gift which is transformed into solitude. The truest solitude is an abyss opening up in the centre of the soul only encountered through 'hunger and thirst and sorrow and poverty and desire'.[9] In a similar manner, one of the lay women of the Community stressed how during her time with the Community she has become aware of a deep need for time alone. 'I'm very greedy for those times of being quiet, just by myself, being with God, being alone.'[10] This drawing to solitude is an invitation to transcend limitations. In this loneliness the deepest activities may begin. It is here that one may discover act without motion, labour that is profound repose, vision in obscurity, and beyond all desire a fulfilment whose limits extend to infinity. Here, it is possible to live in a deep and peaceful interior solitude even in the midst of the confusion of the world. Such a disposition meets the very core of need of those who live and work on the margins. Loneliness when honestly confronted reveals inner emptiness which of its nature can be destructive of personality if misunderstood, but can be vibrant with promise for one who is prepared to explore its dark pain. Thus, loneliness may become a source of human understanding and a source of healing to others who are lost in the darkness of their own sufferings. In this sphere, a contemplative stance towards others is vital because paradoxically, by withdrawing into ourselves, not out of self-pity but out of humility, a space is created for another to be himself on his own terms and potentially to grasp his own life more keenly. 'We can make our minds so like still water that beings gather about us that they may see, it may be, their own images, and so live for a moment with clearer, perhaps ever

---

8   Fieldworker A.
9   Merton T., *New Seeds of Contemplation*, *op. cit.*, p. 62.
10   Fieldworker C.

with a fiercer life because of our quiet.'[11] Paradoxically, true solitude draws individuals into communion with others and in turn true communion with others draws individuals into true solitude. Thus the authentic self can embrace both solitude and other real human beings.[12] A certain depth of disciplined contemplative experience is a necessary ground for fruitful action. Traditionally, contemplation has been associated with the deepening of a person's personal life and the expansion of the capacity to understand and serve others. Far from being essentially opposed to each other, interior contemplation and external activity are two aspects of the same love of God. 'He who attempts to act and do things for others and for the world without deepening his own self-understanding, freedom, integrity and capacity to love, will not have anything to give others.[13]

The example of John of the Cross is again of importance here. John speaks of the important benefits of solitude upon the soul and the attitude of attentive listening to God. Such attentiveness to God is the very heart of the experience of love in everyday life. Here there comes a growing awareness of direct dependence upon God and a realisation that everything comes as pure gift. It is the honest acknowledgement of the existential condition of loneliness in daily life, and the willingness to confront this reality on the interior journey which enables the transformation of loneliness into fruitful solitude.

Contemplative Prayer

The life of contemplative prayer is first of all life and life implies openness, growth and development. According to Merton, it is often more

---

11   Yeats W.B., From his collection of prose – source unknown – an unreferenced hand-written text is in the author's possession.
12   Merton tells us the true solitary is one who 'realises, though perhaps confusedly, that he has entered into…the radical and essential solitude of men – a solitude which was assumed by Christ and which in Christ becomes mysteriously identified with the solitude of God.' Cited in Finley J., *Merton's Place of Nowhere*, Notre Dame, Indiana, Ave Maria Press, 1987, p. 47.
13   Merton T., *Contemplation in a World of Action*, London, Allen and Unwin, 1971, p. 164.

perfect to do what is simply normal and human than to try to act like an angel when God does not will it. Here a daily discipline can be a vital ingredient. This is why the core Hope Community meet regularly for prayer. It gives a dimension and an anchoring to the group without which 'we wouldn't be the same at all.'[14] At the same time for individuals 'prayer is a struggle'.[15] It does appear that the experience of struggle, self-emptying, letting go and subsequent recovery by grace in peace, on a new level, is one way in which lives are transformed through the Paschal mystery. This involves the discipline of interior listening, a difficult ascetical discipline hard to maintain, but vital for that inner journey and for engagement with those who are marginalised.

The heart of such contemplation is always beyond knowledge and reasoned understanding, beyond systems and explanations, beyond our very self, for it reaches out to the knowledge and experience of the transcendent inexpressible God. It is realised only by the sudden gift of awareness, an awareness that will always be incomplete and partial but which is an awakening to the truth of God within all reality. This awakening has a deep resonance in the inmost core of the spirit. A questioning spirit which simultaneously has within it the source of response. In this manner, Merton finds within human beings both question and answer. The question is, itself, the answer and individuals are themselves both. 'It is as if in creating us God asked a question and in awakening us to contemplation He answered the question, so that the contemplative is, at the same time, question and answer.'[16] However, this is not to suggest that contemplation is a solitary activity rather the goal of contemplation is a sharing with others, an overflow of the gift given such that the lives of others are affected and gifted also. Again such an over-abundance affecting the lives of others depends on the degree of any union with God. 'The contemplative is not isolated in himself, but liberated from his external and egotistic self by humility and purity of heart. Therefore there is no longer any serious obstacle to simple and humble love of others.'[17] Indeed, it is in that deepest ground of an individual's being in love, that is found both the individual, other human beings and Christ. Not one of

---

14   Fieldworker D.
15   Fieldworker C.
16   Merton T., *New Seeds of Contemplation, op. cit.,* p. 3.
17   *Ibid.,* p. 51.

these alone but 'all-in-one': thus the same ground of love is found in everything. Merton himself states, 'Whatever I may have written, I think it can all be reduced in the end to this one root truth, that God calls human persons to union with Himself and with one another in Christ.'[18] For Merton there is an important reciprocity in our involvement with others, and this is particular forceful in encounters with the marginalised. This inter-relationship whereby experience of involvement with the people fuels relationship with God was a common experience amongst Hope Community members. 'There are all sorts of flashes, signs from the people of God.'[19] Merton assumed the interconnection of authentic spiritual growth with the challenge to live up to the pragmatic demands of love as necessarily incarnated in those who are marginalised. Here, the contemplative, for Merton, is both prophet and marginal person. 'He does not belong to an establishment. He is a marginal person who withdraws deliberately to the margin of society with a view to deepening fundamental human experience.' Here, the importance of prayer cannot be minimised. It is no coincidence that the emphasis within the weekly programme of the Hope Community is upon prayer both with the residents on a weekly basis, with the Community on a daily basis and the time ascribed by individuals to personal prayer. For the leader of the Community this personal time generally in the early morning is a priority, especially as she is often unable to attend a regular daily liturgy. 'Many times I can't get to mass, but I will pray through the scriptures of the day always.'[20] Prayer if authentic is an acknowledgement of finitude and need, of openness to being changed and of willingness to be surprised. Prayer leads to a greater sensitivity to the plight of others. Such involvement then nourishes the ongoing prayer. Ultimately both interior and exterior life are transformed. 'Only when we are able to 'let go' of everything within us, all desire to see, to know, to taste, and to experience the presence of God, do we truly become able to experience that presence.'[21] The kenotic quality of this prayer, the willingness to stand naked and empty before God leads to an openness to being filled with God's own life, a union which finds its fulfilment in authentic action. Merton saw this mystical

---

18   Merton T., cited in Finley J., *Merton's Place of Nowhere*, *op. cit.*, p. 60.
19   Fieldworker D.
20   Fieldworker A.
21   Merton T., *Contemplative Prayer*, London, DLT, 1987, p. 111.

union as a vital dimension of the holiness of the church. Yet the precondition for such sublime heights is the simple presence of desire. Only in great desire, in earnest prayer and in selfless love can freedom be found. True contemplation is not a psychological trick but a theological grace. 'it is the will to pray that is the essence of prayer, and the desire to find God, to see Him and to love Him is the one thing that matters.'[22] Here openness leads into simple awareness and humble prayer. In prayer the confrontation of poverty and helplessness become evident. Here the true self is secure within humility, and attentive expectancy in faith brings the individual to the brink of the insight of the true self in God. 'Prayer as the distilled awareness of our whole life before God, is meant to lead us to a radical transformation of consciousness in which all of life becomes a symbol. All of life is seen as God sees it.'[23] Contemplative prayer as the integrating agent throughout the whole of life, generating renewed vision, attuning the listening faculty and inspiring action is the experience articulated by Merton and resonant with the experience of Hope Community members.

Emptiness

According to Merton, this contemplative prayer is a transcendent gift. It involves direct docility to the light of truth and to the will of God. It is always the divine initiative at work within human beings. Indeed for Merton, individuals become contemplatives when God discovers Himself in them. 'We must have God dwelling in us in a new way, not only in His greatness but in His littleness, by which he empties Himself and comes down to us to be empty in our emptiness and so fill us in His fullness.'[24] In this case the contemplative stance of receptivity within the active apostolate is the vital focus. Merton cites a paradox of the mystical life as being that an individual cannot enter into the deepest centre of himself and pass through that centre into God unless, 'he is prepared to

22 Merton T., *Conjecture of a Guilty Bystander*, New York, Doubleday, 1989, p. 173.
23 Finley J., *Merton's Place of Nowhere, op. cit.* p. 127.
24 Merton T., *New Seeds of Contemplation, op. cit.,* p. 31.

pass entirely out of himself and empty himself and give himself to the people in the purity of a selfless love.'[25]

The simplicity of infused light leads into those depths that leave an individual inarticulate. For Merton the way to contemplation is an obscurity so obscure that it is no longer even dramatic. Here the importance of poverty cannot be over-emphasised. The true mystical experience of God and renunciation of everything which is not God coincide. 'The surest asceticism is the bitter insecurity and labour and nonentity of the really poor. To be utterly dependent on other people, to be ignored, despised, forgotten.'[26] Such a scenario is a daily physical reality for many of those who live on the Heath Town estate. Here the questions do not revolve around what to forfeit as a spiritual discipline, but what is possible given an increasingly limited income. The result of this is to pose a question for individual members about their own ascetical practices and more deeply about their own interior darkness. 'I found myself having to look at my own...shit.'[27]

The great freedom with which human beings are challenged arouses fear in the face of a potential vacuum that must be filled. This interior emptiness is the seed ground for mature growth and yet it can appear as the prelude to disintegration. According to Merton in the end this fear re-emphasises the importance of renunciation. He refers to this as the 'infinite binding' without which one cannot begin to talk of freedom. Yet such renunciation is not mere resignation or abdication, rather it is an active asceticism into which an individual is drawn by a deepening attachment to the imitation of Christ and the discernment of any motivation for action. This involves a deeper and more interior exercise of the listening faculty. 'There is a higher kind of listening, which is not an attentiveness to some special wave-length, a receptivity to a certain kind of message, but a general emptiness that waits to realise the fullness of the message of God within its own apparent void.'[28] Though, at this time, prayer may seem qualitatively poor in an affective sense, yet its very poverty is real wealth. Its very emptiness is plenitude if open to transformation by God. Indeed Merton asserts that 'the deepest prayer at its nub is a perpetual

---

25   Merton T., *Ibid.*, p. 50.
26   *Ibid.*, p. 194.
27   Fieldworker C.
28   Merton T., *Contemplative Prayer, op. cit.*, p. 122.

surrender to God'.[29] Here, contemplative prayer is a resting in God who constantly draws the heart[30] of an individual to himself.

What Merton consistently emphasises is that the deepest level of the individual is core-related to the crucified and risen Christ. Here lies the mystery of God at work within each one. This for him was the impetus behind the desire to bring into one integrated whole the entire human life. At the same time, he owned the inadequacy of any attempt to articulate the reality of this depth of the interior life. 'The inner self is as secure as God and, like him, it evades every concept that tries to seize hold of it with full possession.'[31] Such manifestation arises in the midst of the ontological poverty of being. Here while empty, individuals are filled. While poor there is at the same time the possession of the Kingdom. The importance of the cross which ultimately transforms the world becomes supremely important. When individuals come to accept the cross within their lives there is the realisation that the inner ontological falsity is healed, and a freeing of that authentic life-giving dynamic which is the action of the Spirit of God within. 'Once we have accepted the cross...then we become able to realise that the world is in ourselves and is good and redeemed. And we can accept in ourselves both the evil and the good which are in us and in everybody else.'[32] Such strong trust in the graciousness of God can enable life to be lived as a marginal person, one whose voice is no longer heard in the councils of the great. Here faith and trust enable a deeper entry into living the paschal mystery. 'This does demand of us a remarkable willingness to entrust our priceless skills, talents possessions, reputation, friends and hopes into the hands of the poor, dishonoured and unappreciated Christ.' However we find this so difficult 'the great temptation is to refuse this ultimate trust lest one

---

29   *Ibid.*, p. 13.
30   'The concept of 'the heart' refers to the deepest psychological ground of one's personality, the inner sanctuary where self-awareness goes beyond analytical reflection and opens out into metaphysical and theological confrontation with the abyss of the unknown.' *Ibid.*, p. 38.
31   'All that we can do with any spiritual discipline is produce within ourselves something of the silence, the humility, the detachment, the purity of heart and the indifference which are required if the inner self is to make some shy unpredictable manifestation of his presence.' Merton T., 'The Inner Experience: Notes on Contemplation' [unpublished] p.6 cited in Finley J., *Merton's Place of Nowhere, op. cit.*, p. 20
32   *Ibid.*, p. 56.

lose all comfort, much respect from others, and a satisfying career, when actually this 'death' through trust maybe the final and fullest growth of person in the Christian'.[33]

Such an entry into emptiness and death is a vital ingredient of any engagement with those on the margins. Here 'leadership' is one of service rather than the exercise of power, to lead people out of confusion and into hope. Yet it is only the one who has had the courage to explore her own inner confusion and has journeyed the way through darkness, emptiness and death into hope who has the ability to undertake this form of leadership. At this juncture compassion is the root of all authority. Such compassion arises from the depths of seeming emptiness and aridity, clinging to nothing of its own, it is enabled to cross boundaries of language, nationality, wealth or poverty, and education. Indeed nothing can be said to be alien for a compassionate individual – no joy or sorrow. For the man or woman of compassion has journeyed far into their own inner emptiness and emerged filled with the divine imperative.

Purification

The God given gifts of contemplative prayer and plenitude amidst emptiness, require an ongoing openness to purification. The Christian mind is a mind that risks intolerable purifications and sometimes, indeed very often, the risk turns out to be too great to be tolerated. Faith tends to be defeated by the burning presence of God in mystery, and seeks refuge from him, flying to comfortable social forms and safe conventions in which purification is no longer an inner battle but a matter of outward gesture. However, those whom God draws deeply to himself have an increased sense of their own sinfulness and a deepening desire that the light of God should illuminate all that impedes that light. Ironically to deny the reality of sin is implicitly to denigrate what may be the noblest qualities of human beings, namely freedom, responsibility to God and commitment to sacrifices for others. Here is encountered the importance of

---

33   Hassel D., *Radical Prayer: Creating a Welcome for God, Ourselves Other People and the World*, New Jersey, Paulist Press, 1984, p. 162.

any prayer of admitted sinfulness which frees an individual from self-righteousness and teaches the ability to live patiently and wisely with shortcomings. Such prayer, 'knocks us off our towering, self-righteous perch, because it produces solidarity or intimacy with our Church of sinners.'[34]

Hassel stresses the importance of living peacefully within limitations and becoming accustomed to a sense of helplessness. Indeed, it is precisely at this point, as already indicated, that there is a new sense of solidarity with marginal people. Here the sharper the pain of poverty the stronger can be the inclusive impetus with regard to those on the margins. The more comprehensive is personal knowledge of inadequacy, the greater the potential to appreciate the working of the spirit of God through prayer and apostolate. Such prayer of sinfulness is filled with gratitude to God and with confident energy for the spreading of the kingdom.

Here is encountered once more the need to risk entry into powerlessness in order that God may operate powerfully. Hassel helpfully elaborates on the nature of such powerlessness. It is not simply one feature, it is a state of soul embracing an insecurity which is also a deeper interior trust in God. It is a choice to be in solidarity with 'Christ's anawim, the dispossessed and marginal people'[35] while at the same time recognising the living tension thus involved. 'In this way, Christ and his people possess me more and more...Inevitably such trusting dependence on God will include tension, misunderstanding, risks, perils.'[36] Such tension is an ongoing feature of the life of the Hope Community members as one thoughtfully indicated. 'There's a lot of struggle in individual members, the struggle to be real. People are made more aware of their real natures, the fact that the only thing they have to fall back on at the end of the day is their real selves.'[37] With the awareness of sinfulness, repentance, according to Merton, is at the same time a complete renewal, a discovery, a new life, and a return to the old, to that which is before everything else that is old. It is a reordering, according to the image and likeness of God,

34   Hassel D., *Dark Intimacy: Hope for Those in Difficult Prayer Experiences*, New York, Paulist Press, 1986, p. 52.

35   *Ibid.,* p. 82.

36   *Ibid.,*

37   Fieldworker E.

which lies as an indelible imprint within the core of human beings. It is a coming home to self, a re-realisation of profound truths, a rediscovery of the authenticity of being. Thus, it is both new and yet resonant with something interiorly inherent within the heart. At the same time it is a consistent commitment to embrace the cross within life, which is above all that deep-seated rebellion against God which lies at the root of all sin. This orientation to falsity thus requires an ongoing humble willingness to bring this to God's healing grace. 'Life is, or should be, nothing but a struggle to seek truth: yet what we seek is really the truth that we already possess.'[38]

Truth becomes available to human beings in the pragmatic reality of life. However if the individual attitude is to take life thoughtlessly, passively as it comes, this is to renounce the struggle and purification which are necessary to gain authentic truth. One cannot simply open the eyes and see. Likewise it has been shown how difficult it is really to listen, hear and understand in any interaction with others, particularly those on the margins. The discipline of listening and of giving attention is a very high form of ascetic discipline which is difficult to maintain. The work of understanding involves not only dialectic, but a long labour of patient attentive waiting, acceptance, obedience to the deep drawing of God through the circumstances of daily life. There is always the temptation acutely prevalent on the margins of falling back into passive abstraction, or frenetic activity thinly disguised as obedience and abandonment. There is the ongoing challenge to live human life to its fullest amidst every changing circumstances.

Paradoxically the path to the fullness of God is one of 'ascetic self-emptying' and 'self-naughting' and not at all a path of self-affirmation, of self-fulfilment or of 'perfect attainment'.[39] Within this way of prayer the gift of discernment is a vital prerequisite along the way, testing the authenticity of all that occurs. Weakness and inadequacy remain upon this journey but are increasingly handed over and integrated as all is made open to the loving compassion of God. There arises a deep personal integration in an attentive watchful listening of the heart. Here the most intense and authentic purification beings. 'The only full and authentic purification is that which turns a man completely inside out, so that he no

---

38   Merton T., *Conjectures of a Guilty Bystander, op. cit.,* p. 184.
39   Finley J., *Merton's Place of Nowhere, op. cit.,* p. 81.

longer has a self to defend, no longer an intimate heritage to protect against inroads and dilapidations'. Full maturity itself cannot be reached unless 'We first pass through the dread, anguish, trouble and fear that necessarily accompany the inner crisis of 'spiritual death' in which we finally abandon our attachment to our exterior self and surrender completely to Christ.'[40] Such purification is an increasingly subtle affair, at times almost imperceptible. Yet it is this ongoing awareness of the need for such activity which reiterates the interior reality of the gospel. Such asceticism purifies and liberates the inner person. Indeed, Merton asserts,[41] inner certainty is in a sense dependent upon such purification which draws to simplicity and sincerity of heart. Here there is a passage through the renunciation of all deluded images of self, those masks and fabrication of everyday living, towards an integration of true identity.

Such ascetic self-discipline is itself subject to grace both for inspiration and to sustain the action. It is vital that this action arises from the depths of human freedom where it is sustained by divine love. Here there is gradually a drawing to deeper and more passive purification which is beyond comprehension but which serves to liberate the deep spiritual power at the centre of an individual's being.[42] Thus there is required that deeper attunement and listening which attentively waits upon the breath of God.

Service of the marginalised may at times be a calling to constant crucifixion. Here, drawn into the paschal mystery, an individual may find self identifying with Christ the fool, the worthless one, in seeking out and serving those who are suffering and risking and sometimes sharing those same sufferings. Yet this is always within the whole paschal mystery and therefore contains within it some sense of resurrection joy. From the darkness light does issue forth, from death life can emerge, indeed from the void of chaos unaccountably emerges the mysterious gift of the spirit sent by God to transform and make all things new. There is a paradox within such paschal mystery prayer, 'Its sweet dryness, full emptiness,

---

40   Merton T., *Contemplative Prayer, op. cit.,* p. 137.
41   *Ibid.,* p. 82ff.
42   'The greatest mystical literature speaks not only of 'darkness' and 'unknowning' but also of extraordinary flowering of 'spiritual senses' and aesthetic awareness underlying and interpreting the higher and more direct union with God 'beyond experience'.' *Ibid.,* p. 106.

teeming desert, light darkness and apparent denial of all intimacy promote a 'homing' prayer at the centre of the praying person's being.'[43] In a not dissimilar manner, Aschenbrenner emphasises that the quality of any action is determined by the graced availability of heart and will to God.[44] For Aschenbrenner, it is important for individuals to learn to plumb the depths of experience to find God without whom being and existence would have no reality. This may at times be in the depth of the experience of pitch darkness or chilling emptiness. Here there is the need to learn to recognise God even upon a dark journey[45] – such is the way of purification.

Freedom

It is the willingness to enter upon the dark interior journey and also engage with one another at the level which can be personally confronting, and which is certain to expose the vulnerability of those so involved, that is also the source of acceptance and bonding both within the Hope Community and for individuals at a personal level. This is why the regular meeting for prayer during a week, and weekly Community meetings are so important and sustain the Community's interaction with the residents of the estate. It is not that such communal interaction and personal prayerful initiatives solve all questions and issues posed by the very life and work of the Community, far from it, but such a commitment enables individuals and the Community to freely confront such questions and

---

43 Hassel D., *Dark Intimacy, op. cit.*, p. 146.

44 'An active apostolic spirituality, never a matter of simple busy activity, is as much a matter of this inner quality of heart expressed in a special human faith presence, as it is a matter of courageous activity and service for God's people.' Aschenbrenner G., *A God for a Dark Journey*, New Jersey, Dimension Books, 1984, p. 92.

45 'Much evidence seems to suggest that we will be led more and more to the Calvary of an apparently dark, empty stillness...And there we must learn to find a God of love and fidelity beyond any power of evil in this world – a God of quiet joy and dogged hope patiently revealed in the eloquent beauty of a Son's faithful obedience in the dark and empty stillness. And that fidelity and obedience is always blessed with Resurrection. It always gives light.' *Ibid.*, p. 179.

honestly engage with the issues which arise. 'The root decision to accept my own life and to obey its demands may challenge my understanding of those demands, my honesty in their regard. The worst temptation...is simply to give up asking and seeking.'[46]

It is not Christian to despair of the present merely putting off hope into the future. Such a negative eschatological view may appear to obviate the necessity of action but has no root in the real contemplative dynamic. There is also a very essential hope that belongs in the present, and is based on the nearness of the hidden God, and of His Spirit, in the present in the face and being of those on the margins. The Christian tradition continually reasserts the integrated nature of contemplation and action. Gradually, by accepting the particular place in the world and tasks as they are, individuals come to be liberated from the limitations of the world and of a restricted half-hearted milieu. Indeed here an individual may come to be content with her own moment of history with whatever depth of obscurity or prominence that might involve.

There is an imperious divine demand for a creative consent at the deepest level of every human being. This creative consent is the obedience of the whole person to the will of God, here and now. The inner 'word' of consent is the coincidence in the Spirit, the identity of an individual's own obedience and will with the obedience and will of Christ. Such is the inheritance and depth of human heritage within the life of grace. It has been described within the Christian tradition as both a 'blind stirring of love' and a 'living flame of love'. Yet this creative consent, is a non-action which informs the most powerful action and overflows into compassion for the poor, and marginalised.

According to Merton, to be truly Catholic is not merely to be correct, according to an abstractly universal standard of truth within a particular denominational form, but also and above all to be able to enter into the problems and joys of all, to understand all, to be all things to all human beings. This cannot be done if there is not a primary personal holistic self-acceptance by an individual which includes the reality of problems and failure. Within such self-understanding may also be found that creative consent and responsibility that unite an individual to God's will and thus to the dynamism of historical transcendence.[47] Here lies the core of

---

46   Merton T., *Conjectures of a Guilty Bystander, op. cit.*, p. 184.
47   See Chapter 7.

interior freedom. For this to be an ever deeper reality in life there is the necessity of a simple daily conversion, as Merton states this, 'If I am not fully free, then the love of God, I hope, will free me. The important thing is simply turning to Him daily and often, performing His will and His mystery in everything that is evidently and tangibly 'mine'.[48] Here a facilitating tool Merton utilises, in words reminiscent of Julian of Norwich, is the 'wise heart'. This hidden dynamism is at work already, the mystery of God within ready to be awakened and by which 'all manner of things shall be well'. To have this wise heart is to live centred on this dynamism and this secret hope. The 'wise heart' remains in hope and in contradiction, in sorrow and in joy, focused on Christ. Such a focus enables the individual to see the mystery of God at work in the humanity of friends and neighbours, children, poor and marginalised. Paradoxically it is those last groups: children and the poor and marginalised who often have a more direct apprehension of being and the quality of those whom they encounter. Sometimes it is given to children and to simple people to experience a direct intuition of being. Such an intuition is simply an immediate grasp of one's own inexplicable personal reality in one's own incommunicable act of existing. An individual's being is given not simply as an arbitrary and inscrutable affliction, but as a source of joy, growth, life, creativity and fulfilment. But the decision to take existence only as an affliction is left to the individual. By contrast in losing touch with being and thus with God, humanity has fallen into a senseless idolatry of production and consumption for their own sakes. According to Merton, the Christian accepts the 'yes' of being with complete joy, docility and abandon because he believes that the 'yes' of being and the 'no' of man's refusal and evasion of being have been completely reconciled in Christ. The Christian choice is simply a complete, trusting and abandoned consent to the 'yes' of God in Christ.[49]

---

48   Merton T., *Conjectures of a Guilty Bystander, op. cit.,* p.189.

49   By contrast, Merton cites what Maritain calls the practical atheism of many Christians. 'They keep in their minds the settings of religion for the sake of appearances or outward show...but they deny the Gospel and despise the poor, pass through the tragedy of their time only with resentment against anything that engenders their interest and fear for their own prestige and possessions...These are terrible and prophetic words, and their light picks out with relentless truth and detail the true face of what passes for Christianity and too often tries to justify itself by an appeal to the Christian past.' Merton T., *Conjectures of a Guilty Bystander, op. cit.,* p. 244.

For Merton, one must live as a Christian, act as a Christian, with a life and an activity which springs from the free unconditional 'yes' of Christ to the Father's will, incarnated in an individual's own free unconditional 'yes' to the reality, truth, and love which are made fully accessible in the Person and in the Cross of Christ. An individual's life and action seek their meaning in a world which has been reconciled with its own truth and its origin by Christ's love for it and for His Father. Thus the Christian response will always be one of implicit or explicit gratitude throughout all the vicissitudes of life. In like manner, Merton cites Bonhoeffer's words that, 'I am sure we honour God more if we gratefully accept the life he gives us with all its blessings, loving it and drinking it to the full, grieving deeply and sincerely when we have belittled or thrown away any of the precious things of life'.[50] According to Merton, what is new in contemporary theology is not the essential message, but the rethinking of it, the rediscovery of insights which had become obscured. These insights awaken the deep truth of human sinfulness and hardness of heart, overcome by the love of God and by His restoration of the world in Christ. The deepest most cogent mystery of contemporary life is that the Lord who speaks of freedom in the ground of our being still continues to speak to everyone. If this is the fundamental presupposition of contemporary Christian understanding, then on the margins it is no use, as Merton states, trying to 'get these people into the church'. Indeed as has already become apparent upon the margins, 'The chief feeling about church is one of alienation.'[51] According to Merton what is needed is to love such individuals with a love completely divested of all formally religious presuppositions, simply as fellow human beings, who also seek truth and freedom. This ready acceptance of individuals in the fullness of their unique humanity has been shown to be the only route for real dialogue, conversation and understanding. Within this process there is the possibility of reciprocal transformation but this appears to lie in the willingness to enter into that mutual vulnerability already discussed.

Such a willingness to listen and enter into the experience of another through mutual openness and vulnerability also leads into the possibility of a deeper encounter with God, by entering into the mystery of the hidden encounter which marks the lives of others in a way that cannot be

---

50   *Ibid.,* p. 316.
51   Fieldworker A.

easily explained or understood. It is evident that God's will is not an external force that presses down on human beings. Rather there is a deep drawing from within the ontological core of human freedom – made free in the image of God. Human freedom contains in itself a demand for infinite freedom which can be met only by perfect union with the freedom of God. Such freedom comes to full maturity in that openness both to God and to other real human beings. By contrast what passes for freedom in contemporary society appears to be the flagrant compromising of authentic freedom. 'Everyone is willing to sacrifice his spiritual liberty for some lower kind. He will compromise his personal integrity [spiritual liberty] for the sake of security or ambition, or pleasure, or just to be left in peace.'[52]

Humility

For Merton the test of authentic humanity is the individual consent to receive the glory of God. Yet the condition for this openness is real humility which paradoxically ushers in the greatest freedom. In Merton's understanding, there appears to be a certain co-inherence of humility with integrity. The former brings with it a deep refinement of spirit rooted in a trusting dependence upon God and facilitating openness to others, and the latter a certain peace accompanying verity of life, which combines with prudence and common sense.

One can only understand God by being in some mysterious way transformed into God. Here the obscurity of faith increases the darker it becomes and for Merton it is in this deepest darkness that human beings most fully possess God on earth. Thus the function of faith then becomes not an attempt to reduce mystery to some rational clarity, rather the need is to integrate the known and unknown into one living vibrant whole, within which an individual becomes more and more able to transcend the limitations of an external self. Here, the summit of one's spiritual being remains a pure mystery to reason. Here that hunger of spirit born of humility is conducive to silence, intellectual solitude, interior poverty, and

---

52   Merton T., *Conjecture of a Guilty Bystander, op. cit.,* p. 83.

limpid obscurity. Life in Christ is life in the mystery of the Cross and participation in the divine mystery. Here the perfection of humility is found in transforming union. 'The humble man receives praise the way a clean window takes the light of the sun. The truer and more intense the light is, the less you see of the glass.'[53] Within contemporary society the Gospel has ceased to be good news. Indeed, according to Merton, it has ceased to be news at all. If this is the case that it is not news, of its nature it must follow that it is not Gospel, for the Gospel is the proclamation of something absolutely new, everlastingly new. The message of the Gospel when it was first preached was profoundly disturbing to those who wanted to cling to well-established religious patterns, the ancient and accepted ways, the ways that were not dangerous and which contained no surprises.[54] The responses of some members of the established churches to the life and work of the Hope Community appear to indicate that this adherence to past securities is still a notable feature of institutional church life.[55] This might be characterised as a renunciation of the world. However, by contrast, Merton cites true *contemptus mundi* as being a compassion for the transient world and a humility which refuses arrogantly to set up the church as an 'external' institution in the world.[56] This clinging to past securities adverts to the crucial importance of tradition, yet such an appeal is often highly selective. As chapter seven illustrated, there is an evident emphasis within the classical spiritual tradition upon the integrated nature of contemplation and action and the peculiar fecundity of contemplation in its outward working in discerned action, particularly amongst the marginalised. Thus the tradition, in this case, would appear to support the risky path of Merton's desire to seek a true integration of the life of the church in the lives of all human beings by an engagement which reverences the mystery of God already at work there. This may

---

53 Merton T., *New Seeds of Contemplation, op. cit.,* p. 147.

54 'One of the great temptations of an over-institutionalised religion is precisely this: to keep man under the constraint of his own and his society's past, so that this safety appears to be freedom. He is 'free' to return to the familiar constraint but this interferes with his freedom to respond to the new gift of grace in Christ.' Merton T., *A Vow of Conversation*, Basingstoke, The Lampe Press, 1988, p. 6.

55 See Chapter 4.

56 'What a shame that all through the church the "will of God" can so easily resolve itself into the will of an Italian under-secretary in the Holy Office.' Merton T., *A Vow of Conversation, op. cit.,* p. 59.

coincide with a mode of presence within the world which does not draw attention to itself in opposition to what Merton terms the 'clerical' presence, which is both official and attention-seeking, issuing forth in 'formal messages of institutional triumph.'[57]

A more modest presence within the society involves: the willingness to stand alongside others, listening to them and thereby reverencing the reality of God at work within them, and acknowledging personal failure and powerlessness. It appears intrinsic to the human condition that individuals fear such powerlessness, and the potential suffering involved. Yet an acceptance of shared human frailty facilitates real contact with the weak, disadvantaged members of society, and only in this way can the communication of good news be made authentic on the margins. Jaspers exemplifies this reality when he poses the choice between opposed philosophical possibilities. 'Will a person enter the limited field of fixed truth, which in the end has only to be obeyed, or will he go into the limitless open truth?' He continues the challenge, 'Will he win this perilous independence in perilous openness as in existential philosophy, the philosophy of communication in which the individual becomes himself on condition that others become themselves.' The cost involved is 'there is no solitary peace but constant dissatisfaction and in which a man espouses his soul to suffering.'[58] Such willingness to embark upon the interior journey of limitless truth is itself a gift of God marked by simplicity: a simplicity that is and has and says everything just because it is simple. Simplicity is integral to real humility. Merton consistently emphasises the importance of this childlike simplicity. This quality is one which the Hope Community members have remarked upon with regard to some of those who live on the estate. It is linked with the lack of illusion prevalent in individuals lives, when effort is focused upon the bare necessities needed for survival. Its effects upon the lives of the fieldworkers is both

---

57   *Ibid.* p. 66 c.f., 'My one real difficulty with faith is in really accepting the truth that the church is a redeemed community and to be convinced that to follow the mind of the church is to be free from the mentality of the fallen society. Ideally, I see this, but in fact there is so much that is not 'redeemed' in the thinking of those who represent the church.' Merton's resolution of the problem consisted in 'Complete obedience to the church and complete, albeit humble, refusal of the pride and chicanery of churchmen.' *Ibid.,* p. 199.

58   Jaspers K. cited *Ibid.,* p. 20.

at the level of a deeper perception of God and in their own life style to adopt a notable simplicity.

Here the mysticism of Weil is once more helpful containing as it does a simplicity which resonates with the experience of the Hope Community and is accredited as authentic by Merton.[59] He recognised her intuition of the integrated nature of suffering and love and her insistence on being identified with the outsider, all those who could not be encompassed within the official church. Such nonconformity, combined with authentic mysticism, he stressed as a powerful symbol for contemporary society witnessing to the reality that the love of God must break all human pride and perforce is drawn to the humble contrite heart. This is the paradox of prayer that individuals are called to learn how to pray and yet receive prayer only as gift. It is only true humility which can wait in open expectation of such a gift. Here at its deepest level the distinction between the presence and absence of God is no longer really distinguishable – it seems that the mystery of God's presence can only be touched by a profound awareness of absence. At this juncture, the disposition called for is a faithful child-like waiting in poverty of spirit, a condition indistinguishable from real humility.

This insight is echoed in the life and writings of Stein. Here she likens this surrender to being led like a child by God and committing all into his care. 'Being a child of God means to be led by the hand of God, to do the will of God, not one's own, to lay all care and all hope in God's hands.'[60] Living in this manner meant for her the grateful receiving of all the circumstances of daily life with both simplicity and humility. In this way the outworking of that desire of the heart echoed in 'Thy will be done' received its most authentic manifestation.

Such an orientation enabled Stein to live through to her death amidst the grotesque reality of Nazi persecution. In a not dissimilar manner, the Hope Community finds itself enabled to live in situations which have included: a riot on the estate, when the Community formed the only safe haven for all protagonists, the occasional violence surrounding local drug-dealing, and the psychotic violence of mentally unstable residents. Combined with this calm receptivity is an attitude of expectant openness,

---

59   See Merton T., *A Vow of Conversation*, op. cit., p. 156ff.
60   Stein E., 'The Mystery of Christmas', cited in Koeppel J., *Edith Stein: Philosopher and Mystic*, Collegeville, Minnesota, The Liturgical Press, 1990, p. 19.

which enables those who work on the margins to engage with the people, who often exhibit great simplicity and spontaneity. A powerful principle, operative throughout the endeavour to be open to the deepest contemplative dimensions and also to the possibilities of discerned action, is for individuals to strive with all human abilities as though all depended upon themselves and yet await the divine gift as though all depended upon God. The lived tension of such a dynamic is difficult but creative. Here discernment becomes again a core foundation for any action. This is particularly operative in what Johnston calls 'mystic nothingness'.[61] Within this consciousness of weakness, which is the prelude to the grace gift of humility, there arises slowly a submission to the spirit of God. Yet this in itself is an art which is only learned over many years. However, gradually there does emerge a delicate sensitivity to the inner motions of grace and such contemplative grace may overflow into discerned action. Here the recognition of gratuitous gift is a quiet movement at the depth of an individual's being. Here too the final kenotic drawing is one which relinquishes all anxiety. Then decision for action is enabled to emerge from the depths of an individual's being where emptiness, darkness and obscurity are prevalent, but where the very emptiness is a guarantee of authenticity and fullness.[62] The way of the interior journey is to discern the leading of the Spirit of God who does not usually lead in clear-cut words and concepts but through inspirations and movements which are dark and obscure, as Johnston indicates, like 'the supraconceptual knowledge of which Dionysius speaks'.[63] This is the true home of the contemplative in action.

> Night is our diocese and silence is our ministry
> Poverty our charity and helplessness our tongue-tied sermon
> Beyond the scope of sight or sound we dwell upon the air
> Seeking the world's gain in an unthinkable experience
> We are exiles in the far end of solitude, living as listeners

---

61   'Mystical nothingness is dynamite. It is the power that moves the universe and created revolutions in human minds and hearts. For mystical nothingness paves the way for the dynamic action of grace – when I am weak, then I am strong.' Johnston W., *The Inner Eye of Love*, London, Collins, 1978, p. 10.

62   'Authentic mystical experience leads to a great compassion for the poor, the sick, the oppressed, the downtrodden, the imprisoned, the underprivileged.' *Ibid.*, p. 132.

63   *Ibid.*, p. 28.

With hearts attending to the skies we cannot understand:
Waiting upon the first far drums of Christ the Conqueror,
Planted like sentinels upon the world's frontiers.[64]

The path of the interior journey, as presented, has a cyclical dynamic. The risk embraced at the beginning is prompted by involvement with those on the urban margins. Openness, temporal commitment, provisionality and messiness are features common to both interior journeying and exterior involvement. Yet the willingness to embark upon this course with the inevitable exposure of vulnerability leads into a mysterious discovery of authentic selfhood. Along the way, loneliness may be transformed into fruitful solitude while the desire for contemplative prayer deepens. As the path becomes darker and more obscure, the inner emptiness may be reflected in the reality of the external situation. Yet the space created within allows a more profound listening to marginalised individuals and apprehension of the divine initiative. This interior emptiness is the seed ground for mature growth but it can appear as the prelude to disintegration. This fear prompts that acknowledged need for purification, and active asceticism into which an individual is drawn by a deepening attachment to the imitation of Christ and the discernment of any motivation for action. A sense of weakness and inadequacy remain upon the journey but ultimately there arises a deep personal integration in an attentive watchful listening of the heart, and an ongoing free creative consent to the divine imperative. This freedom is rooted in and nourished by the grace-gift of humility. This humility involves great limpidity, as such it facilitates awareness of the presence of God in others. Thus the heart of the journey orientates the individual back to that risky involvement with the marginalised, but with an enhanced ability to listen and respond to the presence of God at work amongst the people. Here, there is a deeper appreciation of what Merton describes as 'le point vierge.'[65] 'At the centre of our being is a point of nothingness which is untouched by

---

64   Merton T., 'The Quickening of St. John the Baptist', in *The Collected Poems of Thomas Merton*, London, Sheldon Press, 1978, pp. 199-202.

65   Annice Callahan suggests that this point of poverty and nothingness by which we know God, which Merton calls le point vierge, is what Rahner calls the supernatural existential, a given in our existence.

sin and by illusion, a point of pure truth, a point or spark which belongs entirely to God.'[66]

I have argued that unless there is a more profound human understanding derived from that exploration of the inner ground of human existence, then activity will tend to be superficial and deceptive – particularly in relation to involvement with the marginalised. However, a willingness to enter upon the interior journey leads into an increasingly humble awareness of the presence of God already active on the urban margins.

This has direct implications both for those who work with the marginalised, and also for the church. This is a spiritual hermeneutic for the urban margins. It is rooted in the experience of interaction with the marginalised. Such experience reflectively evaluated propels individuals towards risking the path of their interior journey and ultimately this path leads back to deeper involvement with the marginalised accompanied by an increased perception of the presence of God at work there. Such an interpretation presents a challenge both for individuals and the church: for individuals to risk the engagement upon their own interior journey, for the church to both encourage that individual engagement and to pray for that grace gift of humility to pervade all institutional life such there might be a more receptive attitude to the mysterious presence of God outside the present ecclesiastical boundaries. If this spiritual hermeneutic is to be taken seriously as a potential dynamic for the church at the close of the twentieth century it has serious implications for all engaged in ministry within the church. It prompts the encouragement of the contemplative dimension as a foremost priority in any training for ministry. It gives prominence to engagement with the marginalised as a keynote ministry within the church beneficial for all members in a reciprocal dynamic of transformation. It requires a re-engagement with the classical spiritual tradition and a re-appropriation of the treasures therein for contemporary availability. It may cause the church to be re-invigorated by this dual engagement with its own spiritual depths in the interior lives of its mem-

---

66   'The point which is never at our disposal, from which God disposes of our lives, which is inaccessible to the fantasies of our own mind or the brutalities of our own will. This little point of nothingness and absolute poverty is the pure glory of God in us. It is so to speak His name written in us, it is in everybody.' Merton T., *Conjectures of a Guilty Bystander, op. cit.,* p. 158.

bers, and its own renewed tradition, and with the contemporary manifestation of the presence of God amongst the marginalised.

Conclusion

God is any patient old council tree choked in the cement of city streets,
but showing forth so bravely,
so beautifully in the Spring,
and God is the grass on the waste land beside the factory,
and the town sparrow born of dust and a little dew.
'That can't be right' he said
'Why not?'
'Why – well it's too much, it's too simple!'
'Yes I said 'that's how it goes – too much and too simple!''[1]

'Too much and too simple'. Such a remark could summarise the presence of God at work in the lives, words and actions of the people of the Heath Town Estate. It is 'too much' in that by virtue of their own discovery of the transcendent the people are celebrating grace, but have come to it in and through the sacrament of their own lives. It is too simple in that the operative fact of grace is expressed in ways that are often embarrassingly simple and direct for our more complicated Christian formats. In the face of the enormity of this mystery, that human beings are able to grasp the divine working in the everyday situations of their lives, and confronted by the simplicity of the presence of God at work amongst the people in disconcertingly novel forms, members of the Hope Community are themselves evangelised.

There do exist possibilities for a shared spirituality between those who work on the urban margins and marginalised people. Indeed, the empirical work has revealed that where time is expended in listening to the experience of those who live on the margins, the potential for reciprocal transformation exists. It is the patient commitment of time, the willingness to actively listen and the perceptive attunement which can hear, which are the preconditions for recognition of the presence of God amongst the people. Such fidelity in terms of temporal commitment and the willingness to listen also assists growth in self-esteem and self-

---

1   Myers E., *A Well Full of Leaves*, London, Collins, 1957, p. 138.

confidence. Thus marginalised individuals become increasingly able to give voice to their own ideas, opinions and experience.

In sharing these, there is also an articulation of the experience of God in life. Such a commitment of time and energy stands in marked contradiction to the values of a society which extols a different ethic, where time is money, and time expended – in any sphere of activity – must be shown to have a measurable return.

This is not to argue that all ministry within the church must focus in this way on the personal appropriation of time. However, it is to suggest that any evaluation of ministry needs to give priority consideration to encouraging and facilitating this dimension. Yet the giving of time is only the primary feature. Thereafter there is the need to exercise the faculty of reverential listening. Again, such an emphasis is not to negate the traditional forms of parochial ministry.[2] It is to suggest the possible evaluation of such ministries and the potential for a more developed form of listening to be incorporated or to be able to exist in a complementary form, exercised by diverse personnel.[3]

Conversation and dialogue could also have more life-giving potential for those who work on the margins in interaction with those in ministry at other levels of the institutional church. Here such exchange could serve as positive encouragement for ministerial outreach and fresh stimulus for institutional activity. It is not suggested that such attentive listening be in opposition to other ongoing active involvement in the life of the marginalised. Yet this dimension is a vital ingredient of, and presupposition for, such active engagement. Reflectively evaluated, such profound listening might also lead to significant change within the church at the level of policy making and pastoral practice.

---

2   In giving emphasis to Rahner's concern: that where the church is present, it should be a vital vibrant force, not a presence handicapped by an agenda it cannot possibly fulfil, I have suggested that this implies an evaluation of contemporary parochial needs and the encouragement of new initiatives alongside the possible reform of parochial structures.

3   This may not be the role of the local clergy of the area. However, the clergy may have a role in enabling others to 'listen on behalf of' the churches, and feedback into the churches the insights so received. This might then become not a task associated with any one group but a collaborative venture of laity, clergy and religious. It might also mean a more positive process of collaboration with the laity.

Tracy has argued very convincingly for a natural hermeneutical competence which is universally available. Further research exploring such a possibility amongst the marginalised would continue to make a valuable contribution to urban theology and enrich the self-understanding of the church. In developing Tracy's use of the 'classic' to cover the experience of the marginalised, I argued that in a similar manner to dealing with a text, there are demands which require constant interpretation. Thus it is imperative that there should be ongoing reflection and critical re-appropriation of that experience in the light of the church's contemporary understanding. In order to inform that reflection it would be important to make more available, particularly for those training for ministry, the opportunity of direct involvement with the marginalised.

If it is indeed the case, as Rahner maintains, that human beings in their very essence are a transcendence towards mystery, this is a vital operational principle in engagement with any individual. Here the question arises will the institution continue to cling to known secure ways of relating to those on the margins, ways which serve to alienate rather than include? Or will the church risk the relational mode of listening through those already established contacts on the margins? In so listening will those in authority within the church allow the possibility of transformation by virtue of that experience? In too many discussions of the life of the church two prevalent myths still seem to be an oppressive though often unacknowledged presence, namely: that there is some ideal 'right' model of the church for which Christians are constantly searching, and secondly that once that model has been achieved then the consequent result will be an influx of vast numbers into the church. The first denies the reality of early church history and humanity's defective nature. The second attempts to pre-empt the Parousia. The confrontation of these key myths is necessary if the contemporary church is to move beyond its own boundaries and engage with the urban margins where God is so actively at work.

To enter into such an engagement involves both risk and an openness to the admission of failure. I have argued that such a confession enables a concrete commitment to be made to learn from the experience of those already involved amongst the marginalised.

The facilitating tool for listening critically involves a deepening contemplative stance. This is a particularly acute need if there is to be a real understanding of what is emerging from the marginalised. From that position of essential vulnerability and powerlessness in our own contemplative depths, the clarity of resonance with others – particularly the marginalised – is peculiarly powerful. The divine desire to be unconditionally at hand for human beings in humility and vulnerability – most explicit within the Eucharist – draws individuals who enter upon their own inner journey into an imitative way which is fruitful in action. In this incarnational activity individuals and the institutional church are consistently invited to participate.

It does appear that a sense of church[4] has become so alien to some that it needs to be reclaimed. Yet if this is to be the case the church is called to be attractive, inspiring, challenging and inviting. It is at this juncture that the leader of the Hope Community believes the people of the estate have something to contribute. 'I'm sure the people here have a lot to contribute to the renewal of the church.'[5] This contribution can only be realised if there is a willingness to listen to the experience emerging from the margins and the facilitating tool for this listening is the openness for engagement with the contemplative dimension.

The authenticity of contemplation is to be found in true humility, and the willingness to walk the dark and insecure path is a measure both of the contemplative dynamic which is operative and the grace-gift of humility which has been received. This is applicable both at an individual and an institutional level. A keynote of this way of life is the appreciation of forgiveness. God's gratuitous forgiveness initiates a dynamic which inspires ministry. The individual experience of the awareness of sinfulness and God's forgiveness is a vital feature in distinguishing between the true prophet whose life is formed in the humility of forgiveness and the false prophet. Indeed it is perceptible that the character of apostolic action responds directly to the quality of the

---

4   'Many people continue to grapple with the role of the church in their Christian identity…. And the issue centres on the institutional church…Many, while believing in God and living generous lives of service, either explicitly reject membership in the church or operationally have their religion without any real relationship to the church. For an increasing number of people, practices within the institutional church which they perceive to be unjust are making membership in the church more and more painful and questionable.' Aschenbrenner G., *A God for a Dark Journey*, New Jersey, Dimension Books, 1984, p. 116.

5   Fieldworker A.

experience of being a forgiven sinner. This may also have further far-reaching implications when considering the nature of institutional involvement in this dynamic.

The dimension of a spiritual hermeneutic of this kind potentially provides the ontological grounding for ongoing discernment. What may be most significant for the future is further exploration of the means to enable those fieldworkers who work on the margins, to be more open to, appreciative of, and ultimately willing to be changed by, the reality they experience among the people. A further step is how the institution may make more progress, in its attempts to listen, to hear, and to be open to change by, the reality of God amongst the people, by integrating the experience of those members working on the margins.

A keynote of this interior journeying to facilitate the deeper listening has been the emphasis on discernment. Not a discernment of the heart on the basis of generalised moral criteria but an attunement to the will of God and an endeavouring to seek that will within the circumstances of daily life – inevitably leading to embracing the foolishness of the cross. At this juncture the spiritual tradition's emphasis on purification has been reclaimed for a contemporary spirituality involving a renewed asceticism. Here reconciliation, both individual and communal, proves to be a dynamic for deeper contemplation and propitious action. However, authentic interpretation of either the classic text or the experience of the marginalised depends on the moral authenticity of the interpreter. Yet I have argued that beyond moral integrity, authentic interpretation requires a purification of the spirit. It is within such an ongoing dynamic that discernment – particularly the discernment of motivation prompting action – holds such a key position. It may be that the Spiritual Exercises as a school of discernment have a significant contribution to make here. Further research into this possibility involving those who work on the margins is still to be accomplished.

A spiritual hermeneutic will only be truly radical to the extent that it has classical resonances. It is grounded in the tradition of spiritual fecundity where the deeper the contemplative awareness the more fruitful is the consequent action. Features of importance include the recognition of individual and institutional complicity, failure and helplessness with regard to social realities and the life of the marginalised. This difficult acknowledgement frees both individual and institution from the illusion of false realities dependent upon self-recognition, and encourages the growing risky dependency upon God and other human beings.

Within such a hermeneutic there is the potential for a challenging critique to be made available both to individuals and to institutional structures. There is also the realistic recognition that transformation of this kind takes time. A spiritual hermeneutic does not evolve by a process of osmosis. Of itself it requires a deep commitment to prayer. Contemplation may indeed become a subversive activity as Merton states so clearly. It is also the seed-bed for discernment and the starting point for a counter-cultural liberating position.

Real reconciliation between the church and those on the urban margins will not occur until there is a valuing of the experience of God already at work there. Such a recognition and engagement therewith is fundamental for any social, political or economic initiatives undertaken by the church. The appropriation of this reality may have transformative consequences for the life of the church, while continuing to exclude this from consciousness deprives the church of revivifying resources. Responsible appropriation requires the openness to enter into conversation and to listen through the experience of those who work on the margins. This can only be truly apprehended by bringing to bear on the situation of the urban poor that contemplative dimension of religious experience which prioritises being alongside activity.

Accordingly, this spiritual hermeneutic is vital both for those actively involved with the marginalised and for those in ministry in other areas within the church. Thus individuals may be encouraged to embark upon their own interior journey, in order to guarantee the authenticity of their listening and to facilitate the discernment of action. Such a journey will inevitably require an ongoing purification of spirit, but its potential for creative initiatives, as verified by the spiritual tradition, may be limitless. The necessity for some further formation process is apparent, if there is to be any harnessing of the potential which exists, in the interests of those on the margins and the church. One suggestion might be a two-fold possibility: the first with regard to individual development which might include individual insertion upon the urban margins combined with a nurturing of the contemplative dimension which facilitates profound and critical listening: while the second would look to the institution and the rediscovery of insights which have become obscured, that the God who speaks of freedom in the ground of human beings still continues to speak to all, and in the light of this understanding consideration must be given to possibilities for reflectively evaluating and assisting church social outreach programmes already underway.

A very real possibility exists for revivified life on the margins and a fresh dynamic within the life of the church. By contrast the alternative looks bleak, focusing on an ever diminishing group of devotees, while the spirit may be giving prophetic utterance through the lives, and stutterings of the most vulnerable in the land. The church is challenged to respond – to be a church prepared to take risks, and to enter into the sphere of marginality in forms to which those who live on the urban margins can relate – to be led by the spirit of God beyond its self-imposed boundaries.

> It is not enough for you to be my servant, to restore the tribes of Jacob and bring back the survivors of Israel, I will make you the light of the nations so that my salvation may reach to the ends of the earth.[6]

The discourse continues for you the reader to add your own contribution.

---

6   Isaiah 49 v6., trans. Jerusalem Bible, London, DLT, 1968

Select Bibliography

Ahern G. and Davie G., *Inner City God*, London, Hodder & Stoughton, 1987.

Anderson R., [ed.], *Theological Foundations for Ministry*, Edinburgh, T & T Clark, 1979.

Anderson R., *Historical Transcendence and the Reality of God*, London, Geoffrey Chapman, 1975.

Archer A., *The Two Catholic Churches – A Study in Oppression*, London, SCM, 1986.

Aschenbrenner G., *A God for a Dark Journey*, New Jersey, Dimension Books, 1984

Azevedo M., *Vocation for Mission: The Challenge of Religious Life Today*, New York, Paulist Press, 1988

Barry W., *Now Choose Life – Conversion on the Way to Life*, New Jersey, Paulist Press, 1990

Best S. & Kellner D. [eds.], *Postmodern Theory*, London, Macmillan, 1991

Bishops of England and Wales to the Reports of the National Pastoral Congress of 1980. *The Easter People, Liverpool 1980*

Brown C., *The Social History of Religion in Scotland since 1730*, London, Methuen, 1987

Cabaud J., *Simone Weil: A Fellowship in Love*, London, Harvill Press, 1944

Collins R., *John of the Cross*, Collegeville, Minnesota, The Liturgical Press, 1990

Committee for Community Relations Catholic Bishops Conference of England and Wales *Charity to Empowerment: The Church's Mission Alongside Poor and Marginalised People,* London, 1992

Concilium, 170, 1983

Condemned, A Shelter Report on Housing and Poverty London, Shelter, 1971

Cox J., *The English Churches in a Secular Society*, Oxford, OUP, 1982

Daly G., *Transcendence and Immanence*, Oxford, Clarendon, 1980

De Lubac H., *The Mystery of the Supernatural*, trans. Sheed R., London, Geoffrey Chapman, 1967

Dorr D., *The Social Justice Agenda: Justice, Ecology, Power and the Church*, Dublin, Gill & MacMillan, 1991

Douglas M., *Risk Acceptability According to the Social Sciences*, London, Routledge & Kegan Paul, 1986

Dulles A., *The Craft of Theology: From Symbol to System*, Dublin Gill & MacMillan, 1992

Duquoc C. and Floristan C. [eds.], *Where is God?: A Cry of Human Distress*, 'Gonzalez-Faus J., *We proclaim a crucified Messiah*', [Concilium], London, SCM, 1992

Egan H., *Ignatius Loyola the Mystic*, Wilmington Delaware, Michael Glazier, 1987

Faith in the City: A Call for Action by Church and Nation. The Report of the Archbishop's Commission on Urban Priority Areas, London, Church House Publishing, 1985

Featherstone M., *Consumer Culture and Postmodernism*, London, Sage, 1991

Field F. *Losing Out*, Oxford, Blackwell, 1989

Finley J., *Merton's Place of Nowhere*, Notre Dame, Indiana, Ave Maria Press, 1987

Flannery A. [ed.] *Vatican Council II More Postconciliar Documents*, New York, Costello, 1982

Flannery A., [ed.], *Vatican Council II: The Conciliar and Post Conciliar Documents*, London, Geoffrey Chapman, 1975

Gadamer H. *Truth and Method*, trans. Weinsheimer J., and Marshall D., London, Sheed & Ward, 1989

Gans H. [ed] *Sociology in America*, American Sociological association Presidential Series, California, Sage, 1990

General Synod of the Church of England Publication *Living Faith in the City*, London, 1990.

Gill, R., *The Myth of the Empty Church*, London, SPCK, 1993

Gittens A.J., *Gifts and Strangers*, Mahwah, New Jersey, Paulist Press, 1989.

Glaser B. and Strauss A., *The Discovery of Grounded Theory: Strategies for Qualitative Research*, New York, Aldine, 1967.

Hamilton T., *Solidarity: The Missing Link in Irish Society*, Dublin, Jesuit Centre for Faith and Justice, 1991

Hassel D., *Dark Intimacy: Hope for Those in Difficult Prayer Experiences*, New York, Paulist Press, 1986

Hassel D., *Radical Prayer: Creating a Welcome for God, Ourselves Other People and the World*, New Jersey, Paulist Press, 1984

Hastings A., [ed.], *Modern Catholicism: Vatican II and After*, London, SPCK, 1991

Hastings A., *The Faces of God: Essays on Church and Society*, London, Geoffrey Chapman, 1975

Hauerwas S. and Williman W., *Resident Aliens*, Nashville, Abingdon Press, 1989

Hebdige D., *Hiding in the Light: On Images and Things*, London, Routledge, 1988

Heschel A., *The Insecurity of Freedom*, New York, Shocken Books, 1972

Heythrop Journal, XXV, 1984

Holland J. [eds.]. *Varieties of Postmodern Theology*, New York, New York University Press, 1989

Hornsby-Smith M., *Roman Catholic Beliefs in England: Customary Catholicism and Transformations of Religious Authority*, Cambridge, CUP, 1991

Imhof P. & Biallowons H., [eds.], *Faith in a Wintry Season: Conversations and Interviews with Karl Rahner in the last years of his life*, trans. Egan, H., New York, Crossroads, 1990

Imhof P. and Biallowons H. [eds.], *Karl Rahner in Dialogue, Conversations and Interviews 1965-1982*, trans. Egan H., New York, Crossroad, 1986

Jantzen G., *Julian of Norwich*, London, SPCK, 1987

Jeanrond W., *Theological Hermeneutics: Development and Significance*, London, Macmillan, 1991

Jencks C., *Rethinking Social Policy: Race, Poverty and the Underclass*, Cambridge, Mass., Harvard University Press, 1992

John Paul II, *Centesimus Annus*, London, Catholic Truth Society, 1991

John Paul II, *Redemptor Hominis*, London, Catholic Truth Society, 1979.

John Paul II, *Sollicitudo Rei Socialis*, London, Catholic Truth Society, 1988

Johnston W., *The Inner Eye of Love*, London, Collins, 1978

Journal of Pastoral Care, 37, 1983

Koeppel J., *Edith Stein: Philosopher and Mystic*, Collegeville, Minnesota, The Liturgical Press, 1990

Leech K. & Amin K., *A New Underclass?* London, Child Poverty Action Group, 1988.

Liverpool 1980: Official Report of the National Pastoral Congress, London, St Paul Publications, 1981

Loyola St Ignatius, *The Constitutions of the Society of Jesus*, trans. Ganss G., St Louis, Institute of Jesuit Sources, 1970

Mellor R., *The Inner City as Underclass: A Critique and Restatement*, University of Manchester Sociology Department Occasional Paper, No. 23, 1989.

Merton T., 'The Quickening of St. John the Baptist', in *The Collected Poems of Thomas Merton*, London, Sheldon Press, 1978

Merton T., *A Vow of Conversation*, Basingstoke, The Lampe Press, 1988

Merton T., *Conjectures of a Guilty Bystander*, New York, Doubleday, 1989

Merton T., *Contemplation in a World of Action*, London, Allen and Unwin, 1971

Merton T., *Contemplative Prayer*, London, DLT, 1987

Merton T., *New Seeds of Contemplation*, London, Burns and Oates, 1962

Milbank J., *Theology and Social Theory: Beyond Secular Reason*, Blackwell, Oxford, 1990

Miles M., *Image as Insight: Visual understanding in Western Christianity and Secular Culture*, Boston, Beacon Press, 1985

Munro J., unpublished PhD thesis, University of Edinburgh, 1992

Murray C., *The Emerging British Underclass,* London, I.E.A., 1990

Myers E., *A Well Full of Leaves*, London, Collins, 1957

New Blackfriars, Vol 69, No. 818, July/August, 1988

New Blackfriars, Vol. 73, No. 861, June, 1992

Nichols V., Closing Reflections, Gospel and Culture Conference, 11-17 July, 1992, Swanwick.

Norman E., *Church and Society in England 1770-1970*, Oxford, Clarendon Press, 1976

O'Conner P., *In Search of Therese*, Wilmington Delaware, Michael Glazier, 1987

O'Donoghue N., *Heaven in Ordinarie*, Edinburgh, T & T Clark, 1979

O'Donoghue N., *Mystics For Our Time*, Edinburgh, T & T Clark, 1989

O'Donoghue N., *The Holy Mountain: Approaches to the Mystery of Prayer*, Dublin, Dominican Publications, 1983

Peers E.A., *The Complete Works of St Teresa*, Vol. II., London, Sheed & Ward, 1946

Pelphrey B., *Christ our Mother: Julian of Norwich*, Wilmington delaware, Michael Glazier, 1989

Poloma M. and Gallup G., *Varieties of Prayer – A Survey Report*, Philadelphia, Trinity Press International, 1991

Preston R., *Explorations in Theology 9*, London, SCM, 1981

Puhl L., *The Spiritual Exercises of St Ignatius*, Chicago, Loyola University Press, 1950

Rahner K., *Foundations of Christian Faith: An Introduction to the Idea of Christianity*, London, DLT, 1978

Rahner K., *Ignatius of Loyola*, trans. Ockenden R., London, Collins, 1979

Rahner K., *Opportunities for Faith: Elements of a Modern Spirituality*, trans. Quinn E., London, SPCK, 1974

Rahner K., *The Shape of the Church to Come*, trans. Quinn E., London, SPCK, 1974

Rahner K., *Theological Investigations 3: The Theology of the Spiritual Life*, trans. Karl H. & Kruger B., London, DLT, 1967

Rahner K., *Theological Investigations 4: More Recent Writings*, trans. Smyth K., London, DLT, 1966

Rahner K., *Theological Investigations 6*, trans. Karl H. and Kruger B., London, DLT, 1969

Raper D. [ed.], *Gateway to God*, London, Collins, 1978

Religious Studies Review, Vol. 15, No. 3, July, 1989

Roman Catholic Bishops of England and Wales, *The Easter People*, London, St Paul Publications, 1980, para. 178

Ross A., *Universal Abandon: The Politics of Postmodernism,* Edinburgh, Edinburgh University Press, 1989

Rowland C. & Corner M., *Liberating Exegesis: The Challenge of Liberation Theology to Biblical Studies*, London, SPCK, 1990

Ryan D., *The Catholic Parish: Decline and Development in an English Diocese*, unpublished manuscript, 1991

Schultheis M., DeBerri E. and Henriot P., *Our Best Kept Secret: The Rich Heritage of Catholic Social Teaching*, London, CAFOD, 1988

Sheldrake P. [ed.], *The Way of Ignatius Loyola: Contemporary Approaches to the Spiritual Exercises*, London, SPCK, 1991

Sinetor M., *Ordinary People as Monks and Mystics*, New York, Paulist Press, 1986

Smith A., *Journeying with God: Paradigms of Power and Powerlessness*, London, Sheed and Ward, 1990

Suso J., *Little Book of Eternal Wisdom and Little Book of Truth*, trans. Clark J., London, Faber & Faber, 1953

Townsend P. and Davidson N. [eds.], in Black D., 'The Black Report', Penguin, London, 1988

Tracy D., *Plurality and Ambiguity: Hermeneutics, Religion, Hope*, London, SCM, 1988

Tracy D., *The Analogical Imagination: Christian Theology and the Culture of Pluralism*, London, SCM, 1981

Underhill E., *Mysticism*, London, Methuen and Co Ltd., 1940

Underhill E., *Practical Mysticism for Normal People*, London, J.M. Dent and Sons Ltd., 1940

Veale J., 'Dominant Orthodoxies', in *Milltown Studies*, No., 30, Autumn, 1992

Von Balthasar H., *The Glory of the Lord: A Theological Aesthetics VII*, trans. Davies O., Louth A., McNeil B., Edinburgh, T & T Clark, 1989

Von Balthasar H., *Therese of Lisieux: The Story of a Mission*, trans. Nicholl D., London, Sheed & Ward, 1953

Waddington P., *The Strong Arm of the Law, Armed and Public Policing*, Oxford, Clarendon, 1991

Walsh M., *Here's Hoping!*, Sheffield, Urban Theology Unit, 1991

Weil S., *First and Last Notebooks*, trans. Rees R., London, OUP, 1970

Weil S., *Waiting on God*, Trans. Cranford E., London, Routledge & Kegan Paul, 1951

Whitehead, M., *The Health Divide*, London, Penguin, 1992

Williams R., *Teresa of Avila*, London, Geoffrey Chapman, 1991

Willis P., *Social Conditions of Young People in Wolverhampton 1984*, Wolverhampton Borough Council, 1985

Winch P., *Simone Weil 'The Just Balance'*, Cambridge, CUP, 1989

Wojtyla K., *Sources of Renewal: The Implementation of the Second Vatican Council*, London, Collins, 1980,

Wolverhampton Express and Star, 6 November 1984, and 24 May, 1989

Wolverhampton Express and Star, 8 November 1972

Woods R., *Eckhart's Way*, Wilmington Delaware, Michael Glazier, 1986

Religions and Discourse

Edited by James Francis

Religions and Discourse explores religious language in the major world faiths from various viewpoints, including semiotics, pragmatics and cognitive linguistics. In particular a key issue is the role of figurative speech. Many fascinating metaphors originate in religion e.g. revelation as a 'garment', apostasy as 'adultery', loving kindness as the 'circumcision of the heart'. Every religion rests its specific orientations upon symbols such as these, to name but a few. The series strives after the interdisciplinary approach that brings together such diverse disciplines as religious studies, theology, sociology, philosophy, linguistics and literature, guided by an international editorial board of scholars representative of the aforementioned disciplines. Though scholarly in its scope, the series also seeks to facilitate discussions pertaining to central religious issues in contemporary contexts. The series will publish monographs and collected essays of a high scholarly standard.

Volume 1   Ralph Bisschops and James Francis (eds):
           Metaphor, Canon and Community
           307 pages. 1999.
           ISBN 3-906762-40-8 / US-ISBN 0-8204-4234-8

Volume 2   Lieven Boeve and Kurt Feyaerts (eds):
           Metaphor and God Talk
           291 pages. 1999.
           ISBN 3-906762-51-3 / US-ISBN 0-8204-4235-6

Volume 3   Jean-Pierre van Noppen:
           Transforming Words
           248 pages. 1999.
           ISBN 3-906762-52-1 / US-ISBN 0-8204-4236-4

Volume 4   Robert Innes:
           Discourses of the Self
           236 pages. 1999.
           ISBN 3-906762-53-X / US-ISBN 0-8204-4237-2